Olmans' Guide to Golf Antiques

& Other Treasures of the Game

Foreword by Hale Irwin

By John M. Olman & Morton W. Olman

Market Street Press
Cincinnati, Ohio

Also available from Market Street Press:

The Encyclopedia of Golf Collectibles
by John M. Olman and Morton W. Olman

The Squire: The Legendary Golfing Life of Gene Sarazen
by John M. Olman

Library of Congress Cataloging-in-Publication Data:

Olman, John M.
Olmans' guide to golf antiques & other treasures of the game /
by John M. Olman & Morton W. Olman; foreword by Hale Irwin.
p. cm.
Includes bibliographical references and index.
ISBN 0-972117-02-6 (acid-free)
1. Golf— Collectibles I. Olman, Morton W. II. Title.
III. Title: Golf antiques & other treasures of the game.
GV965.0454 1991
796.352'075— dc20 91-32759

Manufactured in the United States of America

Market Street Press, 325 West Fifth Street, Cincinnati, Ohio 45202

To Scott and Jay and kids everywhere:

May books such as this encourage you
to appreciate and enjoy the craftsmanship
and ingenuity of your forefathers.

ACKNOWLEDGEMENTS

This book could not have been produced without the cooperative efforts of our publishing team. Mary Prince of Impact Publications and Joel Williams of Chelsea Design jointly worked on the page design, typesetting and layout. The dust jacket was designed by Lisa Baranack and photographed by Robert Hale. Kathy Doane used her expert editing skills to ensure that the text would be clear to non-golfers as well as to seasoned followers of the game.

While some of the artifacts illustrated in this book have been in our possession at one time or another, many were generously loaned so that photographs could be taken. We are gratefully indebted to those who unselfishly shared their collections and expertise to enable others to enjoy golf's magnificent heritage: Wayne and Claudia Aaron, Bill Anderson, David Berkowitz, Archie Baird, David Brown, John Capers, Rick Caudill, Peter Crabtree, Bob Curzan, Jack Dezieck, Dick Donovan, Bud Dufner, Art Eden, Jeff Ellis, Mark Emerson, John Fischer III, Nevin Gibson, The Golf Shop Collection, Greg and Barbara Hall, Richard Hamilton, Bob Hansen, Frank Hardison, Ray Hart, Mike Hurdzan, Leo Kelley, Hans Kramer of IMG, Bob Lucas, Millard Mack, Mike Mark, Sid Matthew, John Mross, Joe Murdoch, Bob Gowland at Phillips of Chester, Terry Powell, Jan Russo, Janet Seagle, Steve Shapiro, Eldon Steeves, Bob Thomson, U.S. Golf Association Museum and Library (Karen Bednarski, Nancy Stulack, Andy Mutch and Rand Jerris), Irv Valenta, Bill Wiebold, Paul Wood, and the many dealers and museums who kindly furnished information on their establishments.

A book of this nature depends on illustrations to tell its story. Line drawings were done by Jenny Abell for the club chapter and Pat Kennedy for the display chapter. A special thanks to the following for furnishing photographs: Dorothy Brown of the B.C. Golf House, Bettmann Archive, *The Cincinnati Enquirer*, Weymouth Crumpler of the James River Country Club Museum, Ray Davis and Dick Stranahan of the PGA/World Golf Hall of Fame, Marge Dewey and Saundra Sheffer of the Ralph Miller Library and Museum, *Golf Digest*, The GolfWorks, Joe Hackler of the Old Pro's Table, Mort Hansen, Jr., Jim Larkin, Peter Lewis of the British Golf Museum, Jeff McBride and Rick McCoy.

CONTENTS

FOREWORD

By HALE IRWIN

U.S. Open Champion: 1974, 1979, 1990

Before taking up a new hobby, it's a good idea to do some homework. If you're not familiar with the new activity, then develop an understanding of the basics so that you will have a foundation of knowledge on which to build.

If someone came up to me and said, "Golf seems like such an enjoyable game. I don't know a thing about it, but I'd really like to learn how to play," I would tell them to watch a tournament on television, browse through some golf books or magazines, visit a golf course, learn the objectives and etiquette of the game... And then, with an understanding of the basics, pursue your desire to become a golfer.

As obvious as the axiom of "learning the basics" seems, my wife and I nearly made a major mistake recently when we considered buying some golf art. Instead of progressing from crawling to walking we attempted to start out by running at a full gallop and make an acquisition before doing enough homework.

The purchase consisted of a pair of attractive golf scenes painted in oil on copper rather than on canvas. The antique dealer who showed us the pieces said they were from the 1880s. The paintings were expensive so we told the dealer we wanted some time to think about the purchase. We then decided to get in touch with Mort Olman to see if he could offer any advice. (I knew Mort from my amateur golf days; he ran the U.S. Pro-Am Championship in Cincinnati, which I won with Dale Douglass back in 1967.)

When my wife described the paintings to Mort, he knew exactly what they were. It turns out that the paintings had been done within the last few years by an artist in Italy who sells his work rather inexpensively. Mort said we were not the only ones to be fooled; in 1987, a major British auction house offered a painting by the same artist and dated it circa 1910. Needless to say, we didn't buy the paintings.

Although the artwork was misrepresented to us, the dealer admitted that he, too, had been fooled and intended to get back to his supplier with some pointed questions. The artist isn't totally at fault either; he just happens to paint in a turn-of-the-century style that resembles much of the nicely done art from the period. He even signs his work. But unfortunately, the paintings we were looking at were not dated. After entering the marketplace and changing hands a few times, it's easy to see way they might be mistaken for old works.

The point of this anecdote is that collectors — and dealers, too — really need to educate themselves when getting involved in a new field, especially when it's as hot as golf collecting and especially when so many golf antiques are now worth thousands of dollars. And that's what *Olmans' Guide to Golf Antiques* is all about. Mort and John share their vast knowledge and resources in this book; they show how to collect golf items, what to look for, and how to be a smart collector.

I'm not really a true golf collector, even though I've acquired three gold U.S. Open medals. (And not at auction, I'm proud to say). But I do enjoy the history and artwork of the game. And now that the Olmans have put together this informative guide, I'll be better prepared when considering future acquisitions.

Best of luck in becoming an informed collector!

Hale

Hale Irwin

INTRODUCTION

Since we began gathering information for our *Encyclopedia of Golf Collectibles* during the winter of 1983-84, a lot has happened to the hobby of collecting golf memorabilia. It has exploded!

What once was a lazy pastime shared by a somewhat disorganized conglomeration of golfers who enjoyed the history and nostalgia of golf's bygone eras has evolved into a substantial business. Perhaps we unwittingly had a part in the "coming-out" of this once docile activity.

Our Old Golf Shop was established in 1970 in Cincinnati as a side business when it became apparent that golfers wanted attractive golf lithographs to decorate their homes and offices. We commissioned an artist to paint a few subjects, including ones of Old Tom Morris and Allan Robertson — historic golf figures little known to the average golfer. Word spread about our activity and the prints with their informative descriptions began to sell.

About the same time, some American "golf nuts" formed the Golf Collectors Society. There had been earlier collectors dating back to the turn of the century and before — but there were so few they were hardly noticed. (The genesis of golf collecting is discussed in detail in Chapter Two of this book.) When the new society gathered for their first meeting about two dozen collectors gathered to share their golf interests.

What transpired was a chain reaction. The book collector told the club collector about all the fascinating old golf books just waiting to be discovered by a new generation of golf enthusiasts. And the man with the armful of clubs responded that he had a putter designed by the same Willie Park who wrote golf instruction books in the 1890s. And it turned out that the ball collector had a golf ball made of gutta percha that was popular when the Park putter was made. And so it went.

Finally these collectors had a means of sharing their knowledge and enthusiasm. The more they conversed and corresponded with each other, the more they became addicted to golf collecting.

The Old Golf Shop responded to this surge in interest by expanding its inventory to include more prints and antique golf clubs. Nineteenth century long-nose clubs acquired from St. Andrews, Scotland, were offered for only $200-250 — a steal compared to today's prices.

By 1980, the Old Golf Shop had grown from a sideline into a real business. Golf organizations wanted to use golf mementos for tournament prizes and golfers wanted to adorn the walls of their clubhouses with framed prints. Golf antiques and memorabilia were selling not only for their historical significance, but just because people found them attractive.

However, little research had been performed for the benefit of the collector. In 1968, *The Library of Golf* by Joe Murdoch was published, but other than libraries and book collectors, there was no great demand for Murdoch's labor of love. It took more than 14 years to sell the first and only printing of fewer than 4,000 copies. Now the demand greatly outnumbers the supply and the book routinely sells for an astounding $200-300.

By the mid-1980s, there was a noticeable yearning for information on all old golf objects. After several years of research, we released our *Encyclopedia of Golf Collectibles* at the 1985 PGA Merchandise Show in Orlando, Florida. We have been told that the book has become the "bible" of the hobby.

Our publisher had urged us to include values in our text. We balked at the idea, but finally yielded and provided some broad estimates, such as feather balls in the $1,000-2,000 range and long nose woods valued at $200-1,000. At the time, we were a little embarrassed to admit that a golf ball and club together might be worth as much as $3,000. Today that sum would be a bargain.

We think that through our first book we have had a hand in educating golfers and collectors about golf memorabilia. We listed the makers and artists. We pictured thousands of golf objects. We explained how products were made. Our intention was to share our resources and nurture the hobby.

In the seven years since the publication of our book, golf collecting has grown from a leisure pursuit of hobbyists to include a new type of collector: the speculator. Prized golf antiques now sell for tens of thousands of dollars and one-day golf auctions routinely bring in more than a half million dollars. These investors are largely responsible for causing once ordinary items — like Murdoch's book — to skyrocket in value.

The high prices attract considerable attention outside golf circles . . . the *Wall Street Journal*, *The New York Times*, *The Financial Times* and *Sports Illustrated* have noted the heightened activity.

As a result, our method of doing business has changed. The golf prints, gifts and tournament prizes we used to sell are now handled by a separate company called The Golf Shop Collection. This allows us to concentrate on educating new collectors and helping them and the seasoned collectors buy and sell golf antiques. We manage to do this without an extensive inventory or mail-order catalog. And for all that we seem to know, hardly a day goes by that we don't learn something new about golf history. And hardly a day goes by when we don't hear the woes of a novice collector "taken to the cleaners" by a disreputable dealer.

That is one of many reasons why we decided to write this book and share our knowledge. Compared to other established hobbies, such as stamps, ceramics and artwork, golf collecting is still in its infancy. While some objects depicted on these pages are worth hundreds or thousands of dollars to the ardent collector, there are many times more items that are inexpensive, readily available and entertaining to the average golfer. This means that you don't have to spend a lot of money to break into the hobby. In fact, you don't even have to be a collector to enjoy golf antiques.

The intent of this book is to help you become a smart, informed enthusiast who can appreciate golf artifacts to the utmost and savor the magnificent heritage of the game. Because there are more collectors and higher prices than just a few years ago, the smart collector must acquire not haphazardly, but should concentrate on a particular aspect of the hobby he or she finds interesting. Your goal should be to have fun and enjoy the wonderful hobby of golf antiques.

John M. Olman
Morton W. Olman

Cincinnati, Ohio
December, 1991

CHAPTER 1

ALL ABOUT COLLECTING

The diversity of golf-related items is what makes the hobby of golf antiques so fascinating. This wide range of collectibles has been enhanced mostly during the past century by the creativity of numerous craftsmen and artisans. They have produced a myriad of equipment and decorative items for those obsessed with the challenge and beauty associated with striking a small ball over acres of grassy terrain.

By focusing your efforts, it is possible to create a collection that you and those around you can enjoy. The beauty of collecting golf antiques is that your interests can be broad or specific. This book serves both needs, providing discussions of the primary aspects of the hobby, as well as introducing new ideas for specialization.

Most people, when discussing golf antiques, think of old hickory-shafted clubs for hanging on the wall. But that is just the beginning. There is an abundance of items with golf motifs appropriate for display in every room in the house: paintings, prints and bronzes for the living room; spoons, ceramics and tea services for the dining room; spice tins for the kitchen; lamps and inkwells for the study; decanters and cocktail picks for the bar; windup toys and jigsaw puzzles for the playroom; and books, vintage films, phonograph records and stereoscopes for the den. For the bedroom, there are vintage golf costumes and turn-of-the-century high-top golf shoes, along with personal accessories such as gold buttons, silver hatpins and engraved pocket watches. And for the house itself, there are stained-glass windows, rugs and weather vanes, not to mention sundials and practice devices for the yard. There even are badges and ornaments for the car.

Remember that very few aspects of golf collecting can be mastered; it's a huge realm. Choose an area or aspect that intrigues you. Then study, learn, share and enjoy.

TYPES OF COLLECTORS

There are five primary types of individuals interested in golf antiques: hobbyist, historian, decorator, accumulator and investor. Most have a sincere affection for the game, either as enthusiastic golfers or mere fans. Devout collectors usually are a blend of several categories, whereas any enthusiastic golfer with a few mementos on display could be classified as a decorator.

HOBBYIST

Most collectors of golf memorabilia do so for the enjoyment and camaraderie derived from pursuing the hobby. They are driven by the thrill of the hunt, never knowing when they might unearth a treasure. Some pursue their interests on a daily basis, while others only may allocate a small part of their leisure time to the hobby.

HISTORIAN

It is possible to follow the evolution of golf, with its personalities, equipment and antiquities, and not have an extensive collection of artifacts. Most historians are content to relish golf's glorious past through the printed page. Consequently, most historians have a collection of books and magazines.

1-1 *Signs, books, artwork, ceramics, bronzes, clubs, balls, sheet music, toys, silver — all related to golf and prized by collectors.*

DECORATOR

Often golfers will acquire golf artifacts, such as clubs or artwork, to adorn the walls of a home, office or clubhouse. Although a dedicated hobbyist's primary motivation usually is to exhibit his collection, true golf decorators often have little interest in the historical significance of a collectible. They merely like the game and want to be reminded of it away from the course.

ACCUMULATOR

The accumulator prefers quantity over quality and rarely passes a golf collectible without buying it. Try not to be an accumulator. If you are, consider setting some well-defined collecting goals. In the long run, you'll have more fun and your family and friends will find you and your hobby much more interesting.

INVESTOR

As the hobby of golf collecting has become more popular during the last 20 years, prices have escalated. This invariably has attracted individuals whose primary intention is to profit by the increased demand for golf antiques. True collectors — while always pleased to get a bargain — do not base their purchases solely on price. Their primary interest is in the significance of an object and not what its value may be in the future. However, investors — including dealers and speculators — buy solely for the purpose of reselling.

Hobbyists and decorators occasionally find themselves "investing" in order to justify an acquisition. That's fine. But if someone buys on speculation, with no intention of dealing — especially high-priced items — the consequences can be disastrous should the market take a downward slide.

COLLECTING THEMES

ALL-AROUND

Perfect for the beginning collector. Starting with some clubs, artwork, books and decorative items, all-around collectors usually end up specializing in one of the following themes.

MAJOR CATEGORY

Some collectors dedicate their efforts to one type of collectible, such as clubs, balls, books or ceramics. Each of the major categories is described in detail in the following chapters.

SUB-SPECIALTY

Because it's impossible to learn everything about any of the major categories, many collectors narrow their approach. Club collectors, for example, may specialize in smooth-face irons or patent clubs and art collectors may concentrate on humorous prints.

1-2 *For collectors who prefer quality over quantity, consider these rare golf books:* The Golfers Manual *(1857)*, Golfiana *(1833)*, A Few Rambling Remarks on Golf *(1862)*, Gymnastics, Golf and Curling *(1866) and* The Goff *(3rd edition, 1793). Varying in length from eight to 96 pages, this small collection is valued at more than $50,000.*

PERSONALITY

Sometimes it's fun to pick a famous golfer or group of golfers and seek related memorabilia. Historic figures from the past include Old Tom Morris, Harry Vardon, Francis Ouimet, Walter Hagen and Bobby Jones. Modern heroes include Ben Hogan, Sam Snead, Arnold Palmer and Jack Nicklaus. Nostalgic photos, books, autographs and equipment are fun to collect and display.

EVENT

A prominent golf tournament can be a collecting theme. The memorabilia associated with the Grand Slam events — The Masters, U.S. and British Opens and PGA — is endless. There are programs, books, admission badges, scorecards and a multitude of items pertaining to past champions.

EVOLUTION

Nowhere is the evolution of golf better portrayed than in the antique equipment available to the collector. From the long nose woods and feather balls of the 18th century to the steel shafts and rubber core balls of this 20th century, the changes in equipment provide a never-ending source of fascination. Many aspects of evolution also are exhibited in artwork and books.

TERRITORIAL

Territorial collections deal with the history of a golf locale, ranging from an individual golf club to an entire city, region or country. This type of collecting has contributed to the publication of hundreds of club histories, many of which provide revealing accounts of old-time golf from the grass roots level.

CROSS-COLLECTING

It is possible for golf collecting to overlap other disciplines. Collectors of stamps, art, silver, toys and other broad-ranged items sometimes begin to acquire similar items without a golf motif. Conversely, collectors in other fields might cross over into golf collecting.

MODERN COLLECTIBLES

Most top-notch golf antiques currently available are dated pre-World War II, and this trend will probably continue. However, it is questionable if many golf products of recent times will become future rarities. Because of the mass-produced nature of modern golf equipment, the short-lived oddities will no doubt be of most interest a century from now. (Maybe you shouldn't have given those fiberglass-shafted clubs to the thrift shop!) Although some classic steel-shafted clubs from the 1950s and '60s are already collectible, it is likely that the current proliferation of woods with metal and composition heads will cause persimmon-headed clubs to become a rarity in the not-to-distant future. In the non-equipment area, good books have the ability to maintain interest for generations and, perhaps golf videos may become classics.

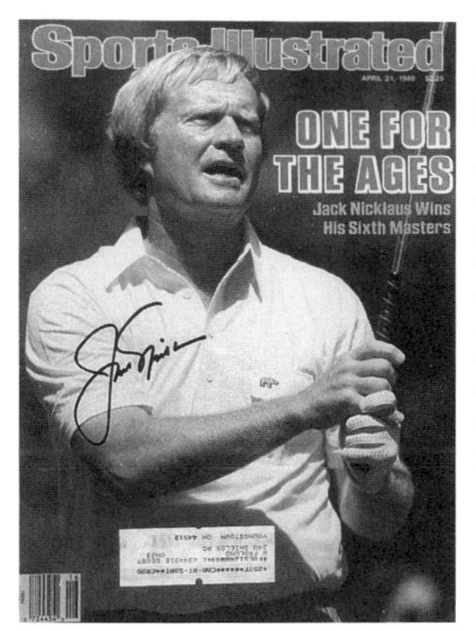

1-3 *Which of today's golf items will be sought by future generations of golf collectors? Probably anything having to do with Jack Nicklaus.*

COLLECTING TIPS

■ The novice collector should make an effort to learn about the evolution of golf and the related artifacts. Before making any substantial purchases, review this book and study some of the references listed in Appendix B (see page 253). Talk to other collectors and dealers and proceed cautiously into the hobby.

■ Don't take up golf collecting as an investment, unless you can risk a loss. Buy items because you enjoy them. At the same time, study the market and get a feel for fair prices. Make your purchases accordingly and if they appreciate in value, pat yourself on the back and consider trading up for better examples.

CHAPTER 2

History of Golf Collecting

Mr. Falconer had no idea what he was starting back in the 1790s when he began collecting golf clubs.

According to the 1793 edition of *The Goff* — the third edition of the first book entirely devoted to the game of golf — this Scotsman had "a greater collection of golf clubs than any person ever possessed; they amounted to several hundreds."

During the nearly 200 years since the revelation of Mr. Falconer's collection, thousands of enthusiasts have joined the ranks. Although Mr. Falconer may have been the "Father of Golf Collecting," his activities are insignificant compared to the pioneers of golf collecting who made their mark during the first half of the 20th century.

If a golf collecting hall of fame were created, the first group of prestigious inductees undoubtedly would include Harry B. Wood and C.B. Clapcott of Great Britain, and Alexander Findlay, Otto Probst, Jack Level and O.M. Leland from the United States. These men shared their zeal for golf history and inspired countless others to cherish the equipment, literature, and artwork of the historic game of golf. Their enthusiasm ultimately led to the formation of the Golf Collectors Society by a group of Americans in 1970 and a worldwide fascination with golf artifacts of all kinds.

Once a neglected facet of the game, articles relating to golf history and collectibles now are regularly published in major golf magazines. And every time there is a notable sale of golf memorabilia, it generates media attention. Golf collecting has definitely come a long way.

Now if we just knew where Mr. Falconer hid all of those 18th-century golf clubs.

THE FIRST COLLECTOR

> Dr JAMES MACKENZIE, phyſician in Edinburgh, is the author of the above ſtanza.—By *Neſtor* we are to underſtand Mr FALCONER of Feſdo, a moſt accompliſhed gentleman. The firſt of theſe lines is not to be taken in a ſtrictly literal ſenſe; the Doctor only means a wiſh that his friend might arrive at that advanced period of human life in full poſſeſſion of all his faculties. Mr FALCONER delighted much in the game of Goff; and was ſuch an adept in it, that he could play off from the Tee, at a full ſtroke, twelve ſucceſſive balls, and lay every one of them within the ſpace of two or three club-lengths from one another: He had, perhaps, a greater collection of clubs than any perſon ever poſſeſſed; they amounted to ſeveral hundreds.

2-1 *Printed in 1793, this paragraph is a footnote to a stanza written by a Dr. Mackenzie in the third edition of* The Goff. *It is the first recorded mention of a golf collector: Mr. Falconer. Falconer apparently was an accomplished golfer in addition to possessing several hundred golf clubs.*

19th-CENTURY REFERENCES

After Mr. Falconer established himself in the 1790s as the first golf collector, there only were a few recorded mentions of golf collecting during the 19th century.

Admiral Drinkwater Bethune, a prominent member of the Royal and Ancient Golf Club (R & A), suggested in 1864 that the club acquire and maintain items of historical relevance. The next mention of a collection in St. Andrews was in 1886, when an advertisement on the cover of a golf annual mentioned that the Union Club had opened a museum. Little is known about either endeavor, but since the members of the Union Club also were affiliated with the R & A and the two clubs merged in 1877, whatever existed in either collection most likely became the basis of the now substantial collection of the R & A.

The next notable reference to golf collecting was an 1891 advertisement in the British magazine *Golf* that offered "a very exhaustive collection" of "Golf Curiosities for Sale." Another advertisement, appearing in 1896, offered 10 bound volumes of *Golf* magazine for sale, complete with the original paper covers "which show the evolution of the game" through the old advertisements. (Even though these volumes only covered the period from 1890 to 1895, it is amusing

William Innes. Portrait of.
J. & W. VOKINS,
Dealers in Drawings
and Works of Art.
May 29th 1896. (Christie's)
14 & 16, G.T PORTLAND STREET, W.
ALSO
10, KING STREET, ST JAMES'S, S.W.
LONDON.

2-2 *Regular auctions of golf memorabilia began in the early 1980s. However, the earliest know auction of a golf item was at Christie's in Great Britain in 1896, when a mezzotint engraving of William Innes, "The Blackheath Golfer," sold for 26 guineas — a rather substantial amount considering that a small house could be purchased for 100 guineas. This label on the back of the framed print probably was inscribed by the successful bidder.*

to note that the seller was very aware of the radical changes that were taking place in the manufacture of golf equipment.)

There also were two classified advertisements placed in 1899 seeking to buy old golf curiosities. One listed "Museum" as a reply. The other was placed by "T.W" of London, probably an aggressive collector since the words "LIBERAL PRICE GIVEN" were emphasized.

Golfing Curiosities for Sale.

FOR SALE.—A valuable and extensive collection of GOLFING SUBJECTS, consisting of pictures, engravings, books, songs, pamphlets, clubs, &c., &c., the whole forming a very exhaustive collection.—For particulars, apply to the Editor of GOLF.

1891

For Sale.

TO GOLF BOOK COLLECTORS AND SECRETARIES OF CLUBS.

FOR SALE.—Fine Set of GOLF in ten volumes, handsomely bound, red and green leather back, with gilt title. Advertisements (which show the evolution of the game) bound up with each volume. Early volumes out of print. The highest offer above seven guineas will be accepted.—Apply, DELTA, care of Editor, GOLF, 80, Chancery Lane, London, W.C.

1896

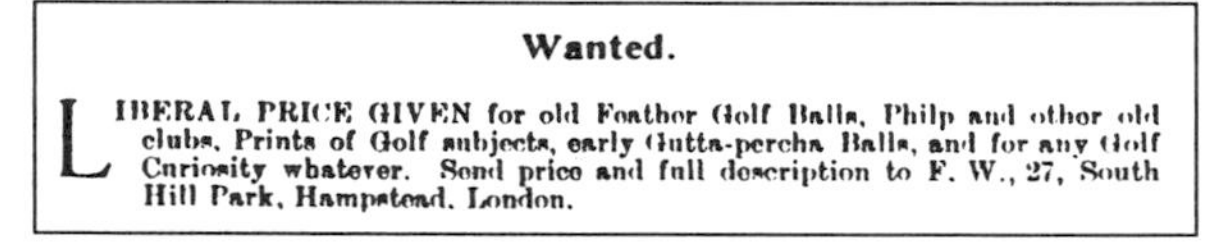

Wanted.

LIBERAL PRICE GIVEN for old Feather Golf Balls, Philp and other old clubs, Prints of Golf subjects, early Gutta-percha Balls, and for any Golf Curiosity whatever. Send price and full description to F. W., 27, South Hill Park, Hampstead, London.

1899

2-3 *These ads from the British magazine* Golf *document collecting activity in the late 19th century. It's amusing to note that the one 1899 ad specified Philp clubs in particular. More than 90 years later, clubs made by Philp remain in great demand.*

GOLF RELICS ON DISPLAY

The most noteworthy display of golf artifacts ever assembled was featured at the 1901 Glasgow International Exhibition, an event that showcased the culture and products of Scotland. The golf exhibit was organized by The Reverend John Kerr, author of the famous *Golf Book of East Lothian* and hundreds of articles on golf. Kerr, who established a substantial collection himself, was so successful in obtaining relics and memorabilia from golf clubs and private individuals that the organizers were concerned that there might not be sufficient display space.

The exhibit depicted all aspects of golf history, from old illustrated tiles to clubs used by royalty. Some of the outstanding items were: the collection of clubs from the Troon Golf Club, thought to be the oldest set of clubs in existence; several silver clubs used ceremonially by the Honourable Company of Golfers as early as 1744; the famous portrait of "The Golfer" done by Charles Lees in 1847; a rare, unused set of clubs crafted by the incomparable Hugh Philp and loaned by noted amateur John Laidlay; a 100-year-old putter from Willie Park Jr. that was use by his father in all of his matches. The most admired group of artifacts was presented by the legendary Old Tom Morris: the famous silver belt awarded to Young Tom after his three successive Open championship victories, Young Tom's putter, clubs used by early professionals Allan Robertson and David Strath, and Old Tom's favorite putter.

PROMINENT EARLY COLLECTORS

Even after the tremendous response to the Glasgow Exhibition, the private golf collector was still a rarity. Most of the displays of historic items belonged to golf clubs. One such private exhibit was assembled by Harry B. Wood, a wealthy chemical manufacturer and merchant from Manchester, England.

It is thought that Wood, the first prominent private collector, started collecting golf artifacts in the early 1890s, perhaps as a result of his friendship with Old Tom Morris and other notable golf personalities from St. Andrews. He wrote about the pleasures of collecting in a series of articles for *Golf Illustrated* in 1908. (These articles and other details about his collection were published in 1910 in his classic *Golfing Curios and "The Like"*.)

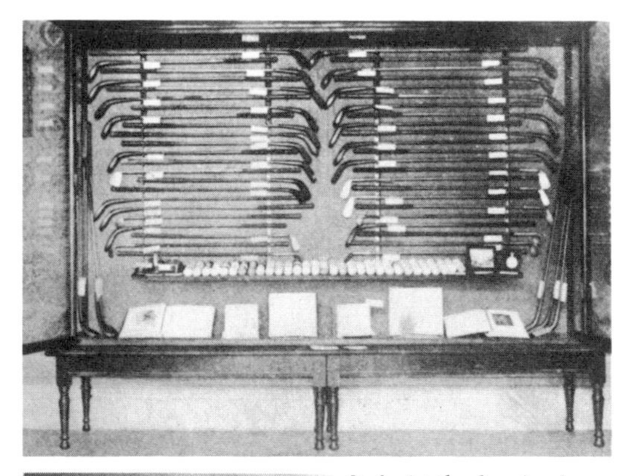

2-4 *At the beginning of the 20th century, Harry B. Wood (left), of Manchester, England, was the first serious collector of golf artifacts. He wrote several articles and a book —* Golfing Curios and "The Like" *— about his famous collection, shown above, circa 1908.*

The Harry B. Wood Collection — books, balls, clubs and other artifacts — was displayed in a large glass case at the North Manchester Golf Club. After Wood's death in 1913, the collection remained at the club. When Wood's son died in 1940, the club assumed ownership, displaying it until 1985 when it was sold. The collection since has been split up and sold to collectors throughout the world.

Why would the club members dispose of such an exquisite collection? With the increasing values of golf antiques, the club was faced with a tremendous security risk. Insurance coverage cost thousands of pounds and the club was going to have to install a sophisticated security system. The membership decided to keep several items from the collection as a small tribute to Wood and to dispose of the remainder.

Although Wood undoubtedly was the most visible collector of all types of golf artifacts during the first part of the century, another Englishman, C.B. Clapcott, established himself as the first eminent collector of golf books. Most of his collection was acquired during the 1920s and 1930s. Clapcott was a student of golf history; he researched the archives of the oldest golf societies and wrote numerous papers on the subject, many of which were published for the first time in *The Clapcott Papers*, a limited edition volume compiled by Alastair Johnston in 1985.

At the turn-of-the-century, Americans found the game of golf itself a novelty, so interest in artifacts was slow to build. One of the first American collectors was Max H. Behr, who declared his interest in a 1906 letter to *Golf Illustrated* in London inquiring about the availability of early golf books. Behr was 24 years old and about to become

2-5 *The legendary Otto Probst, shown in 1965 at 75 years of age, amid his prolific golf collection.*

a fixture in the golfing fraternity. The Yale graduate was a fine golfer — he was runner-up in the 1908 U.S. Amateur — and his fondness for golf literature led to his editorship of *Golf* magazine in New York and later the American version of *Golf Illustrated.* He gave up editing after the death of his wife in 1918 and moved to California where he began to design golf courses and continued his golf reporting. Behr died in Los Angeles in 1955, but not before donating some of his prized possessions to the U.S. Golf Association and the R & A. The remainder of his collection eventually found its way into the hands of a golf book collector in the late 1970s.

One of the most prolific collectors was Colonel R. Otto Probst, an engineer from South Bend, Indiana. Probst began his insatiable quest for golf books and other memorabilia in 1923. One of his major acquisitions was the impressive Clapcott library, which he bought from a London book dealer in 1956 for £350. (Details of the sale are revealed in *C. B. Clapcott And His Golf Library*. See page 257.) Probst had a network of scouts who continually supplied him with merchandise. He also solicited merchandise through magazine advertisements, using the pseudonyms "A.L. Wolfe" and "AagendaA Golf Library." In the 1960s he claimed to have the world's

OLD BOOKS ON GOLF.

To the Editor of GOLF ILLUSTRATED.

SIR,—Could you give me any information in regard to books on golf? What were some of the early ones, and where could I get them? I am trying to make a collection, but it is hard to find anyone up in this matter in this country. I am a subscriber to your estimable paper, which I read with the greatest interest every week. Your kindness in this matter will be very much appreciated.

I am, Sir, etc.,

MAX H. BEHR.

Denobehr, Far Hills, New Jersey, U.S.A., June 19th.

[We published a pretty full Bibliography of Golf in chronological order in our issue of Jan. 3rd, 1902. See also p. 45 of this issue.—ED.]

2-6 *Max Behr, thought to be the first American golf collector, wrote this letter in 1906 to* Golf Illustrated *magazine in London. He developed a fine library and became an established golf writer and golf course architect. Many of the books collected by Behr are now part of the USGA Library in Far Hills, New Jersey — in the same town where he began collecting more than 80 years ago. (Behr moved from New Jersey in 1918 and the USGA relocated there in 1970, making the Far Hills connection a bizarre coincidence.)*

largest collection of golf articles. The PGA of America, impressed by the scope of the Probst collection, purchased it in 1973 and now prominently features the superb library at the PGA/World Golf Hall of Fame. Probst died in 1986 at the age of 96.

Although Probst appeared to buy all the available golf antiques during the middle of this century, he actually had some competition. One of the other collectors was Jack Level from Elmhurst, Long Island, New York. He, too, enjoyed golf books, but had an even greater admiration for golf art and antique equipment. Unlike Probst, who solicited most of his items through the mail, Level loved to rummage through secondhand bookstores and junk shops looking for golf antiquities.

In the 1940s, when he realized that his collection was reaching unmanageable proportions, Level established himself as the first dealer in the hobby. Operating under the name of Golf Book Service from his cramped apartment, the entrepreneur printed price lists — his long-standing price for a long-nose wood or feather ball was $75. He even assembled a 2,500-item golf bibliography, which was never published.

2-7 *Although golf collecting was not an organized hobby prior to the 1970 founding of the Golf Collectors Society, enthusiasts managed to locate each other and correspond. Who knows what rarity prominent collectors Bob Smith and O.M. Leland might have been sharing in this envelope postmarked 1945.*

2-8 *Alexander H. Findlay, also known as Alex or A.H., emigrated to the United States from Scotland in 1887. He was instrumental in introducing golf to thousands through his fine play, by laying out hundreds of golf courses and his business associations with Wright & Ditson, the sporting goods manufacturer, and Wanamaker's Department Stores. Findlay, shown here in 1939, had a fine collection of golf relics which he proudly exhibited during his many travels.*

Other prominent early collectors include Scotsman Alexander H. Findlay, considered to be one of the "fathers of golf" in America; O.M. Leland, former Dean of Engineering at the University of Minnesota, who donated his extensive library to the USGA in 1958 to ensure that Golf House would have copies of the classics; Dr. Robert J. Smith, whose 40-year collection of books and periodicals was privately sold in 1978; Ralph W. Miller, a prominent figure in California golf, whose fine library and collectibles were purchased by the City of Industry, California, in 1976 to form the first publicly owned golf museum (see page 31); John W. Fischer, a former U.S. Amateur Champion and Walker Cup player, who began collecting golf art in

Title	Price
CLARK, ROBERT. Golf: A Royal and Ancient Game	5.00
CLARK and MOTTRAM. Common Sense Golf	3.00
COLLETT, GLENNA. Golf for Young Players	2.50
COLLETT, GLENNA. Ladies in the Rough	2.50
COMPSTON, ARCHIE and ANDERSON, STANLEY. Love on Fairway	3.00
COLT, HILTON. Golfer's Pocket Tip Book	1.50
COLT and ALLISON. Some Essays on Golf Course Architecture	3.00
COMPSON and LONGHURST. Go Golfing	3.00
CORTISSOZ, ROYAL. Nine Holes of Golf	3.00
COTTON, HENRY. Golf	3.50
CROMBIE, CHARLES. Rules of Golf	
CROOME. Technique of Golf	
CROWELL'S HANDY INFOR. SERIES. H[illegible] Play Golf	3.00

2-9 ***Posing with an impressive grouping of rare feather balls is Jack Level, a prominent collector who became the first dealer in golf memorabilia when he set up his Golf Book Service in the 1940s out of his New York City apartment. An excerpt from his 1943 brochure (above) shows some astonishingly low prices for books that now sell for hundreds of dollars.***

the 1940s; Bert Heizmann, a collector/ accumulator extraordinaire, who served the USGA and its museum committee for more than three decades; and Laurie Auchterlonie who, through his family and business connections in St. Andrews, had access to a wealth of golf artifacts.

It is interesting that, other than Auchterlonie who served as Honorary Professional to the R & A from 1964 until his death in 1987,there were no prominent British golf collectors from the Clapcott era until the 1970s. This apparent lack of interest perhaps can be traced to the fact that so many items of historical significance were displayed in clubhouses that they were taken for granted. The Johnny-come-lately Americans, however, were fascinated by the centuries-old heritage of the game and eager to learn more about it. This trend continues today as the majority of the collecting activity centers around American interest in the hobby.

Current golf hobbyists marvel at the prominent early collectors and their vast collections. However, most of the pioneers were not as knowledgeable as their modern counterparts. Consequently, the premier collections today, while usually smaller in size, generally are far superior in quality and depth.

2-10 *Ben Crenshaw, professional golfer and collector/historian, enjoys a 1976 visit with Mort Olman, proprietor of the Old Golf Shop in Cincinnati. Founded in 1970, the shop was the first full-fledged business dedicated to the sale of golf collectibles and artwork.*

COLLECTING ORGANIZATIONS

Although Jack Level suggested that the collectors of golf memorabilia organize as a group in the 1960s, the actual creation of an organization — today's Golf Collectors Society — didn't materialize until 1970. Spearheading the effort were Joe Murdoch, a book collector and oil company advertising executive from suburban Philadelphia, and Bob Kuntz, club collector and industrial sales engineer from Dayton, Ohio. They began by mailing a letter to 63 collectors explaining their intention to create a means by which they could meet and share information about golf memorabilia. They received 27 responses and the Society became a reality. (Initially called the Golfiana Collectors Club, the current name was adopted one year later.)

2-11 *Joe Murdoch and Janet Seagle have been influential in nurturing the golf collecting hobby. Murdoch is the author of several books on golf literature and longtime editor of the* Golf Collectors Society Bulletin. *Seagle, the museum curator and librarian for the USGA for 17 years prior to her retirement in 1989, continues to be a generous source of information for collectors and anyone interested in golf history.*

The Golf Collectors Society, or GCS as it is commonly known, has grown steadily during the past two decades (with the exception of a period or two of organizational instability), and the membership is now approaching 2,000. *The Bulletin*, the group's bimonthly journal was produced for the first 15 years by Murdoch in his straightforward, homespun style. Articles about collectibles, history and events continue to be presented in an informal manner.

2-12 *Many clubs and associations have created museums and historic displays. Two of the first public displays were initiated by the James River Country Club and the USGA in the 1930s. The USGA Golf House Library, shown here in the 1950s at its former mid-town Manhattan location, is now the largest golf library in the world.* *(See page 31)*

The GCS highlight of the year is the three-day annual meeting held each fall in cities around the United States. The meeting features a huge indoor trade show, informative seminars, banquet and the popular Hickory Hacker Open golf tournament where vintage wood-shafted clubs are used.

Even though the GCS boasts of members from 16 countries, a British Golf Collectors Society was founded in 1987 to serve the needs of overseas collectors. There also are various trade fairs and regional get-togethers unaffiliated with either group.

CHAPTER 3

Buying Golf Antiques

The buying and selling of golf antiques has blossomed into a formidable business during the last decade. With several dozen dealers specializing in the field, enthusiasts no longer have to rely on collectors or antiques dealers. Like collectors, some dealers have a diverse range of collectibles, while others limit their scope to equipment, clubs, books or artwork. One major type of dealer doesn't even maintain an inventory — the firms that conduct golf memorabilia auctions sell items placed on consignment by individual owners.

This multitude of commercial ventures doesn't indicate that golf collectors no longer trade, barter, or deal among themselves. It just means that the hobby has developed to the point that it can support a number of full-time golf memorabilia dealers.

Where does this seemingly perpetual stream of golf antiques come from? If you examine the popularity of golf and its tremendous growth — especially from the 1890s until World War II— it is obvious that an enormous amount of equipment, accessories and artwork was created. Old golf memorabilia entering the marketplace comes from several sources: rediscovered material stored or abandoned years ago in attics and basements; golfers and collectors disposing of excess pieces or entire collections; and golf clubs and organizations selling historic items in order to raise funds.

WHERE TO BUY

Where and how you buy depends on convenience, your knowledge of the subject, relationships you may have with sellers and how much you are willing to spend.

If you are short on patience or time, the established golf dealers are your best bet. Tell them what your wants are, and they'll let you know when something comes up. But remember, you'll generally be at the dealer's mercy regarding price.

On the other hand, if patience is one of your virtues, wait until you find the desired article by chance or see it advertised in a dealer's exhibit or catalog. In this circumstance, you have a good chance of negotiating a better price.

If you crave adventure and like to browse, venture outside the golf realm. Flea markets, garage sales, classified ads and antiques shops all provide an opportunity for acquisitions. While the chance for a "steal" is more likely at one of these places than within the golf market, so is the likelihood that you'll see grossly-overpriced items. Some sellers routinely put a steep figure on golf collectibles because they've heard that anything related to golf is highly desirable. Although these vendors sometimes can dupe a novice collector or interior decorator, they rarely get any repeat business and are regarded as a nuisance to the hobby.

PRUDENT BUYING GUIDELINES

If you are considering a purchase from someone who is a dealer, auctioneer or other party in the business of selling old golf items, be sure to check some references to verify his or her credibility. Although most reputable sellers abide by the following guidelines, you should verify their terms before making any transactions.

You should be allowed to closely examine a particular item. If buying sight-unseen from a dealer, you should be allowed several days to inspect your purchase and to return it for a full refund if not satisfied. You also have the right to have a high-priced print or painting removed from its frame or to verify that a mechanical device functions properly.

A dealer should refund the purchase price on any item that was misrepresented with regard to age, authenticity or description. Ask for a detailed sales slip and notice of refund policy if you are unsure of the seller's reputation. An honorable businessperson will not hesitate to oblige. If buying at auction, verify the catalog description with the auctioneer prior to the sale.

If the seller refuses to abide by these terms or if you are buying an item "as-is" or dealing with a private individual, be prepared to take full responsibility for your acquisition.

COLLECTING TIPS

- **If you have to ship an article, make sure it is adequately protected in a strong carton. Consider using a custom packaging service for paintings and other fragile objects.**
- **When making a long distance transaction, always verify with the other party as to who is insuring the shipment. It's a good idea to check with your insurance agent to verify what kind of transit coverage you already may have.**

BUYING FROM A GOLF MEMORBILIA DEALER

Did you ever wonder how dealers replenish their supplies of golf collectibles?

They acquire their inventory from a myriad of sources. Most have a network of "pickers" or scouts who discover merchandise at flea markets, antiques sales and household auctions. These individuals realize that dealers have a better chance at getting top dollar for an item. The picker will, in effect, wholesale it to the specialist for a quick profit.

Dealers also obtain collectibles from collectors who are upgrading or selling off their collections, from estates of deceased collectors, at golf auctions and from other dealers.

Although many dealers in golf antiques are very successful, most are small businesses — with low overhead and few, if any, employees. The typical dealer extensively uses the mail and telephone, and relies on word-of-mouth to generate business. Some issue periodic catalogs, while others have such quick turnover of merchandise that a catalog is of little value.

COLLECTING TIPS

- **A listing of dealers and auction firms can be found in Appendix A (see page 243).**
- **When contacting a golf memorabilia dealer, be sure to include a self-addressed, stamped envelope (SASE) when corresponding or leave a phone message with instructions to return the telephone call collect. Since most golf memorabilia dealers are one- or two-person operations, don't expect the same level of service you'd receive at a fully staffed retail establishment.**

100. **GOLF A PICTORIAL HISTORY** The U.K. edn. of the above book both of which were published at the same time.The only difference being the title on the d/w and title page. £20
101. **HENRY COTTON'S GUIDE TO GOLF IN THE BRITISH ISLES** 1st edn.1959,Pp 124, illus.throughout in colour,green cl.4to.d/w.A coloured illustration of each course together with a plan. £18
102. **THANKS FOR THE GAME** the best of golf with Henry Cotton,1st edn.1980,Pp 176,illus.with photos. brown cl.d/w.Reminiscences,anecdotes,tips,biographical. £18
103. **THANKS FOR THE GAME** as above ex.lib.with library stamp on verso of title page and book plate removed from inside of upper cover. £12

BERNARD DARWIN

104. **GOLF COURSES OF THE BRITISH ISLES** 1st edn.1910,Pp 253,64 cold. and other illus.from the water colour paintings of Harry Rountree.green cl.4to.t.e.g.A good bright copy.There is a slight indentation on the upper cover and some occasional foxing. £400
105. **THE GAMES AFOOT!** Anthology of sport,games and open air,edited by Bernard Darwin.1st edn.1926, Pp (xv) 331, 4 chapters on golf by Sir Walter Simpson, H.G.Hutchinson,John L. Low and Bernard Darwin, green cl.Covers lightly mottled,light foxing,inscription on f.e.p. £16
106. **GREEN MEMORIES** 1st edn.1928, Pp 333, portrait frontispiece and 7 other pages of illus.Quarter morocco spine with original cloth covers.This copy has been respined and has gilt decoration and letter piece on spine. £150
107. **SECOND SHOTS** Casual talks about golf,1930,Pp (viii)178.Portrait frontispiece,light green cl. small 4to.v.g. £70
108. **SECOND SHOTS** Casual talks about golf as above,respined in cloth. £45
109. **SECOND SHOTS** as above complete with a d/w in protective covering.The d/w is worn at top & base £80
110. **OUT OF THE ROUGH** 1st edn.(1932) Pp 336,green cl.spine browned,upper and lower covers faded around edges.Contents good and clean. £55
111. **OUT OF THE ROUGH** 1st edn.(1932) as above,recovered in grey cl.with new end papers. £40
112. **PLAYING THE LIKE** 1st edn.1934,Pp (xii)247,brown cl.first few inches of top of joint very tender,otherwise a good copy,some light staining to base of lower cover. £70
113. **PLAYING THE LIKE** S.B.C.edn.1952,Pp(viii)247,blue cl.with the spine faded but lettering bright. £16
114. **BRITISH GOLF** 1st edn.1946,Pp 48, 8 cold.plates and 27 other illus.bright green illus.boards, d/w. a good copy. £16
115. **BRITISH GOLF** as above without d/w. £12
116. **BRITISH CLUBS** 1st edn.1943,Pp 48,8 cold.plates,20 other illus.blue illus.boards. £12
117. **AT ODD MOMENTS** Anthology selected by Bernard Darwin.1941,Pp 352,brown cl.small post 8vo.The book includes three golfing contributions by Darwin.The f.e.p.contains a note written by a relative of Bernard Darwin referring to the relationship and Darwin's contribution to the Oxford

3-1 *Dealers specializing in golf books generally sell by mail-order catalog. This excerpt showing Bernard Darwin titles is from a catalog produced by Grant Books of Worcestershire, England.*

BUYING AT A GOLF AUCTION

Auction sales comprised solely of golf memorabilia have been conducted since the early 1980s. They provide potential buyers with a large quantity of desirable artifacts — usually more than any individual dealer could assemble at once. The demand for golf collectibles is so great that the three major British firms of Sotheby's, Phillips and Christie's each conduct a golf auction near the British Open each July. (Auction firms are listed on pages 251 and 252.)

The primary goal of an auction firm and its auctioneer is to sell an article for the highest price possible. Although some auction houses sell items they own, most of the lots are consigned by private owners. It is the responsibility of the auction firm to publicize the sale, publish a descriptive catalog with estimated sale prices and provide sufficient viewing time prior to the sale. (Auctioneers are often very gracious and informative in assisting potential buyers, but it is important to remember that their first responsibility is to the seller. Therefore you should be careful not to disclose your detailed buying objectives.)

Golf auctions are efficiently and courteously run — selling about 100 lots per hour. After announcing the lot number and a brief description, the auctioneer verifies that the proper item is being displayed by a porter and promptly calls for bids. Because there is no superfluous commentary as to the beauty or quality of the lot, it is not unusual for an item to sell for thousands of dollars in 20 seconds or less.

"HIDDEN COSTS"

Each of the firms presently conducting golf auctions in the United States and Great Britain charges a buyer's premium of 10% on top of the successful bid. (The winning bid is known as the hammer price. So when referring to an auction sales price, it is important to clarify whether the premium has been included. It can be a substantial hidden cost.) There are also sales taxes that must be paid, except for licensed dealers buying for resale.

Successful bidders at the British auctions are charged Value Added Tax (VAT) of 17.5% on the amount of the buyer's premium only. For Americans buying in Britain, there may be import duties of at least 7% on certain items, plus packing and shipping costs.

These fees can add 20% to 30% to the original hammer price, so proper budgeting should be done prior to bidding.

RESERVES

A reserve is a sum agreed upon between the auctioneer and the seller. It designates the minimum hammer price that the seller will accept for his consignment. If the bidding does not reach the reserve, the item does not sell and is returned to the seller. (Although the bidders are not privy to the amount of the reserve, some locales have laws requiring that the use of reserves be announced.) Since the seller is charged a handling fee whether his item sells or not, it behooves him to set a realistic reserve.

While the use of reserves protects the seller from having to accept a low price, it can keep a buyer from getting a bargain. When the bidding begins, the auctioneer can "bid the reserve" — that is, he can accept an imaginary bid to compete against the bidders in the saleroom. Because the auctioneer is not required to acknowledge that he is bidding the reserve, he often tries to increase the competitive atmosphere in the room my making it appear as if another person is placing the bid. This is referred to as taking bids "off the wall."

This can result in a price being run up with only one person bidding. For example, an item receives an opening bid from the floor of $200. The auctioneer, having a reserve in his ledger book of $400, announces a bid of $250. The bidder nods a bid of $300 and the auctioneer responds $350. Finally, when the bidder goes to $400, the gavel falls. The bidder unknowingly ends up paying twice his original bid, when nobody else expressed any interest in the item.

If this hypothetical sale had been conducted as an absolute auction (with no reserves), the original $200 bid would have prevailed. Auction buyers currently are lobbying for regulations requiring the announcement of reserve amounts so that bidders will be aware of whether they are competing on the open market.

Until an official "prices realized" summary becomes available after the sale, spectators do not know which items did not meet their reserves. Some golf auctions with high reserves have had as much as 22% of the lots go unsold.

ABSENTEE BIDDING

Most auction catalogs contain an absentee bid form that can be submitted through the mail prior to the sale. By completing the form and making a "good faith" deposit, if required, you can authorize the auctioneer to execute bids on your behalf in standard bidding increments up to the maximum amount indicated. If you specify "plus 1" after your price, and the bidding sequence places your maximum figure with another bidder, the auctioneer will enter your bid one increment higher than specified. Bids also can be sent by fax, left in person or, if you are a good customer, phoned in.

Although this process appears to be fair, there are no referees or slow-motion instant replay at an auction. This gives an unscrupulous auctioneer free rein with an absentee bid. Remembering that his primary obligation is to get the highest possible price for the consignor, consider this scenario: you submit an absentee bid of $1,000 for a particular lot that has an unpublished reserve of $600. Assuming there are no other interested bidders, a fast-talking auctioneer can open the bidding at $600, take a few

WHAT IS A PROVENANCE?

A provenance is the documentation of previous ownership of an item — a pedigree of sorts. Every exceptional one-of-a-kind artifact should have a description and statement of authenticity prepared by a respected authority on the subject or by the original owner. This will serve to enhance the value of the item and provide future owners with valuable details.

Articles that were owned by a famous person or that have extraordinary historical significance also should be properly documented (see photo 4-5). Lack of a credible provenance can affect the significance of an item, although sometimes a weak provenance is better than none at all. For instance, a letter from an owner stating the exact circumstances under which he received a golf club from Walter Hagen in 1935 would lend some authenticity to an otherwise ordinary golf club.

bids "off the wall" and hammer it down to you for $900. When you call for the results and find that you won the item for $100 less than your limit, you'll think the auctioneer did you a favor, when in reality, he swindled you out of $300 — in an unethical manner that seldom comes to the attention of legal authorities.

Keep this scenario in mind when submitting an absentee bid. If you are bidding on a high-priced lot, by all means have a personal representative at the auction. The best method is to hire a knowledgeable dealer to act on your behalf. This way, he can examine the item to make sure it is properly cataloged. (Although some catalog descriptions are very detailed, others are purposely vague in an attempt to overlook a defect.) In addition to inspection and bidding, a dealer can arrange for packing, shipping and customs clearing, if necessary.

AUCTION FEVER

Buying at auction can be fun and challenging, but it is imperative that you do ample research in advance, set spending limits and stick with them. Auction fever strikes when you succumb to the heat of battle and are coaxed over your limit by a skillful auctioneer.

COLLECTING TIP

■ Beware that auction prices are not true market values. When auction fever strikes, buyers sometimes greatly overpay for an item. This inflated price does not reflect a value on the open market, but rather an artificial value established by two bidders. Therefore, auction results should not be used as a sole guide to valuing golf collectibles.

MAKER: PAXTON, PETER
CLUB: PUTTER (1854)

USING THIS PUTTER, TOM MORRIS, SR. OF ST. ANDREWS WON THE OPEN CHAMPIONSHIP ON FOUR OCCASIONS. IN HIS TIME, HE WAS RECOGNIZED AS A GENIUS ON THE GOLF COURSE.

3-2 *Unscrupulous dealers are likely to make outrageous claims about an item they have for sale. The club given this description could not have been used by Old Tom Morris — it is left-handed and Morris was right-handed; it is dated 1854 but Peter Paxton, the maker, was not born until 1860; and furthermore, Morris won his British Open titles in the 1860s, whereas the club shown was made circa 1890. So whenever you come across a difficult-to-believe claim, ask for legitimate substantiation.*

MAIL AUCTIONS

In a mail auction, prospective buyers place bids through the mail, based on catalog descriptions. Items best suited for buying sight unseen traditionally have been stamps, coins, books anything that can be easily identified and graded according to condition. Because descriptions of clubs and other golf memorabilia are so subjective, it can be difficult for a buyer to know what he is actually bidding on.

Auctions typically last for several weeks and when the deadline arrives, the auction company compares the bids and awards the lot as if the bidders were present. For example, if two bids are received for an item at $50 and $100, the higher bidder would be charged $60 — one bidding increment higher than the underbidder.

If you participate in a mail auction, verify the credibility of the auctioneer and make sure that you have the option to return an item if you are not satisfied. Also make sure that items are properly packed and insured for shipping.

OTHER SOURCES

Some of the best sources for golf memorabilia are collectors. A common situation occurs when buying a large group of clubs, books, balls or other items — the buyer invariably ends up with duplicates of articles already owned. These items usually are offered for sale or trade at meetings of the Golf Collectors Society or other golf shows. A true collector is happy to rid himself of these excesses for reasonable prices and sometimes even will give articles away, just to help out a fellow collector.

Some collectors, however, are out to make a profit. They are known as "collector/dealers." Several have been known to inflate prices and take advantage of novice collectors, so anyone new to the hobby should do some checking on the various sources before making any substantial purchases.

Flea markets, antiques shows, antiques newspapers and word-of-mouth tips also may result in some great finds. Check the classified ads in your local paper for notices of garage sales and household auctions. You also may want to consult one of the weekly antiques journals for show dates and auction listings: *AntiqueWeek* (P.O. Box 90, Knightstown, Indiana 46148), *The Antique Trader* (P.O. Box 1050, Dubuque, Iowa 52004) or *Antiques Trade Gazette* (17 Whitcomb St., London, England WC2H 7PL).

3-3 *Sometimes golf collectibles can be found where you least expect to see one.* Kay's Edinburgh Portraits, *a two-volume set of engravings and biographies, was first published in 1838 and depicts Alexander McKellar, an avid golfer known as "The Cock of the Green."*

3-4 *All sorts of memorabilia show up at a major golf tournament. These reproductions of vintage photographs were offered for sale on the sidewalk during the 1990 British Open in St. Andrews.*

3-5 *Keep your eyes open for household auctions and garage sales. You never know where antique golf treasures might be hiding.*

SELLING GOLF ANTIQUES

By first understanding how to buy golf antiques, you can get a feel for the selling process. You can sell or trade with collectors or dealers and place items on consignment with auction firms or dealers. If you are philanthropic, you might consider donating unwanted collectibles to a golf club, organization, museum or historical society. (If you intend to take a tax deduction, be sure to get a written appraisal from a qualified source.)

In selecting a method for selling collectibles, you first must decide how much money you want and how quickly you want it. You should talk with a couple of selling sources and then make a deal. Do not shop prices ad nauseum — your unfavorable reputation will spread and nobody will want to deal with you. Be aware that auction firms compete for consignments. Judge them by their reputation and service, not by what they think your article might bring.

3-6 *There are several annual trade shows that feature golf collectibles. They are excellent places to browse, learn, buy and sell.*

SELLING TO A DEALER

Since there are no established "list prices" for golf artifacts, it's not easy for an individual to sell on the open market. When a dealer offers you $50 for an item, you know that he'll probably retail it for $80 to $100. He is entitled to a fair profit and because of his reputation and understanding of the marketplace, he has a much better chance of selling the item than you do. Often a dealer will offer you more than you could ever realize on your own.

The best reason for selling to a dealer is that you'll get your money right away. On the other hand, if you have expensive articles for sale, a consignment or commission arrangement might be a good idea. It may take longer to get your money, but you'll almost always get a better price.

SELLING AT AUCTION

As illustrated in the previous pages, golf auctions can be very profitable for the seller. The items are heavily promoted and are sold before a captive audience. But it also can be risky. The item could sell for a low price or might not even meet the reserve. And since golf auctions only are conducted a few times a year, the time between consignment and receipt of funds can take several months.

Auctioneers charge a selling fee of about 10% of the hammer price. The seller also will be charged for special handling, insurance and often photography and other preferential treatment. You may be able to negotiate the commission rate on a high-priced article — the publicity attained from selling a rare book such as *The Goff* or a $100,000 painting is well worth a fee adjustment to an auction firm.

CHAPTER 4

DISPLAY & CARE

Old golf artifacts are capable of providing endless hours of amusement to those interested in the rich heritage of the game. Objects can be viewed, handled, played with and studied. They can be displayed in the home for the benefit of friends and family or in public settings, such as a country club or restaurant.

But in order to maximize enjoyment and protect their integrity, the items must be properly presented and maintained. It has been found that virtually every material — wood, paper, leather, glass or metal — can be adversely affected by environmental conditions and improper handling. The worst culprits are extremes in temperature and humidity, dust, sunlight and dirty fingers. Acidic conditions, present in many storage envelopes and picture framing materials, will quickly shorten the life of old paper goods.

While some harmful effects are easily detectable, such as fading caused by the sun's ultraviolet rays, it may take years for other types of destruction to materialize. If collectibles are to be preserved for the enjoyment of future generations, it is the responsibility of current owners to exercise proper care. Remember that just because an item already may be 100 years old doesn't mean that it will remain stable for the next 100 years.

The following pages show that proper conservation techniques aren't necessarily expensive or difficult: a little knowledge and some common sense will go a long way in protecting the antiquities of golf.

DISPLAY

For the most part, collectors like to showcase their prized possessions. Fortunately, the majority of golf antiques are suited for wall hanging or tabletop display.

Specimen golf clubs can be individually wall-mounted on a plaque, while large collections are best placed on hooks or dowels that allow for easy access. Creative collectors often fabricate special racks or adapt antique umbrella stands and store fixtures for club displays.

Prints, paintings and ephemera often end up in a picture frame. Don't be discouraged if the framing cost far exceeds the value of the artifact; it's not unusual to spend $60 on a frame for a $10 magazine cover. Proper presentation can make a treasure out of an otherwise ordinary collectible.

4-1 *Restaurants decorated with golf themes vary from the Old Pro's Table, a popular Myrtle Beach (South Carolina) restaurant to a McDonald's franchise in North Andover, Massachusetts. Framed magazine covers and prints can create a pleasant atmosphere without a lot of expense.*

4-2 *Clothing stores often find that decorating with a golf theme can encourage sportswear sales. This 1950 display at Tripler's men's store in New York City was more authentic than most — it featured Lenox ceramics, long-nose woods and feather balls.*

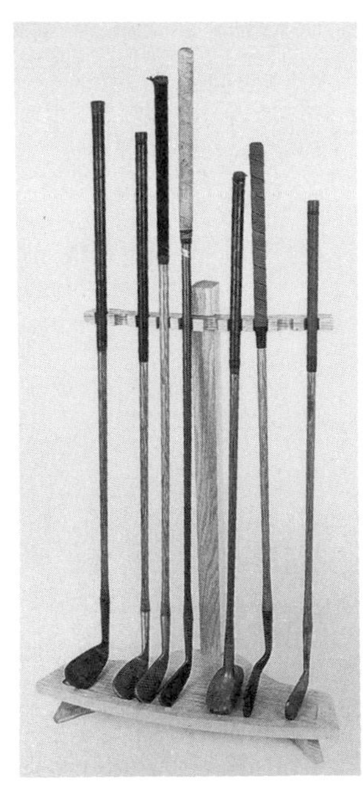

4-3 *Display techniques can be as simple as putting a pair of wooden dowel pegs (or tees) into the wall to support a club. More elaborate display racks can be custom made by a competent woodworker or purchased from a mail-order golf supply company. Antique store fixtures and household accessories, such as glass-enclosed umbrella cases, are perfect for showing off golf clubs. (Before buying a case with a lid, make sure that it is tall enough to hold golf clubs without interfering with the cover.*

COLLECTING TIPS

■ **Do not store photographs, postcards and other paper goods in plastic sleeves or paper folders commonly available from office supply houses. These products usually are not intended for long-term preservation. Instead, visit a photo supply store or stamp dealer and ask for "archival quality" materials. A mail-order catalog source for archival supplies is Light Impressions (439 Monroe Ave., Rochester, New York 14607).**

■ **Display cases for clubs and balls, as well as repair supplies, are available from several mail-order golf equipment suppliers:**

Austad's (800-843-6828)
Golf Day (800-669-8600)
The GolfWorks (800-848-8358)

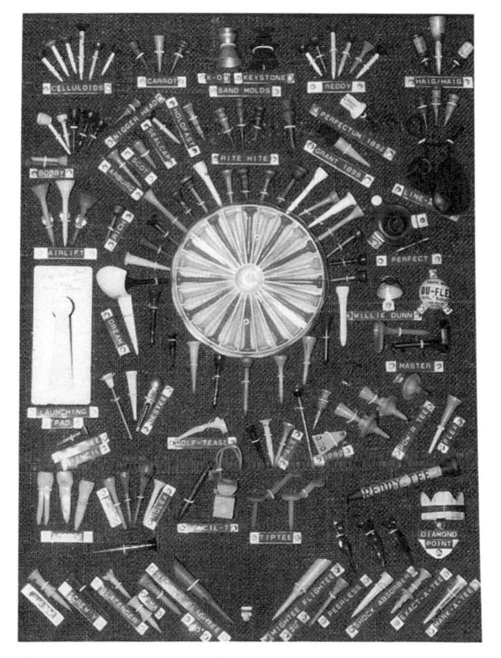

4-4 *An eye-catching display of golf tees. A creative and informative layout makes it easy to share a collection with others.*

PRESERVATION

The preservation of collectibles often is a function of how they are displayed. Any print or paper item should be framed to museum standards, using only acid-free mat board. The extra expense is worth it, even with a commonplace object. Since it may become valuable in the future, it's not worth jeopardizing its integrity by taking a preservation shortcut.

Most golf antiques — clubs, balls, books and items made of paper — will benefit by being kept in locations that are 67° to 73° Fahrenheit with a relative humidity of about 50%. Artifacts also should be kept out of intense sunlight, either direct or reflected. While it is not practical or desirable to keep a collection in total darkness, regular use of window shades and curtains can be extremely beneficial.

Another consideration is cleanliness. Always wash your hands before handling a special artifact. Skin oils can be so injurious that museum curators and conservators often wear special cotton gloves to ensure cleanliness. A periodic dusting of books and other collectibles also is recommended, since dust is abrasive and can harbor damaging fungus.

4-6 *Clamshell containers, custom made from acid-free materials, provide safe storage for rare and delicate paper goods.*

In addition to the physical aspects of preservation, there are other precautions that should be observed. It is wise to discuss the merits of insurance coverage with your agent. Such coverage is designed to supplement your homeowner's policy in the event that damage or theft occurs. A descriptive photographic, written or video inventory of your collection, along with purchase receipts, will go a long way in settling a claim. If you have an extensive collection, instructions as to its disposition upon your death should be included in your will.

4-5 *What better provenance to authenticate an 1830s feather ball than a letter from Old Tom Morris. Mounted together in a shadow box frame, these items together represent one of the ultimate golf antiques.*

COLLECTING TIPS

- **Resist the temptation to grip a rare old golf club and waggle it as you would a modern club. The sudden movement could snap a brittle shaft or cause a weak splice to come apart.**
- **When handling a delicate antique, always support it from the bottom. And never pick up or hold an old ceramic mug or pitcher by the handle — it could break.**

REPAIR

When considering a repair to a damaged collectible, you first must determine the extent of the damage, how the appearance or function has been affected, the potential value of the item and how much time and money you are willing to invest.

Professional restorers and conservators can fix all kinds of objects — damaged paintings and prints, dilapidated books, shattered ceramics, broken clubs — and can fabricate nearly any part that may be unsalvageable or missing. (A golf museum or local art museum should be able to provide referrals.) Simple repairs, however, can be done by the collector, such as regripping or rewhipping a golf club and fixing a paper tear with an archival-quality adhesive tape. (Never use cellophane tape on anything of value.)

4-7 *This stamp on a club shaft is not always a good sign. Laurie Auchterlonie, of St. Andrews, was highly respected for his ability to craft, finish and repair playable clubs during his many decades in the business. However, a number of golf historians feel that he over-restored many 19th-century clubs by excessively refinishing wood heads and replacing time-worn leather grips with new ones.*

4-8 *Creativity can help a repair along. Common hose clamps are great for holding a repair in place while glue sets.*

PUTTING WHIPPING ON A GOLF CLUB

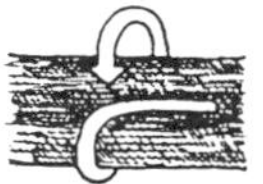

1) To start, place end of whipping at the narrow end of the shaft and begin winding toward the head. (It looks better if you start and finish on the underside of the shaft.)

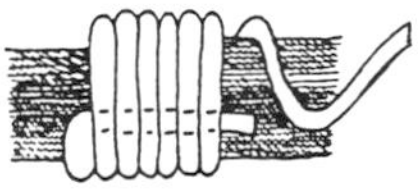

2) Continue winding tightly. After about $^3/_8$ inch, cut off excess "tail" with a knife or razor blade.

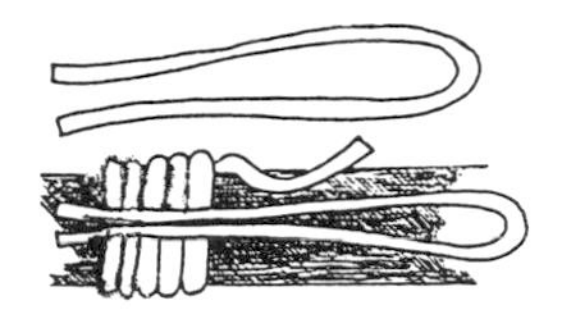

3) About $^1/_4$ inch from the stopping point, place a loop of extra whipping along the shaft and wrap right over it.

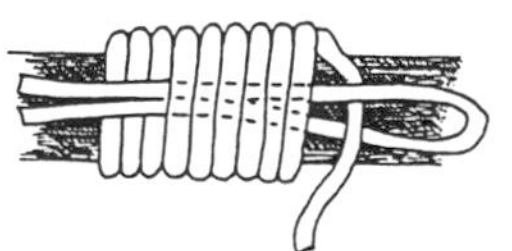

4) Wrap to the finishing point and cut off, leaving a few inches to work with. Place the loose end though the loop.

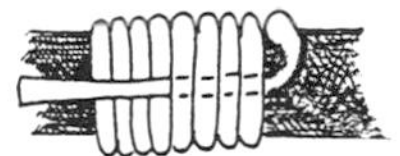

5) Pull ends of the loop to cause the whipping to pass under the previous winds. Give a firm tug of the whipping, making sure that there are no tangles and then trim any excess.

4-9 *Probably the most common golf club repair is to rewhip the neck of a wood. If the original whipping is not reusable, get some of the proper black linen — not nylon — whipping from a club repair shop and follow these instructions. This whipping technique also is good for securing an unraveled grip or a damaged hickory shaft.*

REFURBISHING GOLF CLUBS

It's a good idea to remove grime, rust and built-up finishes from old golf clubs to make them presentable. Often a good cleaning with a soapy rag is all they need. Remember that the charm of old golf clubs is that they look old and possess a patina that only comes with age. Clubs that have been over-restored to an as-new or better-than-new condition are not desirable to the collector. And unless you intend to play with your old clubs, repairs need only be cosmetic.

Most iron-headed clubs made prior to the 1920s were not chrome-plated and will rust. A careful cleaning, however, will make the makers' marks legible without harming the integrity of the clubs. Be aware that the use of a motorized wire wheel, sandblasting, naval jelly or other caustic products will give the heads an unnatural appearance and undoubtedly reduce their value.

The best cleaning method is to apply thin motor oil to the head and then judiciously wet sand with fine emery cloth. A wrap of masking tape around the end of the shaft will prevent it from being damaged. A stiff brush or old dental pick can be used to clean the face markings or maker's mark if desired. When finished, a light wiping with an oil soaked rag will prevent the rust from reappearing. A properly refurbished iron should exhibit an aged patina, rather than a highly polished finish.

Old, thick finishes on wooden heads and shafts may be lightly cleaned with fine steel wool moistened with a chemical wood refinisher (not stripper) obtainable from a hardware store. Never use sandpaper or other abrasive materials on wooden components. The refinisher will remove some of the old varnish and grime, but will leave enough of the old finish to protect the wood. If desired, a small amount of boiled linseed oil or tung oil can be rubbed into the finish.

If a leather grip is tattered, it may be reapplied or replaced with another old one. Loose pieces can be secured with whipping or a small dab of white glue. An old grip gives character to a club, so use a reproduction grip only as a last resort.

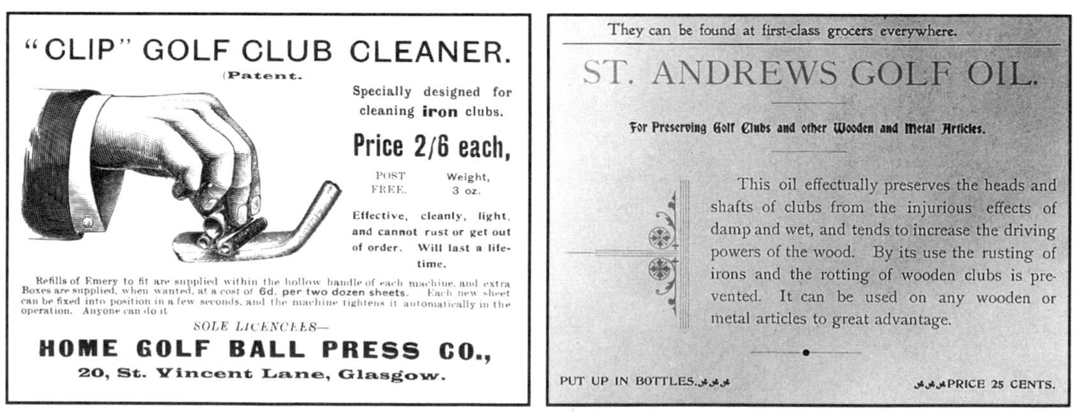

4-10 *The best technique for cleaning a rusty clubhead is the same one practiced when the club was new: a gentle rub with fine abrasive emery cloth. It's best to wet the cloth with a light motor oil to provide lubrication and eliminate scratches. Chemical rust removers may be effective in cleaning garden tools, but they will ruin the patina of an old iron by making it look "too good." And NEVER put polyurethane or other clear finish on a clubhead — a occasional wiping with an oil-dampened rag will keep rust from reforming. The Golf Oil advertised (above) was probably boiled linseed oil, still available in hardware stores and recommended for antique club care.*

CHAPTER 5

GOLF MUSEUMS

If you are captivated by the many rare golf antiques illustrated in this guide, but can't justify the expense of owning any, don't fret — visit a golf museum.

Golf clubs and associations have been acquiring old golf equipment, papers, books and other artifacts for display purposes since the Royal and Ancient Golf Club of St. Andrews (R & A) issued a request for golf-related items in 1864. These collections often have articles related to specific players or noteworthy historical events. Most of the smaller collections are on display at private clubs and are not available for public viewing without special arrangements.

There are, however, nine golf museums in North America and five others throughout the world that are open to the general public. Of the two major governing bodies of golf, the U.S. Golf Association (USGA) and the R & A, only the USGA opens its doors to outsiders. The R & A, though, does share its rarities with its neighbor, the recently opened British Golf Museum.

The least visited, and perhaps the most intriguing, area within the museums is the library. Used primarily by staff and outside researchers, the casual visitor rarely takes the time to look at the fascinating books and magazines devoted to golf. Although many of the volumes are under lock and key, the librarians and curators usually are willing to share the literary gems. Unlike most books at public libraries, the ones at golf libraries may not be borrowed.

The major golf museums and libraries, open to the public, are listed on the following pages. Because of funding through governing bodies and special fund-raising golf tournaments, most facilities do not charge admission.

UNITED STATES

American Golf Hall of Fame
P.O. Box 100
Foxburg Country Club
Foxburg, Pennsylvania 16036

Phone: 412-659-3196
Kitty Christy, Director
Hours: 8 a.m.-6 p.m. seven days a week

Although the idea for the American Golf Hall of Fame was conceived in 1954 by members of one of the nation's first golf clubs — the Foxburg Country Club, founded in 1887 — it was not until the 1960s that the concept materialized.

Club member Ken Christy was visiting Scotland and, while in St. Andrews, met clubmaker and historian Laurie Auchterlonie. The two shared thoughts on how a hall of fame and golf museum could become a reality.

Shortly thereafter, the project was underway. Auchterlonie was entrusted with the task of assembling a collection of golf memorabilia, and Christy enlisted the aid of newsman Lowell Thomas, architect Robert Trent Jones, pro Joe Kirkwood and other golf luminaries to function as a selection committee for the hall of fame. Finally in 1965, the museum opened on the second floor of Foxburg's log cabin-style clubhouse.

The hall of fame flourished for about a decade, then lost momentum as some of the directors died or went on to other projects. Although there has not been an induction ceremony since 1980, the display recently was rearranged to include space for the Tri-State PGA Hall of Fame. (Due to increased public awareness and financial resources, the PGA/World Golf Hall of Fame in Pinehurst, North Carolina, has assumed the role of golf's "official" hall of fame. See page 30.)

The museum, funded and maintained primarily by proceeds from an annual pro-am golf tournament, has displays pertaining to each of the inductees as well as a fine collection of antique golf clubs and other artifacts. The nine-hole golf course (open to guests) is situated in a rural setting overlooking the Allegheny River, about an hour-and-a-half drive northeast of Pittsburgh.

James River Country Club Golf Museum
1500 Country Club Road
Newport News, Virginia 23606

Phone: 804-595-3327
Weymouth Crumpler, Curator
Hours: 9 a.m.-9 p.m. Tuesday-Sunday

In the early 1930s, a group of golfers in Newport News, Virginia, approached shipbuilding magnate Archer M. Huntington to discuss plans to build a golf course overlooking the James River. The wealthy philanthropist replied, "I am not much of a golfer, but if you people are interested in museums, I will be glad to endow one for your clubhouse."

Not only did Huntington put up the money — as he already had done with a dozen other museums — he also enlisted John "Jock" Campbell, a Scotsman employed at his shipyard, to sail to the British Isles in 1932 to search for golf antiquities. Campbell purchased approximately 80 fine old clubs, including ones crafted during the feather ball era by such masters as Simon Cossar and Hugh Philp. He also acquired balls, books and artwork,

5-1 *John "Jock" Campbell spent several months in 1932 searching the British Isles for golf antiquities to form the nucleus of the James River Country Club Golf Museum in Newport News, Virginia. He served as curator until his death in 1936.*

all of which went on display in a special wing of the James River Country Club when the museum opened during the winter of 1932-33.

The James River collection has continued to grow, although the antique clubs acquired by Campbell are still the main attraction. Featured with the 18th-century Cossar putter are clubs made by each of the five generations of the McEwan family of clubmakers, the bag and clubs used by Harry Vardon in winning the 1900 U.S. Open and three clubs used by Bobby Jones (including a brassie used during his heyday from 1926 until 1930).

5-2 *The Ralph Miller Golf Library/Museum near Los Angeles is unique because it is the only major golf collection owned by a municipality.*

Ralph W. Miller Golf Library/ Museum
P.O. Box 3287
One Industry Hills Parkway
City of Industry, California 91744

Phone: 818-854-2354
Marge Dewey, Manager
Saundra Sheffer, Librarian
Hours: 8:30 a.m.-5 p.m. seven days a week

Situated in a uniquely configured business/industrial/recreational area in the San Gabriel Valley, just east of Los Angeles, is one of the finest golf libraries in the world. The Ralph W. Miller Golf Library/Museum is part of the Industry Hills Recreation and Conference Center, an elaborate complex owned and operated by the City of Industry.

Thousands of books owned by the late Ralph Miller make up the nucleus of the collection. Miller, a prominent figure in Southern California golf until his death in 1974, was a pioneer in the field of golf collecting, having started in the 1930s.

All of the books are cataloged according to the Library of Congress classification system. (New books entering the nation's library systems are cataloged in this manner, however this is the first time that older golf books have been classified by the modern method.) The staff also is preparing a computerized index of old magazine articles that will enable researchers to easily access historic information.

Although commonly referred to as the "Miller Library," it is important to note that the two large rooms also contain displays of historic artifacts, memorabilia and artwork. The most visually striking aspect of the facility, however, are the elegant cabinets made of Honduran mahogany.

Francis Ouimet Museum
190 Park Road
Weston, Massachusetts 02193

Phone: 617-891-6400
Robert P. Donovan, Executive Director
Hours: 9 a.m.- 4:30 p.m. Monday-Friday

Established in 1975 to honor the popular U.S. Open and Amateur champion, the Ouimet Museum is more than a shrine to one man. Accompanying the Francis Ouimet memorabilia and modest golf library is a regional golf museum with displays pertaining to Massachusetts golf history.

The museum is part of Golf House, the headquarters of the Massachusetts Golf Association, the Women's Golf Association of Massachusetts and the administrative offices of the Ouimet Caddie Scholarship Fund. The fund, established in Ouimet's honor in 1949, has awarded more than $5.5 million in undergraduate assistance to golf course employees.

Golf House is adjacent to the clubhouse at the Leo Martin Memorial Golf Course, a municipal facility on the west side of Boston.

PGA/World Golf Hall of Fame
P.O. Box 1908
PGA Boulevard
Pinehurst, North Carolina 28374

Phone: 919-295-6651
Dick Stranahan, Curator
Hours: 9 a.m.-5 p.m. every day,
March 1-Nov. 30

Although the PGA/World Golf Hall of Fame primarily is known for its recognition of nearly 60 golf achievers, it also is the home of one of the premier collections of golf artifacts.

5-3 *The Ryder Cup room at the PGA/World Golf Hall of Fame in Pinehurst, North Carolina, chronicles the history of the biennial professional team competition between the United States and Europe (formerly Great Britain). The display features a replica of the gold Ryder Cup and photos of every team since the competition began in 1927.*

The facility was constructed by a real estate development firm to honor golf greats, relate the heritage of the game and, of course, to attract tourists to the famous Carolina golf locale. Its opening in 1974 attracted lots of attention as President Gerald Ford presided over the dedication ceremony.

A few years after the grand opening, disaster struck — the novelty of the project wore off and the developer ran into financial difficulties. The future of the project was in jeopardy until 1983, when the Professional Golfers' Association of America (PGA) was brought in to control the operation. Ray Davis, a veteran golf collector and historian, was hired to organize the vast array of artifacts. (Davis has stepped down from the position of curator, but still serves as a consultant to the hall.)

In 1986 the PGA finally full ownership and added its name and financial resources to the institution. In doing so, the PGA was able to showcase its own collection, which included the Probst, Clapcott and Tilley libraries — all of which had been stored in a warehouse.

The facility has been rejuvenated, with considerable renovation to the buildings and extensive landscaping. Encompassing 25,000 square feet of exhibit space in two attached buildings, the primary display areas are devoted to: Hall of Fame enshrinees, a 160-foot-long golf history wall, an old clubmaker's shop, Ryder Cup Room, Auchterlonie Collection of antique clubs, major tournament showcase, original golf art and the PGA Library of 6,000 books. Also featured are special exhibits devoted to allied golf associations, including the various professional tours, American Society of Golf Course Architects, Golf Writers Association of America, Golf Coaches Association and National Golf Foundation.

Jude E. Poynter Golf Museum
College of the Desert
43-500 Monterey Ave.
Palm Desert, California 92260

Phone: 619-341-0994
Hours: 9 a.m.- 4 p.m. daily

While admittedly not a collection of rare golf artifacts, the Jude E. Poynter Golf Museum is a sincere attempt to relate the history of the game. The museum was created in 1990 through the generosity of Jude Poynter, a golf collector, retired movie theater executive, senior golf administrator and former senior golf champion. The 3,000-square-foot display occupies a new building along with the Victor J. LoBue Golf Institute — a unique two-year program that prepares students to manage all aspects of country club operations. Both are part of the College of the Desert, located near Palm Springs in the golf-laden Coachella Valley of Southern California.

More than 1,200 clubs, artifacts, books, photos and prints make up the museum's collection, which is intended to familiarize students and visitors with the history of golf. Featured displays include: photos of every Ryder Cup Team, tools for making feather balls, a case of Bobby Jones memorabilia and a collection of replicas of clubs used by famous players (donated by former President Gerald Ford).

USGA Museum and Library
Golf House
P.O. Box 708
Liberty Corner Road
Far Hills, New Jersey 07931

Phone: 908-234-2300
Karen Bednarski, Curator
Hours: 9 a.m.-5 p.m. Monday-Friday,
10 a.m.- 4 p.m. Saturday-Sunday

Several golf associations have named their headquarters "Golf House." The original Golf House was at the Leith Links in Scotland and was used by the game's first organized club — now known as the Honourable Company of Edinburgh Golfers — from 1768 until about 1831. In recent times, the Golf House moniker most often is associated with the museum and offices of the USGA.

The impetus to create a golf museum came in 1935 from George W. Blossom, Jr., former president and longtime committee member of the USGA, who suggested that the organization assemble a museum and library. His plan was enacted and donations began to accumulate at the association's New York City headquarters. The items were not displayed formally until 1951, when the USGA moved to larger quarters in a five-story, converted residence at 40 East 38th St. This building officially became Golf House and was large enough to allocate two floors to the growing collection of golf artifacts and books.

The Golf House collection flourished for two decades under the watchful eye of USGA Executive Director Joe Dey, until growing pains forced another move. In

1972, the governing body of American golf transferred its offices, museum, library and the name, Golf House, to its present address — a 62-acre estate in Far Hills, New Jersey, about an hour's drive from Manhattan.

The move also marked the appointment of Janet Seagle, a USGA staff member, to full-time curator. She single-handedly developed the collection and brought it to its current state of organization. Seagle relinquished her post in 1989, but continues to work on special projects for the USGA.

The current Golf House is actually a converted mansion. Constructed in 1919, the red brick, white columned, Georgian style structure is an architectural masterpiece. It was designed by John Russell Pope — of Jefferson Memorial and National Archives fame — and provides a spacious, but cozy, setting in which to admire the world's most comprehensive collection of golf art, memorabilia and literature. (Continued growth of the USGA required the construction of a separate administration facility next to Golf House in 1985. The historic golf treasures can now be enjoyed in the serenity of the 73-year-old dwelling without the hustle and bustle of office workers.)

To describe the USGA collection would take too many pages. Simply stated, the collection has more than enough items to illustrate all aspects of the evolution of golf: from a Rembrandt etching to Bobby Jones' medals to Ben Hogan's 1-iron to the famous golf club used on the moon. The USGA Library contains virtually every golf and significant golf-related book among its 9,000 works. More than 40,000 historic photos are being cataloged into a computer data-base. And both permanent and temporary exhibits utilize artwork, memorabilia and equipment to trace the evolution of the game.

5-4 *The magnificent facade of the USGA Golf House graces the cover of* Coming Home to Golf, *a 25-minute videotape that traces the history of the game with a walking tour through the museum.*

Most artifacts have been gifts of famous players or their families, or have been donated by golf collectors and other friends of the USGA. The cornerstones of the Golf House collection are the antique clubs donated by T. Suffern Tailer, the vast library donated by O.M. Leland, the artwork collected by former U.S. Amateur Champion Johnny Fischer and the medals given by the immortal Bobby Jones.

CANADA

B.C. (British Columbia) Golf House
2545 Blanca St.
Vancouver, British Columbia V6R 4N1
Canada

Phone: 604-222-4653
Dorothy Brown, Executive Director
Hours: noon-4 p.m. Tuesday-Sunday

The B.C. Golf House is operated by the British Columbia Golf House Society, an enterprising group of Canadian golf aficionados. The Society was formed in 1987 when a contingent spearheaded by avid golf collector Mike Riste came up with the idea of converting an about-to-be-demolished golf clubhouse into a provincial golf museum. (The building previously had been used by the adjoining University Golf Club, which moved into a larger facility in 1985.)

Fueled by donations of money, building materials and labor from the government, local businesses and individuals, the renovation of the single-story bungalow began. In 1989, after two years of mainly volunteer work, B.C. Golf House opened its doors. Most of the 1,200-book library, clubs and collectibles were contributed by Riste and other area collectors.

5-5 *The B.C. Golf House overlooks the University Golf Club in Vancouver.*

The main exhibit area traces the evolution of golf from the "Dutch Era" to the "Era of TV Golf." Two other rooms are dedicated to British Columbia golf history, which dates to 1892. The museum stresses a hands-on approach with its artifacts and encourages visitors to try out various hickory-shafted putters on a practice green located outside the building.

Royal Canadian Golf Association Museum & Canadian Golf Hall of Fame
1333 Dorval Drive
Oakville, Ontario L6J 4Z3
Canada

Phone: 416-849-9700
Karen Hewson, Curator
Hours: 9 a.m.- 4:45 p.m. Monday-Friday, plus selected weekends

Organized golf began in North America with the founding of Royal Montreal Golf Club in 1873 — about 15 years before the game became established in the United States. The Canadian version of "American" golf, therefore, is the predominant theme of the Royal Canadian Golf Association (RCGA) museum. It is located at the association's headquarters, near Toronto, at Glen Abbey Golf Club, the permanent site of the Canadian Open.

The museum and accompanying hall of fame were established when the RCGA moved to its current home in 1975. One area of the museum is devoted to the history of the Canadian Open, an event won by such stars as Tommy Armour, Walter Hagen, Sam Snead and Byron Nelson. Also of particular interest are the exhibits detailing the evolution of golf equipment and the research library.

Overseas

British Golf Museum
Bruce Embankment
St. Andrews, Fife KY16 9AB
Scotland

Phone: 0334-78880
Peter Lewis, Museum Director
Hours: Vary with season, call to verify.

It was a long time coming, but there finally is a golf museum in St. Andrews, the home of golf. In 1990 — after years of political controversy — the British Golf Museum opened across the street from the R & A clubhouse. Tucked into a hillside overlooking the sea, the contemporary-style building of concrete and stone contains 6,500 square feet of exhibition area.

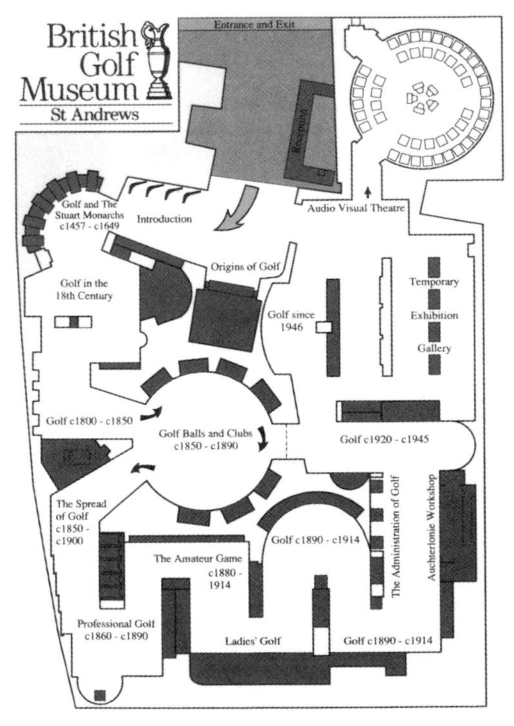

5-6 *This floor plan of the British Golf Museum lets visitors walk their way through the evolution of the game.*

5-7 *The touch-screen video displays at the British Golf Museum are especially popular with the younger generation.*

The 16 separate galleries are a combination of ancient and high tech. In telling the history of golf, interactive touch-screen displays are utilized. These modern wonders allow visitors to select audio-visual descriptions and accounts relating to the clubs, balls and other rarities on display. There are even short quizzes on golf history that can be taken by just touching the video screen.

Those choosing not to interact with the computer technology can sit back in the theater and watch great golf moments from the past come alive on the large screen. There always is a special visiting exhibit on display such as a collection of championship trophies or prized portraits on loan from the USGA Museum. Unfortunately, there is no golf research library for public use at the museum (or anywhere else in the British Isles).

The British Golf Museum is strikingly modern in this venerable old town. What the collection lacks in decorative golf collectibles, such as artwork and ceramics, it compensates for with the marvels of electronic displays. And because it is associated with the R & A, the museum will continue to have access to a vast array of memorabilia. Don't leave St. Andrews without taking a peek.

5-8 *Archie Baird in his Heritage of Golf museum in Gullane, Scotland. During the 19th century, this region was a center of golf activity and home to the famous Park, Dunn and McEwan families.*

The Heritage of Golf
Gullane Golf Club
Gullane, East Lothian EH31 2BB
Scotland

Phone: 087-57-277
Archie Baird, Curator/Owner
Hours: By appointment only.

The Heritage of Golf is not a typical museum. Although privately owned and operated, it is publicly shared. The museum is the brainchild of Archie Baird, a retired veterinary surgeon and inveterate collector of golf artifacts. (Even his wife Sheila is a descendant of the famous Park family of golfers, clubmakers and ballmakers.)

The museum shares a building with the pro shop at Gullane Golf Club and is known in golf collecting circles simply as "Archie's." Baird describes it as "compact yet comprehensive." Located less than a half-hour drive east of Edinburgh in the golf-rich county of East Lothian, the museum is nearby such historic sites as Musselburgh, Muirfield and North Berwick.

Since 1980, Baird has been explaining the evolution of golf, using his homemade displays of old equipment, artwork and other artifacts. He prefers that visitors phone ahead so that he can plan his frequent golf games accordingly. But if you drive by and notice a dog patiently waiting outside the door, then the Scotsman is undoubtedly inside.

Japan Golf Association Museum
7-3, Hirono, Shijimicho
Miki-shi, Hyogo-ken 673-05
Japan

Phone: 07948-5-0123
Miki Fujioka, Curator & Deputy Secretary General of JGA
Hours: 9 a.m.-3 p.m. Tuesday-Sunday, closed January-March and July-August

The most extensive golf museum in a non-English speaking nation is located in Japan, west of Osaka. It was established by the Japan Golf Association in 1978, primarily through the efforts of the late Mowa Settsu, a prolific golf collector and golf author.

The attractively designed two-story museum, which opened in 1982, is complete with a copy of *The Goff,* long nose woods by Philp and McEwan, feather balls, the noted Nishamura golf book collection and an extensive collection of Japanese golf memorabilia.

In 1986, a unique fund-raising effort was undertaken to help cover museum expenses. By asking golfers to donate 10 yen (about 5¢) each time they played during the year, several hundred thousand dollars was raised.

5-9 *The Japan Golf Association published this 140-page guidebook about its golf museum in 1987. Although the text is in Japanese, the excellent photographs are accompanied by English captions.*

Australian Golf Museum
155 Cecil St.
S. Melbourne, Victoria 3205
Australia

Phone: 03-6997944
C.A. Phillips, Executive Director
Hours: 9 a.m.-5 p.m. Monday-Friday

It's no secret that Australians know how to play golf — Peter Thomson, Kel Nagle, Greg Norman and Ian Baker-Finch have won a total of eight British Open Championships.

Even though the Australian Golf Museum was not started until 1987, golf is not new to the country. David Robertson — brother of Allan, the noted 19th century professional and ballmaker — reportedly sailed to Australia from Great Britain in 1848 and was responsible for introducing golf to the island continent. And golf equipment companies, such as Spalding, have had manufacturing facilities down under since the days of hickory shafts.

The museum owns some wonderful memorabilia, including clubs used by many world famous Australian golfers. Funding is provided by the Australian Golf Union.

Danmarks Golfmuseum
Bogevang
7100 Vejle
Denmark

Phone: 05-82-50-01
Eric Halling, Curator
Hours: By appointment only

Although golf has been played for over 100 years in Denmark — the Copenhagen Golf Club was founded in 1898 — Danish golf history is not very extensive. There are now more than 70 golf courses, but as recently as the 1960s, there only were 20 to 30. Still, there is enough interest to support Denmark's Golf Museum.

It is contained in four rooms of a small house in the coastal town of Vejle. The museum is supported by contributions from most of the Danish golf clubs, including the Danish Golf Union.

COLLECTING TIPS

■ **When visiting a golf museum, ask the curator if there are any artifacts you can examine close up. It's quite a thrill to grip an antique club crafted by a noted clubmaker or to peruse a 100-year-old golf book.**

■ **Some golf museums have gift shops that sell reproduction art-work, books and various souvenirs. A purchase not only provides a memento, it helps sustain the museum's collection.**

C-1 *Old Tom Morris, near his shop along the 18th hole of the Old Course at St. Andrews. An original watercolor by Thomas Hodge, painted in 1885.*

C-2 *A mid-19th-century watercolor by Charles Lees, best known for his 1847 painting of a famous golf match in St. Andrews (shown on page 139).*

C-3 *A photogravure in sepia published by* Golf Illustrated *in 1910 to commemorate the 50th anniversary of the British Open and to honor the Triumvirate of Harry Vardon, James Braid and J.H. Taylor. These professionals dominated British golf at the turn of the century, accounting for 16 Open victories between 1894 and 1914.*

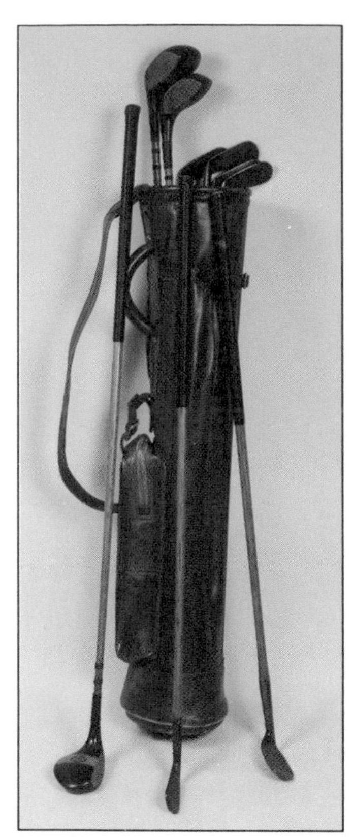

C-4 *A mint condition set of wooden-shafted clubs from the 1920s, complete with leather golf bag.*

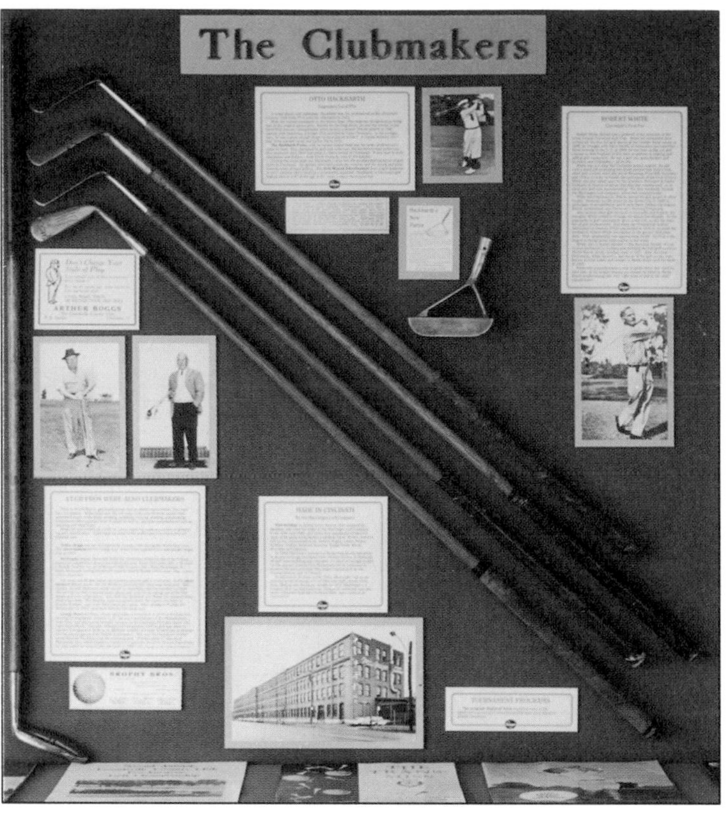

C-5 *Nostalgic displays of golf memorabilia can provide an entertaining account of club, local or regional golf history. This assemblage depicts notable makers and sellers of golf clubs who plied their trade in Cincinnati, Ohio. Included are clubs and facts on Robert White, Otto Hackbarth and the MacGregor Golf Company.*

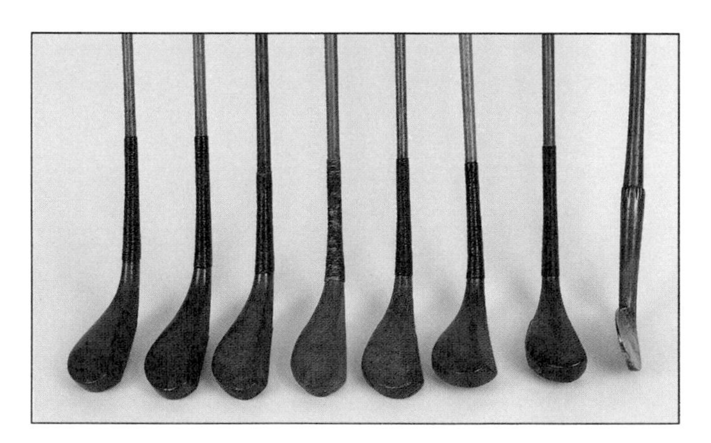

C-6 *A typical set of clubs used in the feather ball era, circa 1840. From left: play club, long spoon, mid spoon, short spoon, baffing spoon, wooden niblick, putter, iron.*

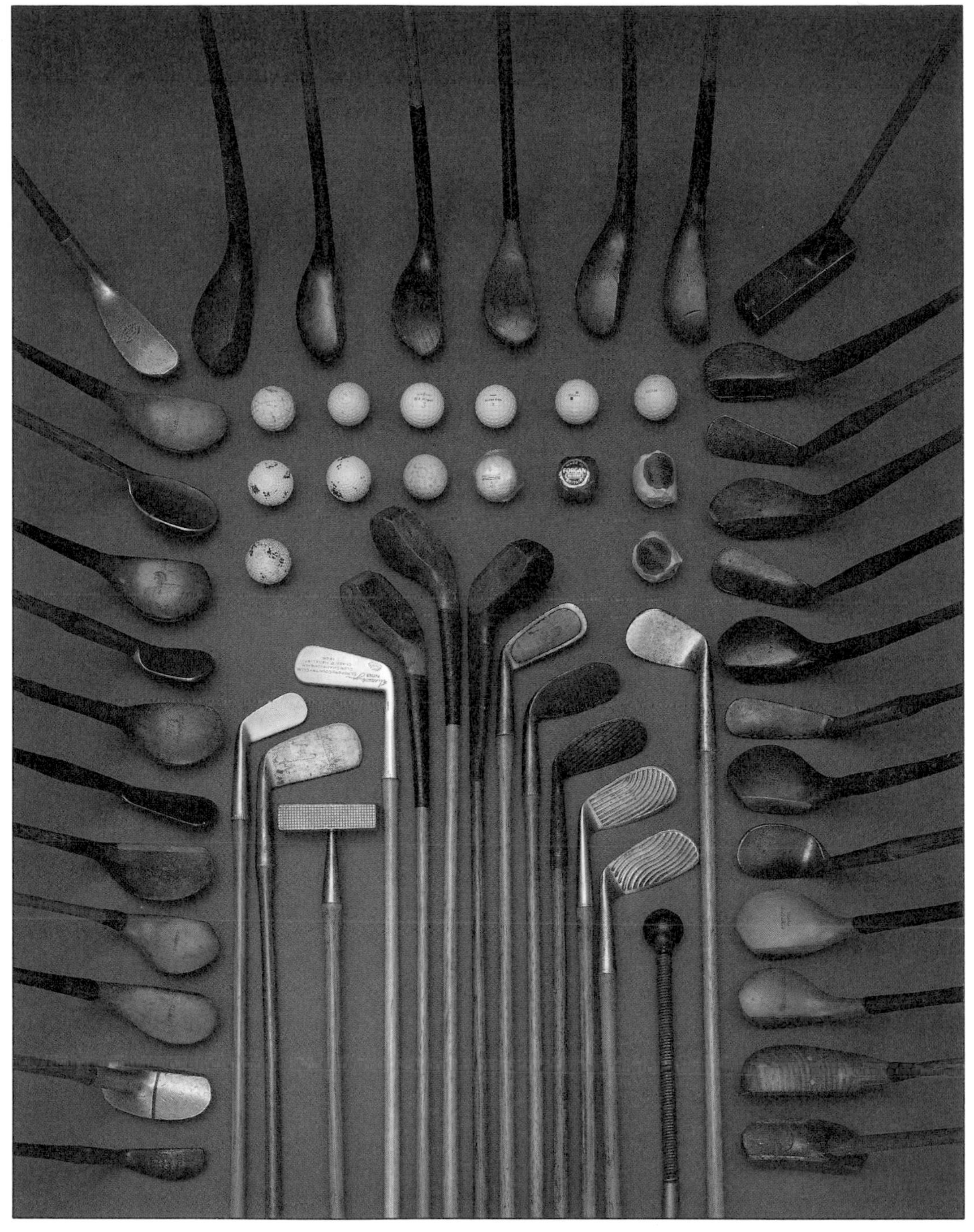

C-7 *An impressive assemblage of rare and unusual clubs and balls dating from the 1870s to the 1930s.*

C-8 *A collection of classic books on American golf (left) and British golf (right).*

C-9 *Since the 1890s, many card and board games have been devised to provide indoor entertainment for golfers.*

C-10 *The original art (top row) for the printed cigarette cards (bottom row) issued by Cope Brothers, circa 1897. Measuring slightly more than 2 inches high, the detailed paintings of Old Tom Morris, Young Tom Morris and Allan Robertson are a sampling of the 50 illustrations painted by John Wallace (a.k.a. George Pipe-shank) for the series.*

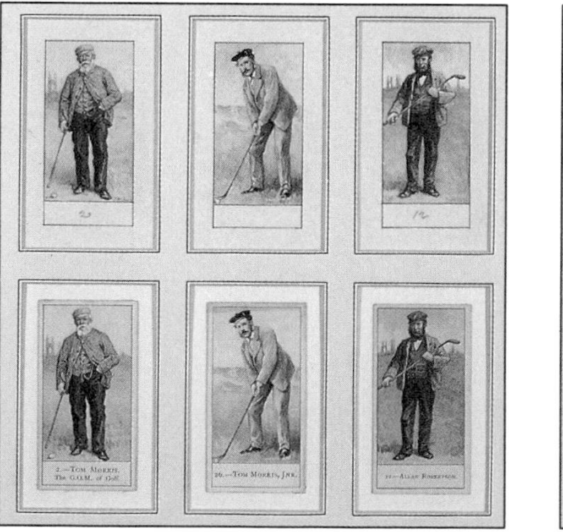

C-11 *Advertising leaflet promoting a book assembled in 1916 by Clare Briggs, noted cartoonist and avid golfer.*

C-12 *Three rare golf balls: a Tom Morris feather ball, circa 1850; a Paterson Composite smooth gutty ball, circa 1848; and a knife-cut gutty ball, made by Allan Robertson not long before his death in 1859. Although feather balls are thought by many to be the rarest of all balls, the early gutty balls actually are more difficult to find.*

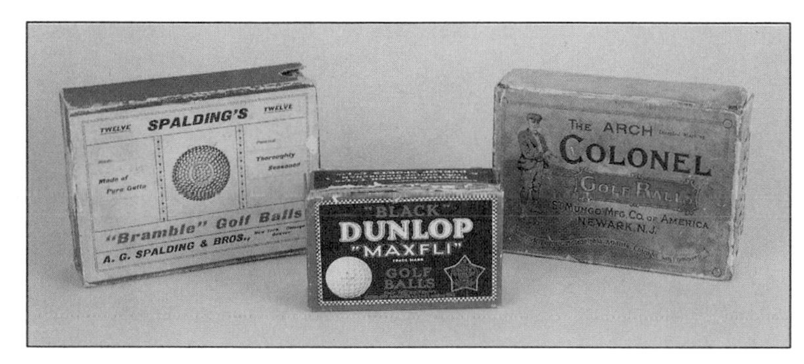

C-13 *Golf ball boxes often had attractive graphics, but are hard to find since most were discarded. Beginning with gutty balls in the 1890s and through the 1930s with rubber-cored balls, Spalding was the predominant ball manufacturer. Dunlop and St. Mungo were popular brands of rubber-cored balls in the early 1900s.*

C-14 *Before the current peg-type golf tee was universally accepted in the 1940s, tees were made in countless styles using various materials.*

C-15 *The premier illustrators of the 20th century —Harrison Fisher, Norman Rockwell, James Montgomery Flagg and others — often portrayed golf themes for* The Saturday Evening Post, Collier's, Ladies' Home Journal, Punch, McCall's *and other non-golf publications. This disappointed golfer was painted by Lawrence Toney.*

C-16 *Old golf magazines contain a wealth of stories, trivia and ads that illustrate how golf was enjoyed by previous generations. They also provide accounts of the spectacular play of golf greats, such as Harry Vardon, Walter Hagen and Bobby Jones — right as they happened.*

C-17 *An actual program from the first Masters Tournament in 1934. Although tournament founder Bobby Jones insisted that the event be called the Augusta National Invitation Tournament because he felt that the Masters designation was too pretentious, he finally relented to the wishes of the press and the community and the current name formally was adopted in 1938.*

C-18 *Golf auctions and sales allow collectors the opportunity to purchase a wide variety of collectibles at a single location. Potential buyers should spend ample time in examining and comparing items during the preview time.*

C-19 *This scene, measuring about 1 square foot, is part of a stained-glass window, made circa 1895 in Great Britain.*

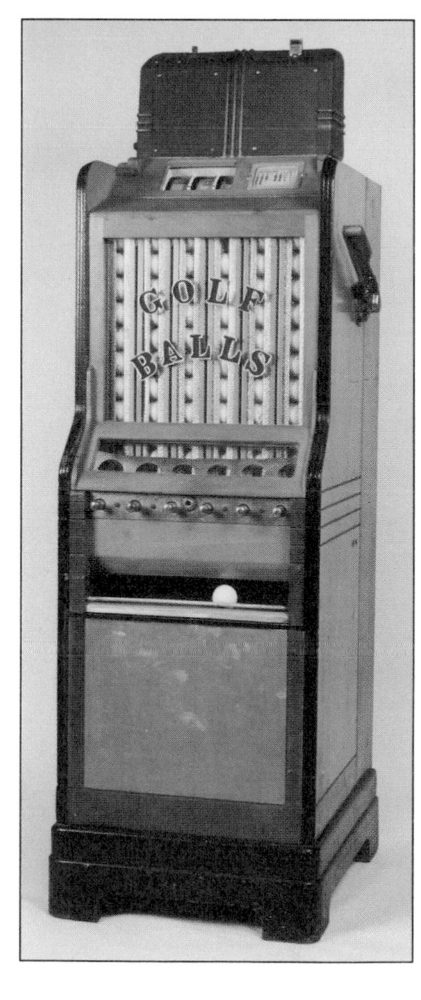

C-20 *Golf professionals once kept slot machines in their shops to supplement their income. Elaborate machines, such as this Jennings floor model from the 1930s, accepted quarters and paid off in golf balls, according to how the dials lined up.*

C-21 *A selection of fine ceramic golf mugs from the early 1900s. From left: Doulton Lambeth, Lenox, Royal Doulton Series Ware, Copeland Spode and O'Hara Dial.*

C-22 *Silver items have been used for golf prizes ever since 1744, when the Provost of Edinburgh presented a silver club to the Company of Edinburgh Golfers for their competition at Leith Links. Shown above is a selection of finely detailed antique silver that includes trophies, spoons, hatpins, hors d'oeuvres picks, buttons and a cigarette case.*

C-23 *A golfer doll, measuring 22 inches high. Made in the early 20th century, it features real hair, custom-tailored clothing and handmade golf clubs.*

CHAPTER 6

CLUBS

Without a doubt, wooden-shafted golf clubs are the most prevalent golf antique. Considering that there were more than five million golfers in the 1920s and that each might have owned 10 clubs, that means more than 50 million clubs possibly existed during that period alone. It's no wonder there still are so many around!

But regardless of age or rarity, the old-fashioned charm of wooden-shafted clubs fascinates modern golfers — especially those who avail themselves of today's computer-designed, high-tech clubs. The trick in studying and collecting old clubs is to differentiate the special ones from the ordinary. Some clubs, such as those from the feather ball era are treasured for their scarcity, while others are desirable for their influence on the history or evolution of the game. The latter group includes putters like the Schenectady and Calamity Jane models that, although mass-produced, are sought by collectors.

Because the majority of valuable old clubs have wooden shafts, this chapter primarily covers clubs made up until the 1930s, when steel became the preferred shaft material. (Later clubs aren't considered antiques yet and lack the craftsmanship associated with older examples.)

Be careful when dating a club. It is not unusual to find a club that was made years after it was in common use. In 1910, Old Tom Morris' shop in St. Andrews advertised that they would replicate old long-nose clubs — 20 years after they went out of vogue. So be wary when examining a club that may be old, but perhaps not as you might think.

To the uninitiated, all wooden-shafted golf clubs might be lumped together into the general category of "old clubs." There are, however, distinct classifications of clubs based on style and age. By learning to use the proper designations and nomenclature described on the following three pages, your appreciation of antique clubs will be greatly enhanced.

PARTS OF A WOOD

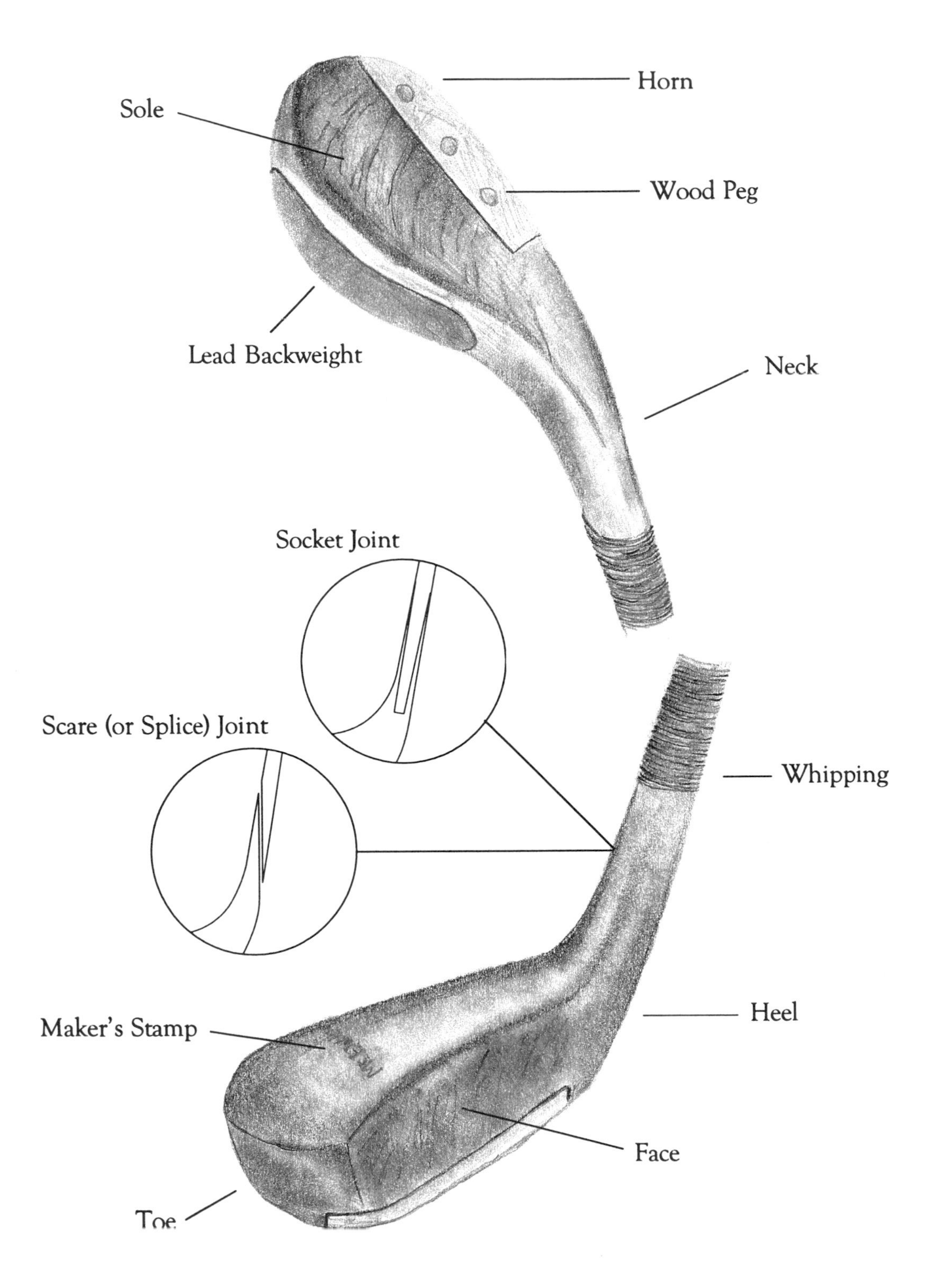

Parts of an Iron

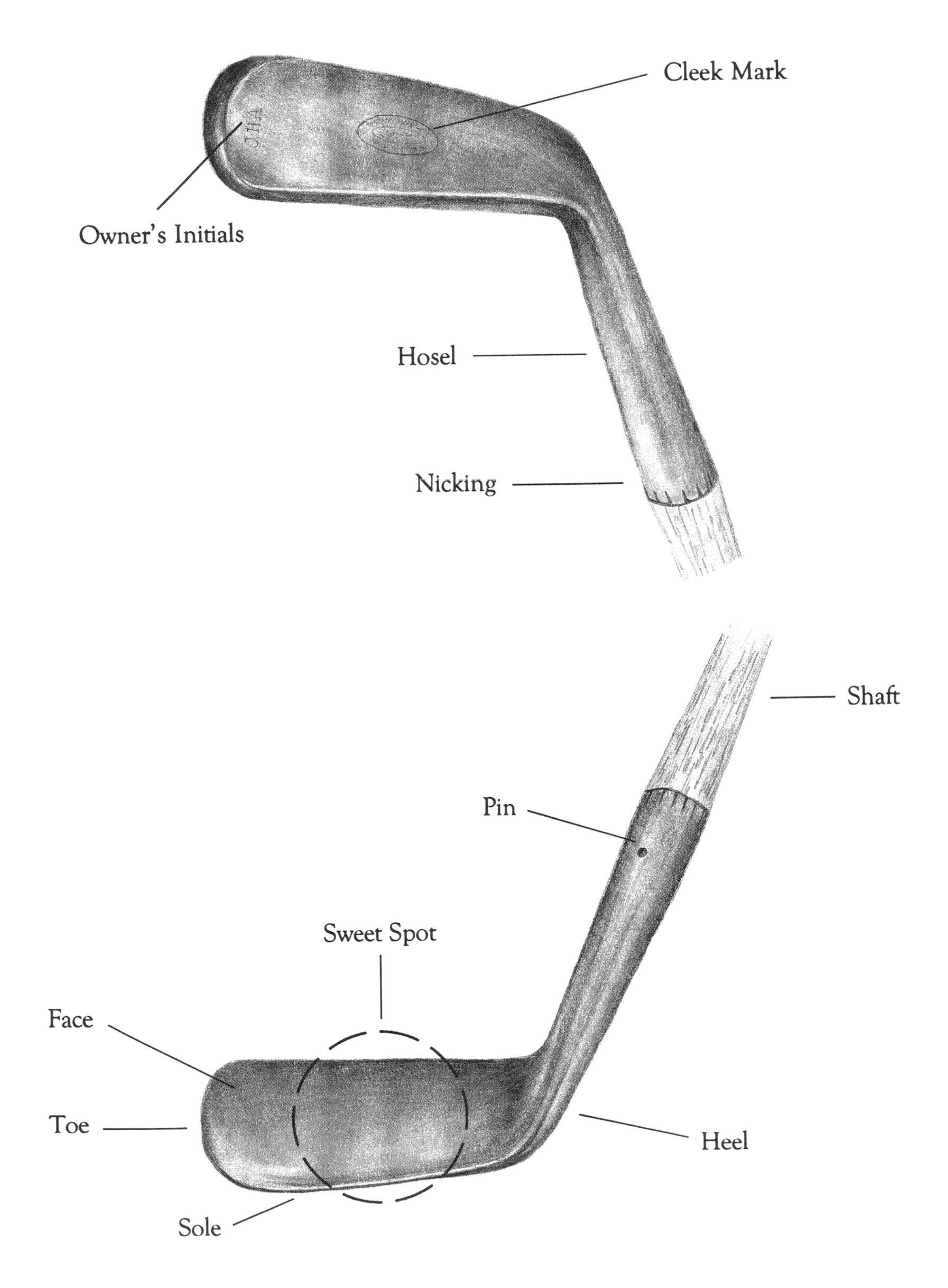

Classification Of Wooden-Shafted Golf Clubs

WOODS

LONG-NOSE – page 49
(pre-1890)

Long, slender head, often with hooked face • spliced joint to shaft • large lead backweight poured into head cavity • strip of horn at leading edge of sole • feather ball clubs (pre-1860) are more graceful and lower in profile • gutty ball clubs (1850-1890) have thicker necks, shorter head length in later years • face repairs made with leather.

TRANSITIONAL – page 54
(1880s-1920s)

Same features as long-nose, but considerably shorter heel-to-toe length • bulger style with slightly convex face became popular by 1890, standard by 1900, lingered on until 1920s • except for the splice joint, later heads resemble modern club shape and may have fiber face inserts • brass sole plates on fairway woods.

SOCKET-HEAD – page 56
(1890s-1930s)

Resembles modern pear-shaped wood except for wood shaft • neck of club drilled to accept shaft • metal sole plates and face inserts were common by 1920s.

PATENT WOODS – page 66
(1890s-1930s)

Unusual head shapes, use of aluminum and other materials • non-traditional methods of attaching the shaft to the head • most clubs marked "patented" or "patent pending" • any major design deviation from the normal style of the period also qualifies for this class.

IRONS

BLACKSMITH-MADE – page 52
(pre-1890)

Clubheads hand shaped from bars of iron • thick, heavy hosels with uneven nicking • earlier clubs (pre-1860) may exhibit crude workmanship and concave faces • hosels not drilled, but hammered around a mandril so seam may be visible • smooth faces and little, if any, marks on back of head.

CLEEK-MARKED – page 57
(1880s-1920s)

Usually has several cleek marks and other stampings on back • often marked "hand-forged" • pre-1900 clubs have smooth faces; later clubs have irregular hand-applied punch marks or scoring on face • most clubs made after 1900 have stamped face markings and may be chrome-plated or stainless steel • usually marked with old-fashioned club name like "mashie" rather than a numeral.

MASS-PRODUCED – page 62
(1920s-1930s)

Factory made, matched sets, usually with numbers • usually chrome • no true nicking, but rather uniform, decorative knurling • may have matching socket-head woods.

PATENT IRONS – page 70
(1890s-1930s)

Unusual or exaggerated features, including deep grooves, unorthodox hosel shapes and protrusions or other odd methods of weight distribution • may be marked "patented" or "patent pending"

LONG-NOSE WOODS

(Pre-1890)

Long-nose wooden clubs, with their slender heads and long, whippy shafts were used by golfers from the earliest known days of golf in the 15th century until the late 19th century. Although this style of club was used for more than 400 years — longer than any other piece of equipment, including the feather ball — relatively few pre-19th century clubs remain.

This can be attributed to several factors: the clubs were easily broken; for a long time golf was played only by a limited number of people, primarily on the east coast of Scotland; and few people saved old clubs.

6-1 *In this circa 1850 photo, Watty Alexander, a popular St. Andrews caddy, holds a typical set of clubs used during the feather ball era: eight woods and one iron. Note that Alexander's pockets are full of spare balls and that golf bags had not been invented.*

To the casual observer, most long-nose woods look similar. To the club connoisseur, however, it is the slight differences that make them so intriguing. Heads were made from apple, pear, thorn, beech and other woods and range in color from a light blond to a black stain. The hand-turned shafts also exhibit varying shades and grain patterns. They were fashioned from several woods, including ash, greenheart, redheart, purpleheart, hazelwood, lancewood and hickory.

Even the protective strip of ram's horn, held in place with wooden pegs on the leading edge of the clubface, had its own unique coloration.

Combine all of these diverse attributes with the patina of old wood, a thick sheepskin grip and twine whipping blackened

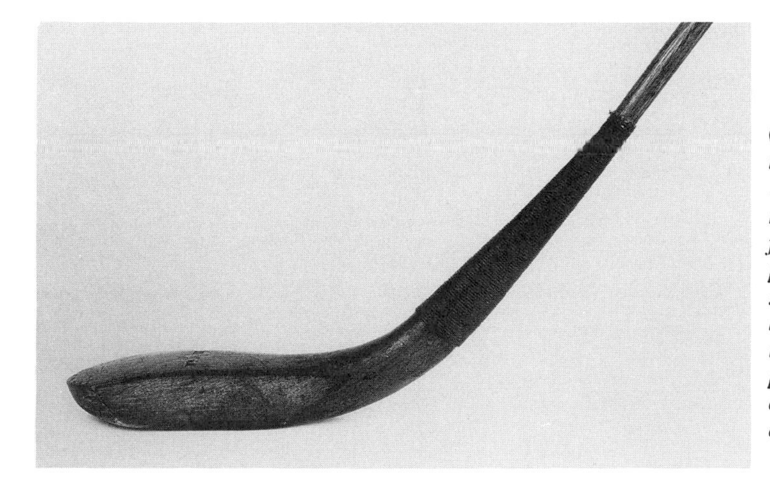

6-2 *This play club (driver) made by Willie Dunn, Sr. in the 1840s typifies the long, slender head characteristic of the feather ball era. Clubhead profiles were gradually shortened and thickened beginning in the 1850s, when the harder gutty ball became popular. By the end of the century, the long heads had evolved into the compact "bulger" style used today.*

with pitch and varnish, and you'll immediately realize the mystique of these venerable clubs. To think that a golfer once took full swings at the ball with such a finely crafted piece of woodwork is almost beyond belief.

Long-nose woods were used with feather balls except for from the 1850s until about 1890, when the gutty ball became the ball of choice. During the feather ball era, the fragile nature of the ball dictated that the golfer play primarily with wooden-headed clubs and utilize a long, sweeping swing. For this reason a set of clubs — not a matched set as we know it today — was comprised of a play club (driver), about six "fairway" woods, one or two irons and a wooden putter (see photo page 38). The clubs had varying lofts, shaft flexes and weights (which was determined by the amount of lead placed in the back of the head).

During the gutty ball era, the clubs were strengthened to accommodate the hardness of the ball. The necks became thicker and the heads had a stockier appearance. Sections of leather often were inserted into clubfaces needing repairs or to soften the impact. This frequently can be seen on feather ball clubs that were used with gutties.

PLAY CLUBS were used for teeing the ball off from a small mound of sand (see page 105). Most of the clubs used for hitting the ball off the ground were called spoons. There were LONG SPOONS, MID SPOONS, SHORT SPOONS and BAFFING SPOONS, listed according to the length of shot they were capable of producing. The wood with the highest loft was the WOODEN NIBLICK (see book dust jacket). PUTTERS also came in varying lofts for hitting approach putts and short putts.

The makers of long-nose woods came from two different backgrounds. Some were

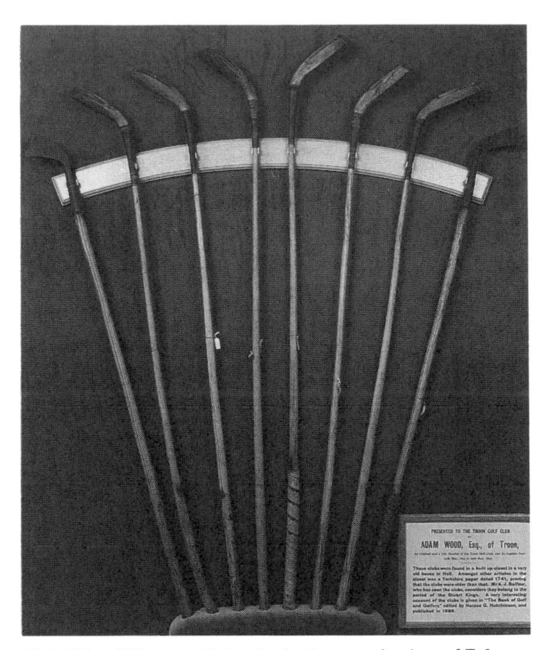

6-4 *The "Troon clubs," dating to the late 17th or early 18th century, are considered to be the oldest documented set of golf clubs in existence. They were discovered in 1898, with a newspaper dated 1741, during the remodeling of a house in the English seaside town of Hull. They were presented to the Troon Golf Club (now Royal Troon) by Adam Wood, a past captain of the club.*

6-3 *Hugh Philp (1782-1856) was considered to be the Stradivarius of clubmaking. Originally a woodworker in St. Andrews, he was appointed clubmaker to the R & A in 1819 and made clubs for many of the early professionals, such as Allan Robertson and Tom Morris. This sketch by Arthur Weaver was taken from an old photograph.*

craftsmen, skilled woodworkers who also made cabinetry, spoked wheels, archery bows and fishing rods. The notable craftsmen were Hugh Philp, the McEwan family, Simon Cossar, Robert Forgan, J. Jackson, Alexander Patrick and James Wilson.

The other type of clubmaker evolved in the 19th century. They were the golf professionals. Not to be confused with modern club or touring pros, the ancient golf professionals had multiple responsibilities. In addition to competing in challenge matches, they cared for the golf course and often made clubs and balls. Some of more famous professionals who made clubs were Willie Park (Sr. and Jr.), twins Willie and Jamie Dunn and Old Tom Morris.

By the early 19th century, all of the clubmakers were stamping their names into the clubheads they produced. Since the more successful makers had apprentices and assistants, there is no guarantee that the clubmaker actually made a club which bears his name. Just because a club has no maker's name, however, does not indicate that it is pre-1800 — the mark may have worn off.

6-5 *Clubs made by James McEwan (1747-1800) are the earliest known to have been stamped by their maker. His stamp (left) included a distinctive thistle flower. James, the first of four generations of McEwans to make long-nose clubs, set up business in 1770 at the links in Bruntsfield, near Edinburgh. By the 1890s, the family business was being run by his grandson Douglas in Musselburgh (right).*

6-6 *Robert Forgan (1824-1900), shown here in his later days, learned to handcraft clubs from his uncle Hugh Philp. Upon Philp's death in 1856, Forgan took over the business and shaped it into the largest clubmaking concern in St. Andrews. In 1863 when he was appointed clubmaker to the Prince of Wales, Forgan began stamping all of his clubs with the Prince's coat of arms: a plume of feathers.*

BLACKSMITH-MADE IRONS

(Pre-1890)

Prior to the widespread acceptance of the gutty ball in the 1850s, the use of iron-headed clubs was minimal. The feather ball was easier to manipulate with the long-nose woods, so irons were only used to get out of difficult lies. Because the irons were not as prone to breaking and since golfers owned only two or three, there was little demand. Consequently, not many were produced.

The noted clubmakers during the feather ball era were woodworkers who left the fabrication of irons to local blacksmiths. The blacksmiths heated iron bars in their forges and then hammered them into shape on anvils. The clubmakers completed the clubs by installing shafts and grips and probably sold the finished product to golfers.

Early irons had specific functions, unlike modern sets, which offer an even progression from one club to the next. The CLEEK was a long-faced iron, similar to a 3-iron, that could be used for long shots or

6-9 *There were two Robert Whites from St. Andrews who were important in golf history. One was born in 1857 and placed this ad in an 1892 golf magazine. The other, born in 1874, was a teacher, proficient golfer and had an interest in agronomy. He emigrated to the United States in 1894 and, because he knew far more about golf than most Americans, started to lay out golf courses. He also worked for Slazenger's Sporting Goods Store in Boston and served as golf professional and greenkeeper at numerous courses throughout the Midwest. He was elected first president of the PGA of America in 1916, was a founder of the American Society of Golf Course Architects in 1948 and was instrumental in developing the first golf course in Myrtle Beach, South Carolina. Although this Robert White was not a clubmaker, he did sell clubs with his name stamped on them, such as this one (right), made during his tenure at Cincinnati Golf Club in 1896-8.*

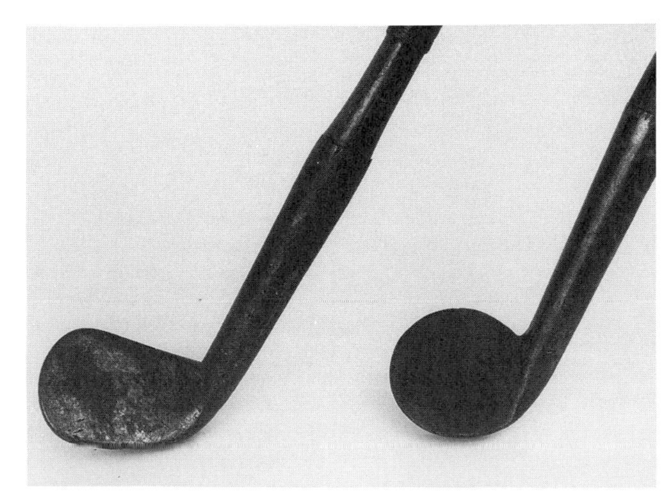

6-10 *These two clubs of different vintages served a similar purpose: to extract the ball out of a deep rut or a wheel track. The club with a larger head (left), is a rut niblick. It frequently is mistaken for a track, or rut iron (right), which has a head barely larger than the diameter of a golf ball and were made prior to the mid-1880s.*

approaching. The LOFTER or SAND IRON was a heavy, large-faced, medium loft club, often with a concave face. The TRACK or RUT IRON had an extremely small head — about the size of a golf ball — and was an effective way to hit out of a hole or wheel track.

In the 1850s, golfers found that the durable gutty ball allowed them to swing aggressively with their iron clubs, a feat not possible with the delicate feathery. This increased use of irons, coupled with an influx of new golfers, resulted in several Scottish blacksmiths specializing in the forging of clubheads. They soon became known as cleekmakers.

Until John Gray of Prestwick and the Carricks of Musselburgh began stamping their names on clubs in the 1850s, irons bore no identifying marks. Other blacksmiths-turned-cleekmakers, who plied their trade through the end of the century, were: George Nicoll, James Anderson, Robert White, Robert Wilson and Willie Wilson. Although the names of wooden clubmakers, such as McEwan, Forgan and Morris, may be found on early irons, they did not forge the clubs themselves.

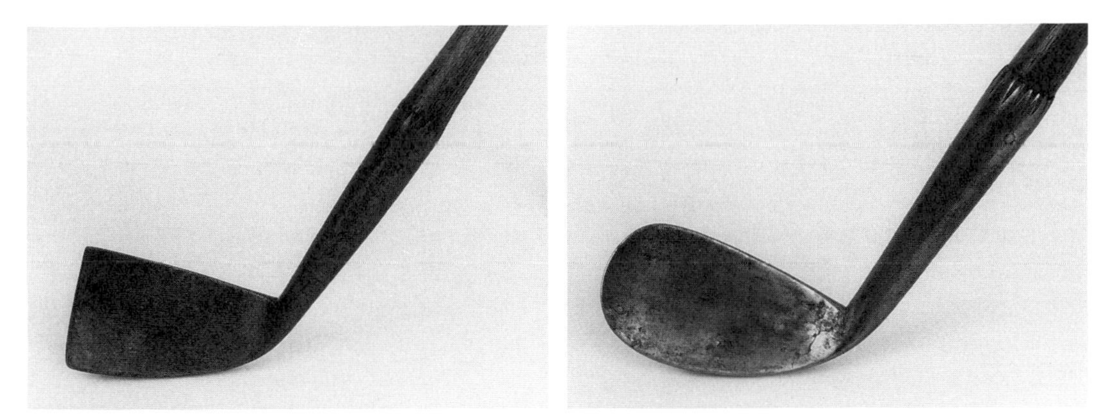

6-11 *Early irons are characterized by thick hosels with deep nicking, a dished face and crude — by modern standards — craftsmanship. The square-toe iron (left) was made circa 1760; the round toe iron circa 1800.*

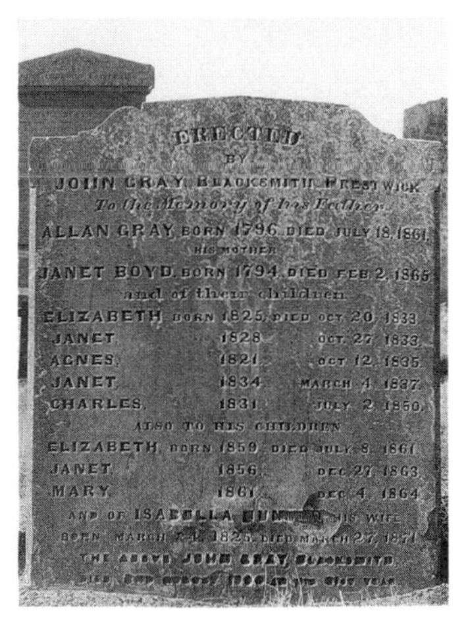

6-12 *Until the middle of the 19th century, iron-headed clubs were forged by blacksmiths. John Gray, a well-known clubmaker from Prestwick, is remembered by this grave marker that identifies him as a blacksmith.*

6-13 *Two notable names that appeared on clubs during the mid-19th century were Gray and Carrick. John Gray began forging heads in Prestwick in 1851 and stamped various versions of his name on clubs. Most of the Carrick clubs were made by cousins Alex and Archibald Carrick, third-generation blacksmiths from Musselburgh. They operated the firm of F. & A. Carrick, a business started by their fathers. Carrick clubheads — the later ones carried an "x" trademark — were made until the business closed in 1904.*

TRANSITIONAL WOODS

(1880s - 1920s)

The transitional period of wood clubmaking was at its peak at the end of the 19th century. It marked the progression from the traditional long-nose clubs of the feather ball days to the current pear-shaped woods.

When golfers gave up the feather ball for the gutty in the 1850s, clubmakers had to strengthen the long-nose wood to withstand the impact of the harder ball. They did so by increasing the thickness of the neck. A further refinement was made in the mid-1880s, when clubmakers reduced the length of the clubhead from heel to toe. This compact head became known as the semi long-nose wood. Like all transitional clubs, the head was attached to the shaft by the time-proven splice joint.

Another club that evolved during this period was the bulger. Popularized by Willie Park, Jr. during the late 1880s, the bulger was similar to the semi long-nose, except that the clubface had a heel-to-toe bulge, rather than the slight concavity, or hook, evident in all previous wooden clubs. Modern club manufacturers still utilize this feature — referred to as bulge — for superior ball control.

The 1890s was a time of fierce competition among clubmakers. Mechanization of their shops brought club prices down and interest in the game soared. Inventive genius, combined with advances in technology, resulted in the design of many out-of-the-ordinary clubs. Those oddities, with their unusual designs and shaft splices, are classified as patent clubs (see page 64).

One new design that emerged eventually brought an end to the transitional period. It was the socket-head wood. With a bulger shape and drilled neck, these new clubs were well-suited to mass production (see page 62). Clubmakers offered both styles, but by 1915 the more expensive, handcrafted spliced clubs were considered antiques. Only a few diehards, such as Walter Hagen and Bobby Jones, used the venerable spliced bulgers into the 1920s.

6-14 *The use of transitional spliced-head woods spanned several generations — from Willie Park, Jr. (1864-1925) (right), to Bobby Jones (1902-1971). Jones (far right) was still using a large-headed "Dreadnaught" driver when he won the 1923 U.S. Open. Most of the other players had already converted to the modern compact woods which featured a socket-style joint.*

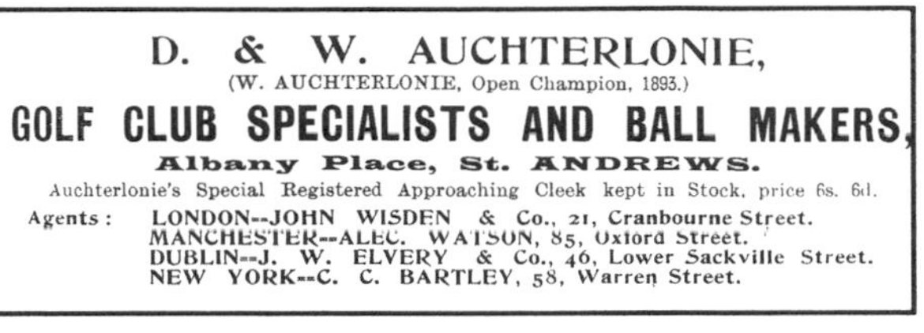
D. & W. AUCHTERLONIE,
(W. AUCHTERLONIE, Open Champion, 1893.)
GOLF CLUB SPECIALISTS AND BALL MAKERS,
Albany Place, St. ANDREWS.
Auchterlonie's Special Registered Approaching Cleek kept in Stock, price 6s. 6d.
Agents: LONDON--JOHN WISDEN & Co., 21, Cranbourne Street.
MANCHESTER--ALEC. WATSON, 85, Oxford Street.
DUBLIN--J. W. ELVERY & Co., 46, Lower Sackville Street.
NEW YORK--C. C. BARTLEY, 58, Warren Street.

6-15 *Willie Auchterlonie, the 1893 British Open champion, stands in the doorway of the golf shop he operated in St. Andrews with his brother David. Willie was appointed honorary professional to the Royal & Ancient Golf Club in 1935. The family name is well-known in golf. Willie's son Laurie, was a noted 20th-century clubmaker; another brother, Laurence, lived in Chicago and won the U.S. Open in 1902; a cousin, Tom, opened a golf goods business in St. Andrews in 1919 (which still operates today).*

6-16 *The development of transitional spliced-head woods took place from the mid-1880s to about 1900. The shape of these spliced heads evolved from the long-nose style of the feather ball period and most of the gutty ball period (left) to the shorter semi-long nose clubs of the mid-1880s (middle) and finally to the compact bulgers that were introduced in the 1880s and were popular for about two decades.*

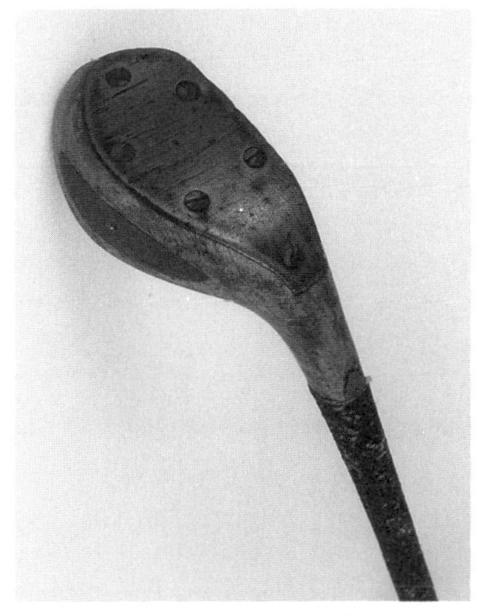

6-17 *The brassie — named for its attached brass sole plate — became fashionable in the 1880s as a durable, small-headed fairway club. In the 1920s, when matched sets with club names became popular, the brassie became synonymous with a 2-wood — regardless of whether it had a brass soleplate.*

SOCKET-HEAD WOODS

(1890s - 1930s)

The most common antique wood-headed club is the socket. The drilling of holes in the clubhead to accept the end of the shaft, rather than the traditional splice joint, was pioneered in the early 1890s, primarily on exotic patent clubs (see photo 6-47). By the middle of the decade, however, clubmakers were producing ordinary woods with this revolutionary feature.

The joints were fashioned in various forms. Some of the sockets were drilled completely through to the sole, while others were only about 2 inches deep. The shafts were secured with glue and were tightly whipped with twine. Experiments were made with threaded joints, but the straight bore was simple to drill and performed adequately.

6-18 *When the copy lathe was introduced in the 1890s, manufacturers were able to mechanically duplicate clubheads from a steel or wooden model called a master. The firm of C. Spinks was a pioneer in the fabricating of both clubheads and shafts by machine rather than with hand saws and planes. Shafts made of American hickory were commonplace by the mid-1800s, and by the end of the century, American persimmon was replacing beech, apple, thorn and other woods as the preferred clubhead material. Spinks delivered their rough turnings to clubmakers and professionals who performed the final shaping, weighting and finishing by hand.*

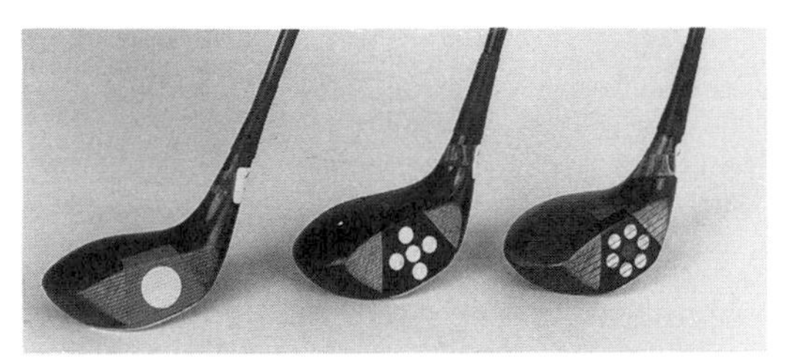

6-19 *The most attractive factory-made clubs from the 1920s and '30s are the "fancy-face" clubs – those embellished with inserts of ivory, mother-of-pearl and other decorative materials. Most fancy-face clubs were made with hickory shafts. However, these clubs – made by Spalding, Wilson and Kroydon – feature early steel shafts.*

Although the socket-head was better suited to mass production, clubmakers continued to make splice-headed clubs into the 1920s to satisfy the demands of golfers from "the old school." (Today's club manufacturers appear to follow a similar route as metal and other materials become the preferred material for "wood" heads.)

The early socket-heads, circa 1895, featured the traditional protective horn insert at the bottom of the clubface. After the turn of the century, metal soleplates and face inserts were incorporated into the clubhead. The wood-shafted era of socket-headed clubs ended about in the mid-1930s, when hickory shafts became obsolete.

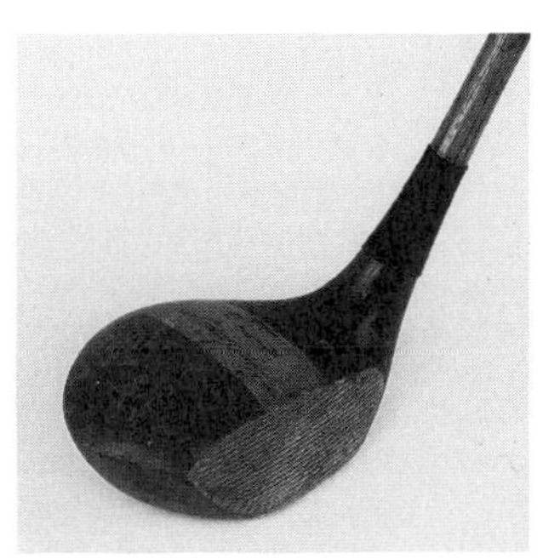

6-20 *Socket-head woods from the early-20th century are still plentiful and most are rather plain in appearance. Some heads, such as this Gene Sarazen model made by Wilson in the 1920s, had two-tone finishes.*

CLEEK-MARKED IRONS

(1880s - 1920s)

When iron-headed golf clubs were no longer handmade by blacksmiths and before their mass production in 20th-century factories, they were made by cleekmakers. Many were blacksmiths who turned to clubmaking full time. They forged clubs with huge steam-powered (and later electrical) mechanical hammers. By 1900, clubs were shaped by hammering the heated iron blanks between two pre-shaped dies. Finishing was accomplished with grinding and polishing wheels.

Exactly why these men were called cleekmakers and not ironmakers is unknown. (The term cleek had long been used to describe a narrow-bladed iron club.) Nevertheless, the independent Scottish and English ironmakers from the 1880s until the 1920s were referred to as cleekmakers and the identifying marks they stamped onto the backs of clubheads were known as cleek marks.

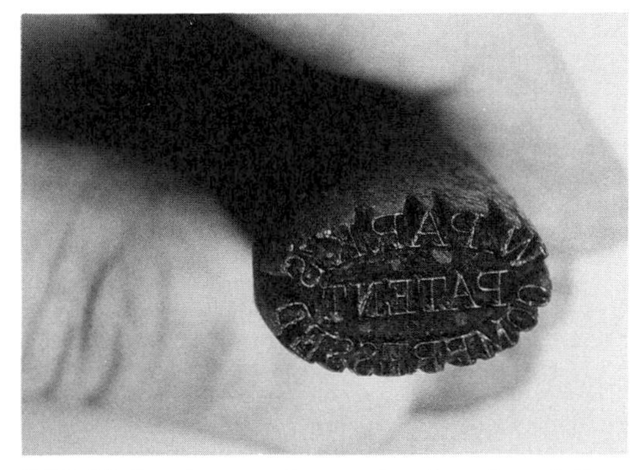

6-21 *Clubmakers used a casehardened steel die to impress trademarks into the surface of their products. This stamp was used in Willie Park, Jr.'s shop.*

COLLECTING TIPS

■ **With the exception of patent clubs (see page 64), most irons from this era are similar in appearance. Therefore, it is the cleek marks on the back of the clubs that are of greatest interest to collectors. It's a challenge to see how many different marks and names can be found and identified.**

■ **It's also fun to see how many different face markings you can discover. Dozens of different combinations of lines, dots and other patterns were used until the current groove pattern became the standard in the 1930s.**

The cleek marks ranged from simple outlined figures, such as stars or animals, to intricate designs. Some makers just stamped their name, a custom practiced by makers of wooden-headed clubs. Cleekmakers also

6-22 *The star cleek mark was used by William Gibson from 1895 until 1930 to identify the clubheads he supplied to numerous clubmakers and professionals. Since his forge was in Kinghorn, a small town near St. Andrews, he was known as "Gibson of Kinghorn." This differentiated him from Charles Gibson, a noted clubmaker at Royal North Devon Golf Club.*

sold clubheads to golf pros and other retailers who would complete the club by adding a shaft and grip. These assemblers also had a name stamp, so many clubs exhibit a cleekmaker's mark and a seller's mark. Until matched sets of clubs became prevalent in the 1920s, players would buy individual mid-irons, mashies, niblicks and other clubs and would assemble a set that felt good.

The collecting of different cleek marks has become a major aspect of club collecting. Although there are more than 150 known marks, only about a third are commonly found today (see pages 60-61). By the 1920s, small cleekmaking firms disappeared and only those capable of mass production survived. The survivors included the large clubmaking firms of Tom Stewart, George Nicoll, R. Forgan & Son, Spalding and MacGregor. Although the use of cleek marks continued into the 1930s, they were primarily for decoration rather than identification.

6-23 *There were several unrelated Anderson families who made golf clubs during the 19th century in Scotland. The two larger ones were D. Anderson & Sons of St. Andrews (shown here) and the Andersons from nearby Anstruther. David Anderson (seated, center) founded the family firm with his five sons in 1895 and sold golf clubs and balls until the 1920s. David's father was the legendary David "Old Da" Anderson, a contemporary of Old Tom Morris, who cared for the links and made feather balls. Old Da's eldest son, Jamie, won successive British Opens in 1877, '78 and '79 and had his own clubmaking business in St. Andrews.*

6-24 *Most of the bronze and brass clubheads were putters produced by Spalding at the turn-of-the-century. Many collectors polish the heads to a distinctive shine.*

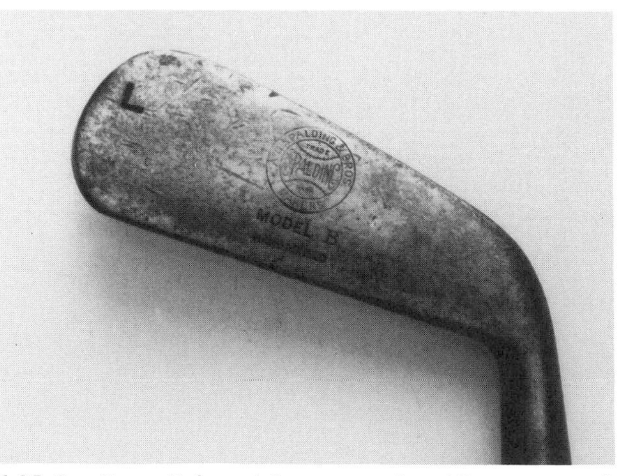

6-25 *Smaller or lighter clubs were produced for women and children. They usually are designated by an "L" for ladies or "J" for juvenile.*

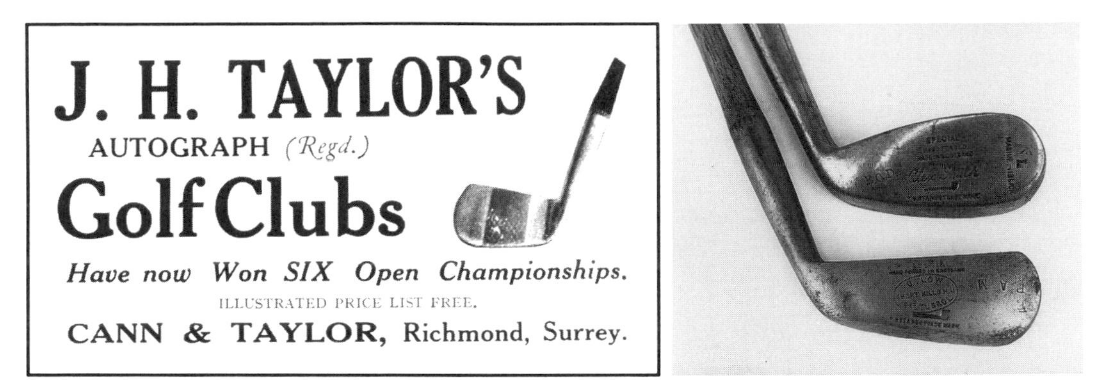

6-26 *The appeal of collecting clubs from the 1890s through the 1920s is the names of famous golfers and golf courses that often were stamped in addition to the cleek mark. Whereas modern players often have an autograph model made by a large manufacturer, five-time British Open champion J.H. Taylor owned his own company (left). The two clubs (right) have the pipe mark, indicating they were forged by Tom Stewart. The top one was sold by Alex Smith, a transplanted Scot who won the U.S. Open in 1906 and 1910. The bottom club came from the pro shop of George Low at Baltusrol Golf Club, the site of numerous major championships.*

6-27 *Drop-forging, a process that permitted heated bars of iron to be shaped into clubheads using a powerful mechanical hammer and hollow dies, was introduced in the mid-1890s. Modern forged irons still are made by this process, which had replaced hand-forging by 1920.*

6-28 *The firm of George Nicoll was located in the town of Leven, near St. Andrews, from its inception in the 1880s until its demise in the early 1980s. They used a hand as their cleek mark for many decades, beginning in the 1890s.*

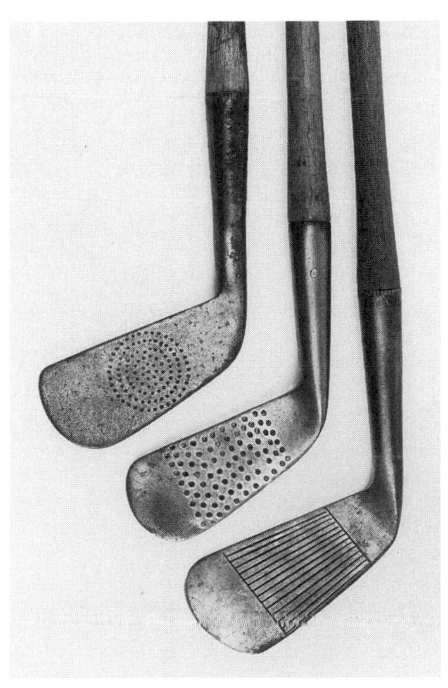

6-29 *Iron clubs had smooth faces until the late 1890s, when hand-punched dots — the forerunners of today's grooves — were applied in various patterns to enhance backspin. By 1910, machine-applied patterns were common as smooth-face irons became obsolete.*

COMMON CLEEK MARKS

Many clubmakers, club assemblers and retailers stamped iron clubs with a unique identifying symbols known as cleek marks. This custom was practiced from the mid-19th century until about 1930.

Although there are more than 150 known cleek marks, more than 90% of the marked irons were stamped with one of the 44 shown here. (Some makers simply stamped their name instead of a symbol.)

ALEX ANDERSON
Anstruther, Scotland
One of many Andersons to make clubs (5/8" dia.).

ARMY & NAVY STORES
London
A department store that sold golf equipment.

B.G.I.
Bridgeport, Conn.
The Bridgeport Gun Implement Co.

CHARLES BRAND
Carnoustie
Other makers used similar rampant lion.

G. BRODIE BREEZE
Glasgow
A golf retailer.

R.H. BUHRKE CO.
Chicago
Mass-produced clubs post-1920.

BURKE GOLF CO.
Newark, Ohio
A prolific manufacturer, founded in 1910.

BURKE GOLF CO.
Newark, Ohio
Most clubs carried their name as well as a mark.

GEORGE BUSSEY & CO.
London
Made and sold a fine line of golf equipment.

CANN & TAYLOR
England and U.S.
Most clubs also stamped with J.H. Taylor's name.

F. & A. CARRICK
Musselburgh
One of the first to stamp irons, circa 1855.

CLAN GOLF CLUB CO.
London
One of several makers to use thistle mark.

COCHRANE'S LTD.
Edinburgh
The bowline knot.

COCHRANE'S LTD.
Edinburgh
Known for making balls and giant niblicks.

ROBERT CONDIE
St. Andrews
MacGregor also had a similar rose mark.

ROBERT CONDIE
St. Andrews
The rare fern used on hand-forged irons.

J. & W. CRAIGIE
Montrose, Scotland

R. FORGAN & SON, LTD.
St. Andrews
Prince of Wales feathers, used 1880s-1901.

R. FORGAN & SON, LTD.
St. Andrews
Crown used 1901-8, after Prince became King Edward.

CHARLES GIBSON
Westward Ho!, England
Professional at Royal North Devon Golf Club.

WILLIAM GIBSON
Kinghorn, Scotland
"Gibson of Kinghorn" used the star 1895-1930s.

JAMES GOURLAY
Carnoustie, Scotland
Another anchor was used by Stadium Golf Co.

JAMES GOURLAY
Carnoustie, Scotland
The Gourlays use several crescent moon marks.

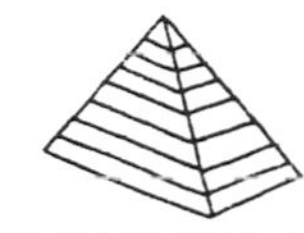

J.B. HALLEY & CO.
London
The pyramid used by the popular retailer.

HENDRY & BISHOP
Edinburgh and Leith
The firm wholesaled club-heads around the world.

HILLERICH & BRADSBY
Louisville, Kentucky
A mass producer of golf clubs.

HARRY C. LEE CO.
New York
The acorn mark of this large importer.

MacGREGOR GOLF CO.
Dayton, Ohio
J. MacGregor was a fictitious maker's name.

MacGREGOR GOLF CO.
Dayton, Ohio
MacGregor's variation of the rose. See Condie.

CHARLES L. MILLAR
Glasgow
Millar and others used thistles.

TOM MORRIS
St. Andrews
Mark came into use after Morris' death in 1908.

GEORGE NICOLL
Leven, Scotland
One of the famous hands, used 1890s-1920s.

BEN SAYERS
N. Berwick, Scotland
The robin mark used by this fine player.

ANDREW HERD SCOTT
Elie, Scotland
Prince of Wales feathers used 1902-10.

A.G. SPALDING &BROS.
England; Scotland; U.S.
The baseball mark used on American clubs.

A.G. SPALDING &BROS.
England; Scotland; U.S.
Anvil mark used primarily in Dysart, Scotland.

A.G. SPALDING &BROS.
England; Scotland; U.S.
The American version of Spalding's hammer brand.

STADIUM GOLF CO.
London
Gourlay made a modified anchor brand for Stadium.

TOM STEWART
St. Andrews
The famous pipe mark came in several styles.

TOM STEWART
St. Andrews
The serpent appeared on ladies and juvenile clubs.

URQUHART'S, LTD.
Edinburgh
Mark appears on the firm's adjustable clubs.

JACK WHITE
London and Scotland
The sun is attributed to Sunningdale Golf Club.

WILLIAM WINTON
London and Montrose
A major supplier of clubheads to professionals

WRIGHT & DITSON
Boston, Massachusetts
The one-shot brand of this Spalding subsidiary.

MASS-PRODUCED IRONS
(1920s - 1930s)

By 1920, most golf clubs were mass produced in factories by Spalding, MacGregor, Wilson and other large companies. Even longtime Scottish clubmaking firms, including R. Forgan & Sons and Ben Sayers, mechanized their operations in order to meet the demand for clubs.

Clubs of this era are characterized by matched sets — clubs marked in numerical order or with names, such as mid-iron, mashie and niblick. Most heads were chrome plated to prevent rust and had line-scored faces. Although some exhibited cleek marks, the marks primarily were used for decorations in conjunction with the manufacturer's name, rather than as a method of identification, popular with earlier clubs.

Except for the switch to steel shafts in the 1930s, club designs remained relatively unchanged from the 1930s until the 1960s. Most refinements were in manufacturing techniques and quality control, so clubs from this time are undistinguished and

6-32 The Forgan name is synonymous with fine clubmaking in St. Andrews. The business that began with Robert Forgan (see photo 6-6) at the helm in the middle of the 19th century continued to serve golfers until the 1960s with clubs such as this late 1930s steel-shafted Tommy Armour model. Their shop, shown here in 1952, overlooked the 18th hole of the Old Course. Although the building now is home to the St. Andrews Woolen Mill, the Forgan name lives on in the brass letters set in the sidewalk near the front door.

6-31 *Buhrke (not to be con-fused with Burke) was a bag manufacturer that subsequently produced clubs and balls.*

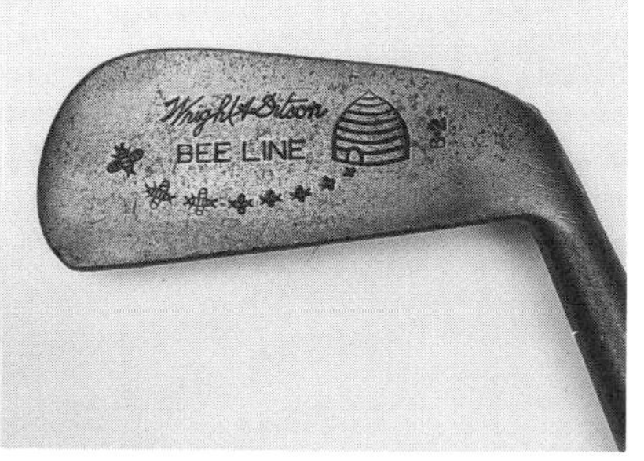

6-33 *Was the Bee Line of lesser quality than an "A" Line? Wright & Ditson originally was an Boston sporting goods retailer, co-founded by George Wright, a 19th-century baseball pioneer. The firm sold hand forged clubs as early as the 1890s. By the turn of the century, they were acquired by Spalding, who manufactured Wright & Ditson clubs in the same factories as their Spalding brands. The Bee Line was made circa 1915-30.*

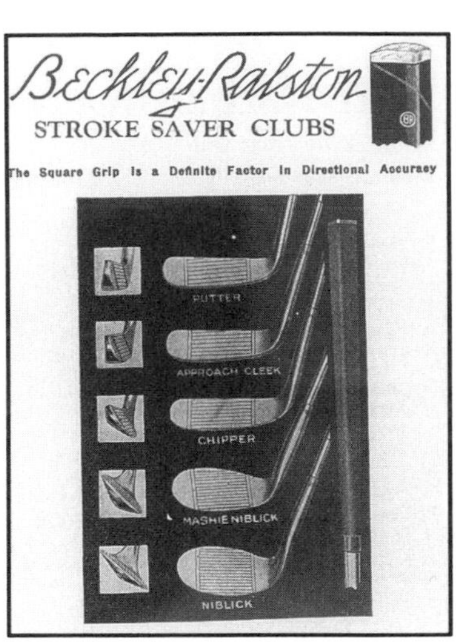

6-34 *Beckley-Ralston of Chicago specialized in making putters and utility clubs. Their trademark feature was a long, square leather grip designed to promote "directional accuracy."*

6-35 *Many contemporary golfers are familiar with "Iron Byron" and other high-tech mechanical devices that manufacturers use to test golf clubs and balls. Similar machines were employed in the days of hickory shafts, such as this weight-driven contraption at the Burke Golf Company in Newark, Ohio.*

inexpensive to collect. Therefore, these mass-produced, hickory-shafted clubs are best suited for use as playable classics or as "wall-hangers" — clubs that are good for decorative purposes.

6-36 *The Crawford, McGregor and Canby Company began making clubs in the late 1890s. During the 1930s, the company started marking clubs with a "Mac" prefix instead of "Mc" for a Scottish flair. After several years of the dual spelling, the corporate name was changed to MacGregor.*

COLLECTING TIP

■ **The sequential numbering of golf clubs was not universally adopted until the 1940s. The traditional 19th-century and older Scottish names for clubs were modified into the following terms which were popular well into the 20th century:**

WOODS	**1**	**driver**
	2	**brassie**
	3	**spoon**
IRONS	**1**	**driving cleek or iron**
	2	**mid iron**
	3	**mid mashie**
	4	**mashie iron**
	5	**mashie**
	6	**spade mashie**
	7	**mashie niblick**
	8/9	**niblick**

PATENT CLUBS

(1920s - 1930s)

Some of the more popular antique golf clubs are those with extraordinary features, better known as patent clubs. As the name implies, these clubs were so unique to have been granted patents or were "patent pending." The antique examples covered in this chapter are wooden-shafted and were made in Great Britain from the 1890s through the 1920s.

Patents were awarded to individuals who devised clubs with unique shapes, improved performance or had other novel features. There are several hundred patent clubs; some were extensively manufactured

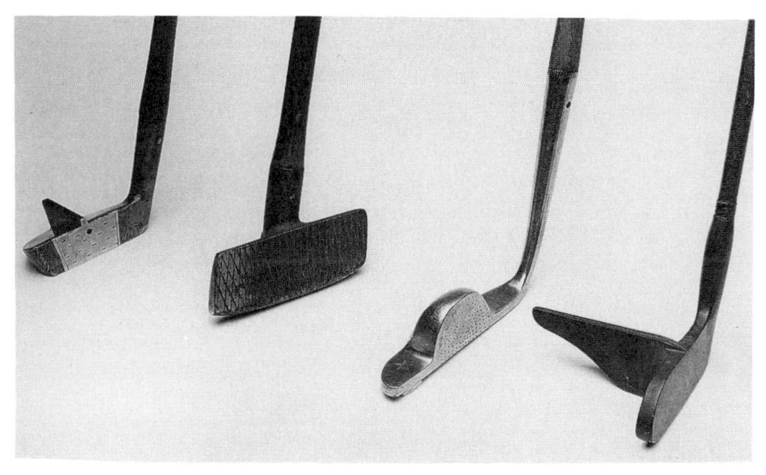

6-37 *Some of the oddest looking patent clubs are putters. From left: bronze Nesco model, with a steel face and aiming aid; Gouick Dundee center-shafted putter; Gibson of Kinghorn enlarged sweet spot putter; Crosby "T" head directional putter.*

6-38 *Official patent registration documents—an inventor's dream and possibly a manufacturer's gold mine. This is the U.S. patent awarded to James Ross Brown for his famous slotted irons in 1905, two years after he received his British patent. (See photo 6-66)*

PATENT PUTTER—NEWLY OUT.

DEADLY ON THE GREEN.

GOLF says : " Mr. Aitken is working on the correct lines for a Putter, by presenting a deep, straight face behind the ball, and in allowing it to have the full benefit of impact with the striking surface of the club. We have tried the Club, and can speak in this sense from actual experiment.

In Iron or Gun Metal, 6s. 6d. each, Carriage Paid.

A. AITKEN,
Golf Club and Ball Maker,
BARNTON GOLF COURSE, near EDINBURGH.
London Agent: FRANK BRYAN, 38, Charterhouse Square, London.

6-39 *As shown in this ad from the 1890s, the patent aspect was an effective marketing tool.*

and are commonplace today while others had such a short production life that only one or two examples were made. The fact that most were ruled illegal by golf's governing bodies actually adds to their collectibility.

A number of patent clubs — considered newfangled or far-fetched when introduced decades ago — had features which now are considered ordinary. These included: "woods" with heads made of metal and other non-wood materials, center-shafted and offset hosel putters, perimeter clubhead weighting, alignment aids incorporated into club design and, of course, the most significant change of this century — steel shafts.

Of all the types of golf clubs, putters deviate the most from traditional designs. Since the putting stroke is comparatively short, the club is not subjected to the physical demands of speed and torque that are associated with a full swing. This allows the clubmaker to produce a club emphasizing balance, feel and appearance that will enable a golfer to properly aim and execute the short rolling shot.

Because patent clubs make such extraordinary conversation pieces, golfers like to collect them. Some of the popular models, such as Smith or Fairlie anti-shank clubs and deep-groove irons, were made by the thousands and are inexpensive to obtain. Mills aluminum putters also are plentiful. On the other hand, rake irons, one-piece woods and other clubs, of which only a few remain, can be worth several thousand dollars. There are the one-of-a-kind examples that connoisseurs yearn for.

The following pages explore the fascinating realm of these non-traditional clubs in the major categories of woods, irons and putters.

6-40 *Patent clubs can be found in all shapes and sizes. Some designs were incorporated into production models, while others proved impractical for one reason or another. The major drawback of this club was finding a caddy capable of carrying it.*

PATENT WOODS

Many patent woods are prized because they were made of materials other than wood or have the heads attached by methods that deviate from the traditional scare or socket joint. Some incorporate unusual shapes and designs.

The most plentiful examples were the aluminum clubs, especially those made under the Mills patent by the Standard Golf Company of Sunderland, England. Whereas the insides of modern metal "woods" are filled with material similar to Styrofoam, the Mills clubs had wooden centers. These innovative clubs were so popular in the late 1890s that the company designed entire sets: from driver to niblick. Spalding and several smaller companies also were active in the production of aluminum clubs.

One of the most desirable patent woods is the one-piece wood, with the shaft and head made from a single block of wood. These remarkable clubs were made from the mid-1890s until just after the turn-of-the-century. Most examples were American made and are stamped Dunn, BGI or Spalding.

6-41 *Anti-slicing clubs have always been a popular gimmick. One wonders if repeated use would require the purchase of anti-hooking clubs. Frank Johnson — not to be confused with club inventors Claude Johnson and T. Johnston — had a small golf business in London during the first decade of this century.*

6-42 *Some golf club patents are purely cosmetic. These woods made by Gibson of Kinghorn sport initialed soleplates that signify spoon, brassie and driver.*

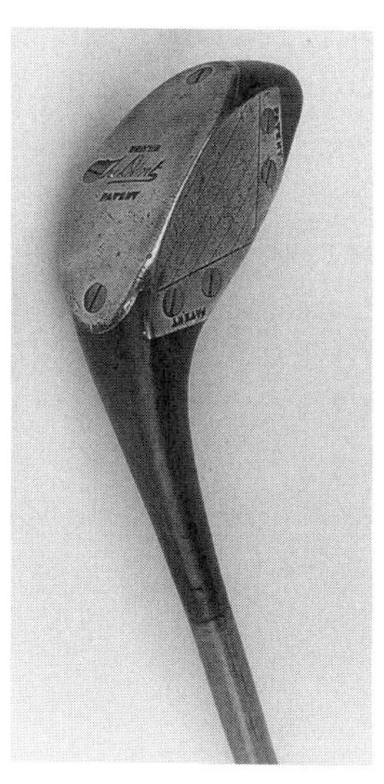

6-43 *The Dint patent wood appears structurally sound, with a one-piece brass soleplate and clubface.*

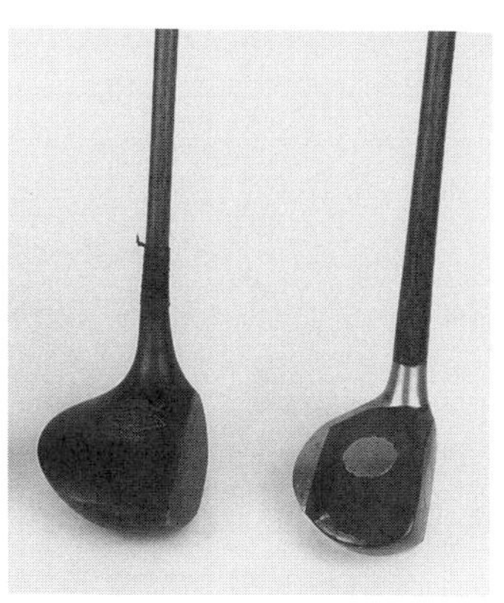

6-44 *Unusual shafting configurations on old clubs included the Velometer (left) and one of several methods that combined metal and wood for cosmetic and performance reasons.*

6-45 *The theory of the center-shafted Simplex clubs from the turn-of-the-century (left) and the Crooker patent Streamliner steel shaft clubs from the 1930s is to place the shaft behind the sweet spot in order to eliminate club twist. The Simplex clubs — made in eight lofts, from driver to putter — were intended to be used as a set. However the Streamliner, which was marketed in America by MacGregor, only came in 1-, 3- and 4-wood styles.*

6-46 *Spalding offered this Model R mallet-style wood with a brass faceplate, but no soleplate at the turn-of-the-century.*

6-47 *Claude Johnson's wood with an integral metal socket for the shaft was patented in 1893.*

COLLECTING TIP

■ **If you come across a bulger-style driver without whipping and can't see a clear line where the shaft enters the head, don't assume that you have a one-piece club. Odds are that you don't. Because club necks were sanded smooth to blend into the shaft, it can be difficult to see the transition. The best way to verify one-piece construction is to check the roundness of the neck. Socket-head clubs tend to be circular in cross-section, while one-piece clubs generally are oval.**

6-48 *Modern utility clubs mimic some of the clubs patented in the early 20th century. Park's Pikup (above) utilized "rails" on the soleplate to quickly move the club through deep grass. The Dunlewy patent wood and iron by the Stadium Golf Company (right) used V-shaped soles to contend with difficult lies.*

NON-WOOD HEADS

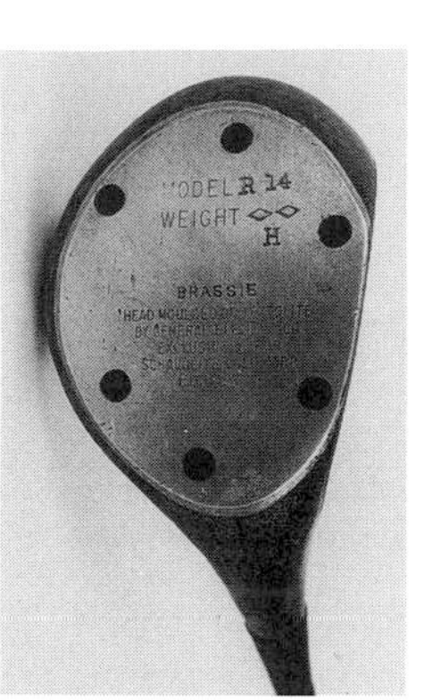

6-49 *Although non-traditional materials such as graphite and ceramics now are being utilized as clubhead materials, the concept is not new. The Schavolite Golf Corporation offered heads in the 1940s molded from durable Textolite, a resin developed by the General Electric Company.*

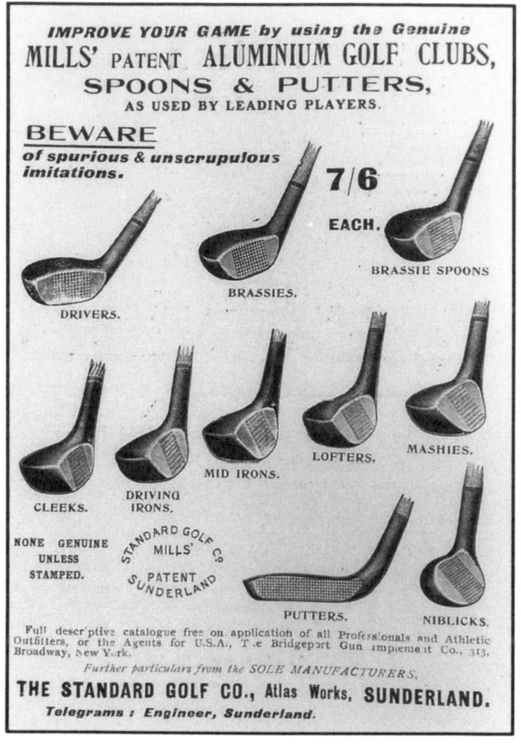

6-51 *Englishman William Mills was a pioneer in the design of metal woods. His 1896 patent for an aluminum head with a wood core enabled the Standard Golf Company to become a major international supplier of clubs. This 1903 ad shows a fraction of the numerous driver, fairway club and putter options. Manufactured until World War II, the often imitated, wood-filled heads were available with steel shafts in the 1930s. Many of the putter styles were named after and used by famous professionals, including James Braid and Ted Ray.*

6-50 *Inserts were first placed in the striking face of woods to repair damage. By the early 1890s, clubmakers tried to improve the performance of their products by experimenting with various insert materials. The Ramsbottom patent (left) is an aluminum club with a dovetailed brass insert and the Mill's club (right) had an aluminum body with a wooden face.*

6-52 *Willie Dunn, Jr. and his nephew John D. Dunn — members of the famous Scottish family of ball and clubmakers — moved to the United States at the end of the 19th century and were influential in developing the budding golf industry. This club, a 1903 Dunn patent, was similar in construction to the innovative Haskell golf ball that had been introduced a few years earlier. This club actually contained tightly wound rubber strands that were intended to impart extra energy to the golf ball. In spite of its supposedly magnificent attributes, the club was not popular with golfers.*

WOOD SPLICES

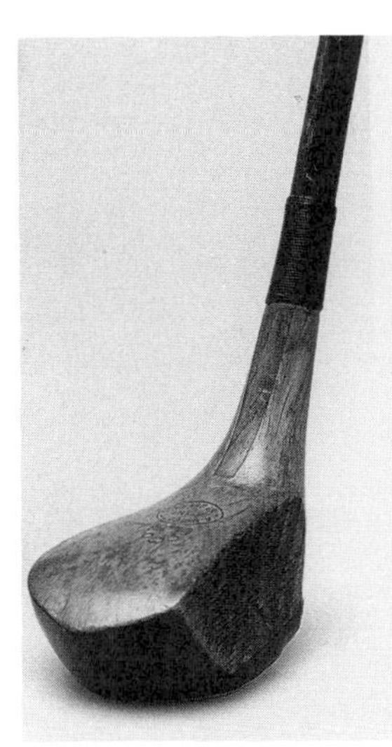

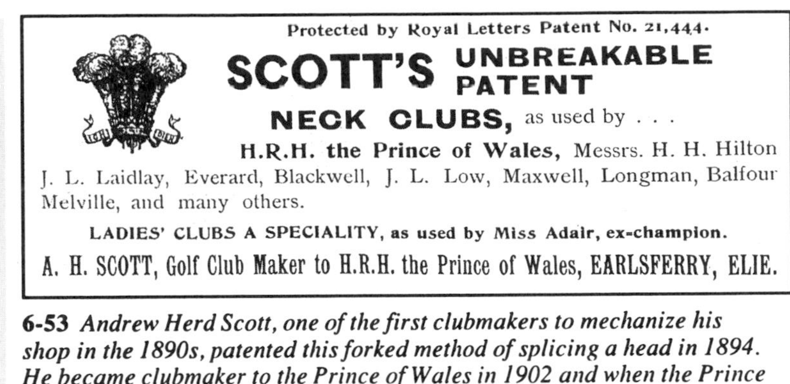
Protected by Royal Letters Patent No. 21,444.
SCOTT'S UNBREAKABLE PATENT
NECK CLUBS, as used by . . .
H.R.H. the Prince of Wales, Messrs. H. H. Hilton J. L. Laidlay, Everard, Blackwell, J. L. Low, Maxwell, Longman, Balfour Melville, and many others.
LADIES' CLUBS A SPECIALITY, as used by Miss Adair, ex-champion.
A. H. SCOTT, Golf Club Maker to H.R.H. the Prince of Wales, EARLSFERRY, ELIE.

6-53 *Andrew Herd Scott, one of the first clubmakers to mechanize his shop in the 1890s, patented this forked method of splicing a head in 1894. He became clubmaker to the Prince of Wales in 1902 and when the Prince became King George V in 1911, Scott became clubmaker to the King. (Forgan had made clubs for the previous monarch, Edward VII, both as king and as Prince of Wales.) Both clubmakers were permitted to mark all of their clubs with the insignia of the king's crown or prince's feathers while holding the royal appointment.*

Golfers Old AND Golfers New!
WE HAVE CLUBS
TO SUIT YOU ALL,
JOHN D. DUNN'S celebrated one-piece club, drives "sweetly" and adds 20 yds. to a drive.
Whether Experts or Beginners, Devotees of the Game, or Devotees of Exercise.
Caddy Bags, Balls, Etc.
— MANUFACTURED BY —
THE BRIDGEPORT GUN IMPLEMENT COMPANY,
— SOLD BY —
HARTLEY & GRAHAM, 313 Broadway, New York.
AGENCIES: 300 W. 59th St., N. Y.
533 Fulton St., Brooklyn, N. Y.
162 Columbus Ave., Boston, Mass.
Wholesale Agents for Massachusetts, Maine, New Hampshire and Vermont.
DAME, STODDARD & KENDALL, BOSTON.

6-54 *The Bridgeport Gun Implement Company (BGI)—a firearms company and one of the first American club manufacturers—was making several unique woods nearly a century ago. Their V-type forked splice (right) and their club with no splice at all—the rare one-piece wood patented in 1894 (far right)—are both museum quality antiques. In spite of their quality workmanship, the company only made golf clubs for about 10 years.*

6-55 *This delicate multiple splice ran a foot up the shaft as the whipping indicates.*

PATENT IRONS

Many patent irons were utility clubs, designed to extricate the ball from a troublesome lie or to achieve a certain type of shot. Golfers would add a couple of these clubs to their arsenal, much the way modern players use wedges or specialized fairway woods.

Although many of these clubs were offered in various lofts, using a complete set of patent clubs might have been an admission of poor golfing skills. After all, who would have the nerve to carry a bag full of anti-shank irons? Certain clubs, such as the Bussey irons with their brass heads and iron hosels or the Maxwells with their perforated hosels were more likely candidates for regular use.

Some of the best known of all patent clubs are the most exotic ones, such as the Brown Patent Perforated Irons (see photo 6-66). Patented in 1903, these clubs often referred to as rake or water irons — are famous for their fancy perforations and slots in the clubface. James Ross Brown, a blacksmith from Montrose, Scotland, designed the clubs to reduce the interference of long grass or sand between the ball and clubface.

Although golf collectors were long familiar with Brown's clubs, the rest of the golfing world only discovered their existence recently when a "Major" model iron apparently sold for more than $80,000 at a 1989 golf auction in Glasgow. Veteran followers of the golf collecting scene suspected that an error had been made since the club was in poor condition and therefore worth no more than a few thousand dollars. Magazines and newspapers throughout the world reported the astounding sale. Except that there was no sale. Evidently, two parties were recklessly bidding by telephone and although the club "sold" for the unheard-of sum, reportedly it was never picked up or paid for.

ADJUSTABLE CLUBS

6-56 *The All-One adjustable iron had only three settings. What appears to be an endorsement in the advertisement from noted amateur Chick Evans is probably a borrowed quote that refers not to the adjustable club, but to the fact that he won the 1916 U.S. Open while carrying only seven clubs.*

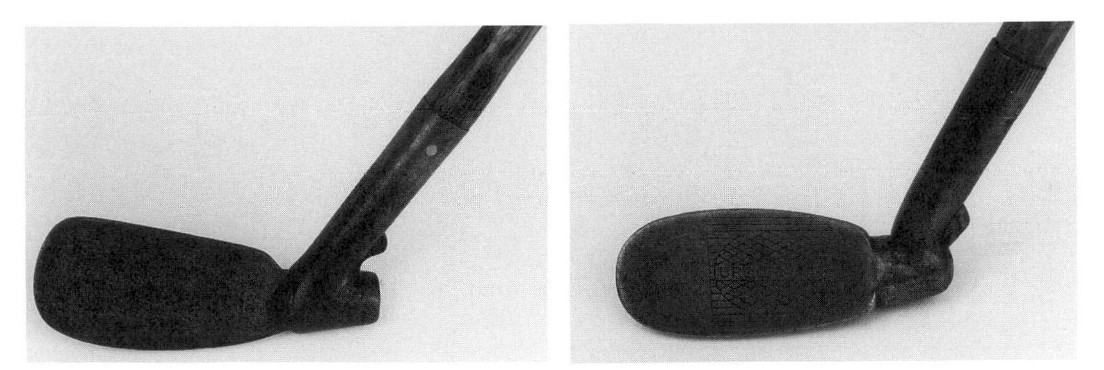

6-57 *Urquhart's Ltd., of Edinburgh, was a family business that pioneered the adjustable loft golf club in the early 1890s and was awarded numerous patents for additional enhancements. The smooth-face club (left) was made circa 1895, while the other club with the scored face and improved locking mechanism was made about eight years later. These novelty clubs were the only clubs made by the firm, which ceased production in 1906.*

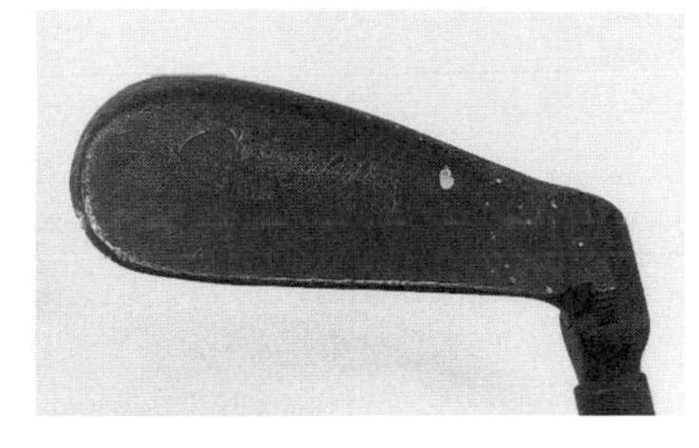

6-58 *The Novakclub adjustable club was made in San Francisco during the 1920s and had an early steel shaft. Note the external gearing.*

CLUBFACE STYLES

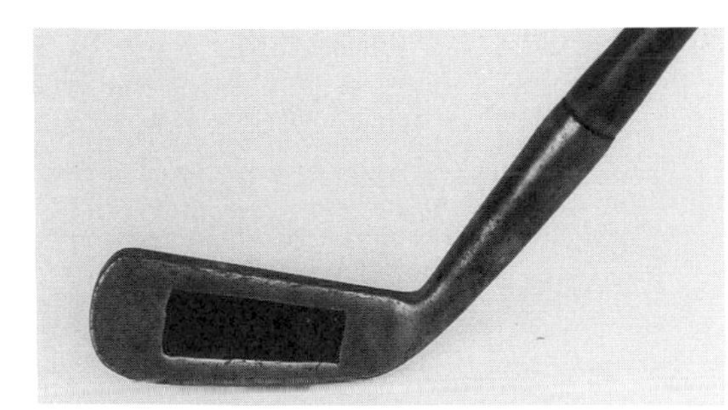

6-59 *Irons with leather inserts for "softer feel" were promoted by the highly regarded Nicoll company of St. Andrews in the 1890s. This particular club was retailed by Robert Black Wilson, a local golf professional.*

6-60 *The Anderson crescent head mid-iron. Since it has no hosel, the brass pin that retains the shaft penetrates right through the clubface.*

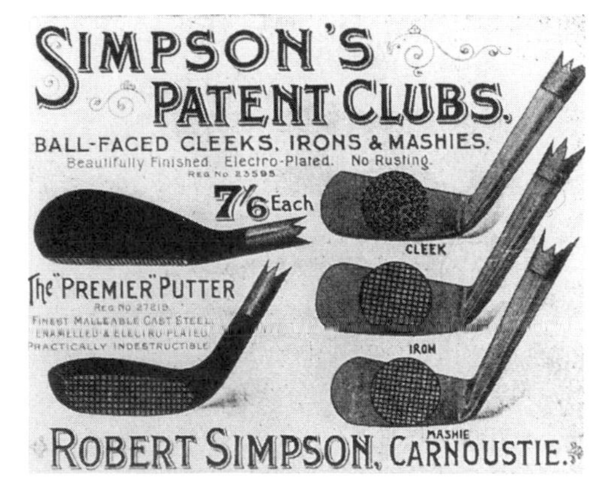

6-61 *Robert Simpson, of Carnoustie, patented an iron in 1903 that featured an oversize circular sweet spot stamped to resemble a golf ball. Perhaps even more significant was that his clubs were some of the first to be electroplated to guard against rust — a procedure that was about two decades ahead of the rest of the industry.*

6-62 *The forerunner of the 60°, square-grooved wedge must have been Kroydon's Banner brand 50° niblick with vertical square grooves.*

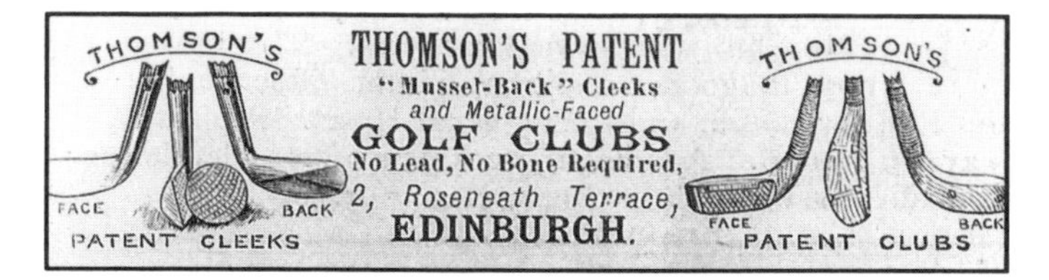

6-63 *Although Thomson's patent for an iron with a convex or "mussel" back was granted in 1891, he received little protection for his departure from the traditional flat-back design. His idea for concentrating clubhead weight behind the sweet spot was reconfigured and copied many times. Modern club manufacturers regularly run advertisements that misconstrue the original meaning of this club shape — one that resembles the shell of the mussel mollusk. They incorrectly use the homonym "muscle" to describe similar irons.*

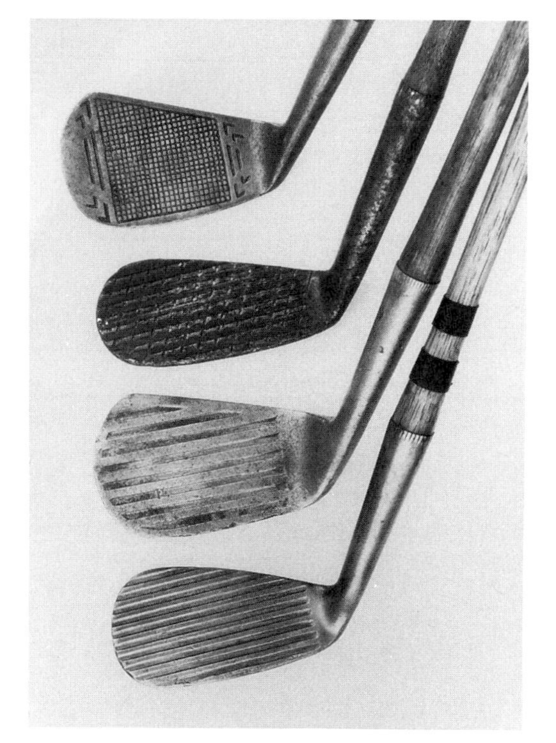

6-64 *When face markings became commonplace at the beginning of the century, all types of unusual patterns were presented to golfers. The deep-groove irons that made their debut in 1914 brought on controversy similar to the recent arguments over clubs with square grooves. Opponents of the unorthodox clubs claimed that the excessive backspin produced by the grooves was making the game too easy. Finally, after Jock Hutchinson won the 1921 U.S. Open with deep-groove clubs, they were declared illegal and soon went out of production. Pictured is a sampling of clubs that carried trade names such as Dedstop, Stopum, Shur Stop, Holdem and Bakspin.*

COLLECTING TIP

■ **The following nine clubs are essential to a collection of patent irons. All were made in sufficient quantities to satisfy the wants of today's collectors. However, increased demand has caused values to escalate considerably during the last decade. They are grouped below in order of rarity, with the rarer clubs at the top of the list. (Because of fads or market manipulation, the hard-to-find clubs are not always the most expensive.)**

Cran (photo 6-65)
Spring-faced (photo 6-65)
Urquhart (photo 6-57)

Giant niblick (photo 6-73)

Carruthers (photo 6-72)
Deep-groove (photo 6-64)
Fairlie (photo 6-71)
Smith (photo 6-71)

Maxwell (photo 6-68)

6-65 *The American sporting goods firm of A.G. Spalding & Bros. first offered golf goods in 1892 after a young employee named Julian Curtiss (left) bought some clubs while on a trip to Scotland. For the next 50 years, Spalding was the premier manufacturer of golf clubs and balls in both the United States and Great Britain. Two of their notable club innovations were the Cran cleek (center), patented in 1897 with its wood insert, and the spring-faced iron (right) with a semi-hollow head, patented by W. Ross in 1893. Although both clubs were in production for several decades, they are highly prized by collectors. Curtiss, shown above in later years with some relics, eventually became president of the Spalding company.*

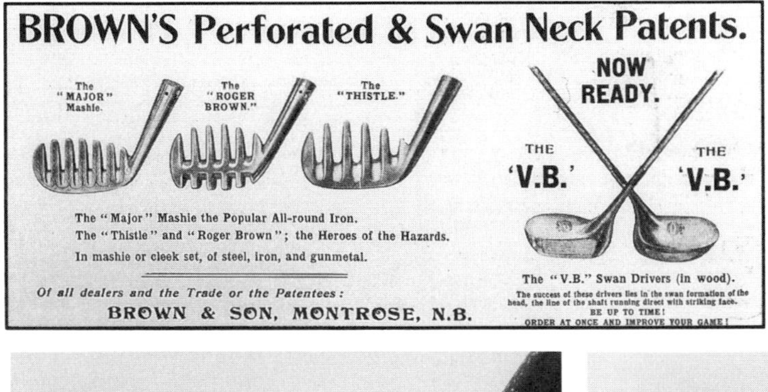

6-66 *Brown's patent perforated irons were made in at least nine different styles in the early 1900s. This "Major Niblick" rake iron was designed to reduce the interference of sand, grass or water between the ball and clubface. Several makers tried to duplicate the look, but none had the attractive filigree of the originals, made by Winton. (Also see photo 6-38)*

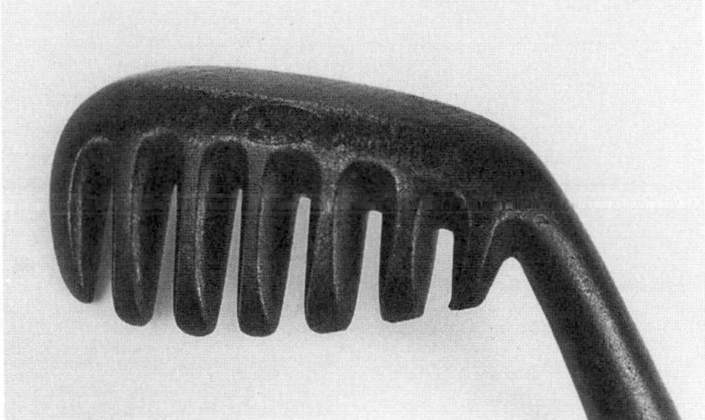

PATENT HOSELS

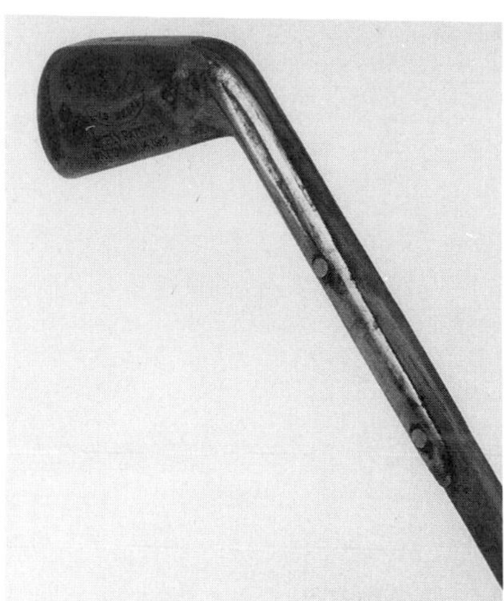

6-67 *The Seely clubhead had two tangs that extended up the shaft and was held in place by two pins. The hickory shaft was very susceptable to damage from moisture.*

MAXWELL IRONS.

Made in the following Models: Cleek, Mashie Cleek, Driving Mashie, Driving Iron, Medium Iron, Mashie Iron, Jigger, Ordinary Mashie, Deep-faced Mashie, Baxpin Mashie, Putting Cleeks and Wry-necked Putters. Fitted with the best Selected Hickory Shafts. Used by most of the Leading Amateurs and Professionals. Records already broken—

JACK WHITE at Sunningdale, and BEN SAYERS, Jun., at Wimbledon.

To be obtained from the Inventor: BEN SAYERS, Jun., ROYAL WIMBLEDON GOLF CLUB, Wimbledon, S.W.

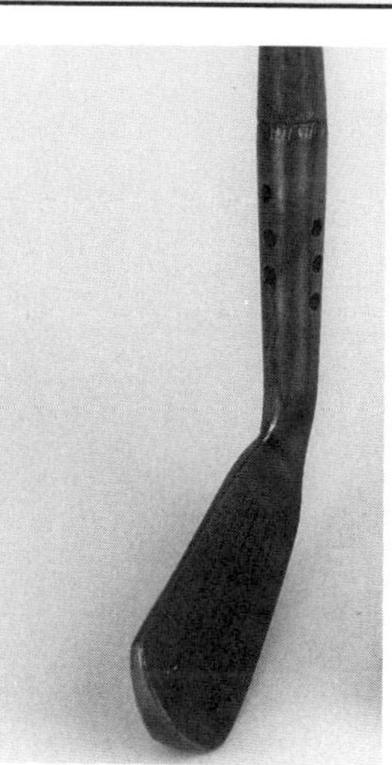

6-68 *Clubmakers tried all kinds of methods to remove excess weight from iron hosels. The popular Maxwell patent of 1910 (left) had a series of holes drilled in the hosel. Although some were made by makers such as Sayers (above) most examples are stamped with the star cleekmark to signify that it was made by Gibson of Kinghorn.*

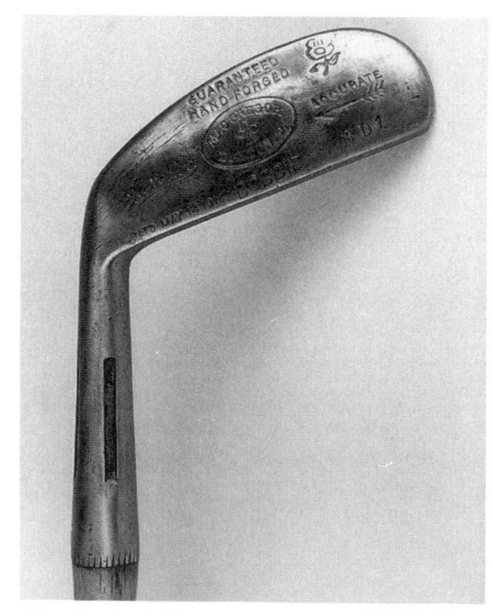

6-69 *The Bobbie patent iron of 1918 had a slotted hosel and rounded sole. Made by MacGregor, this club was stamped with several of the company's cleekmarks.*

6-70 *Some patent clubs came from areas normally not associated with golf. John Dwight, of Des Moines, Iowa, invented several golf clubs in early 20th century, such as this "Direction" anti-shank club. Sometimes a shaft stamp (above) can be very revealing.*

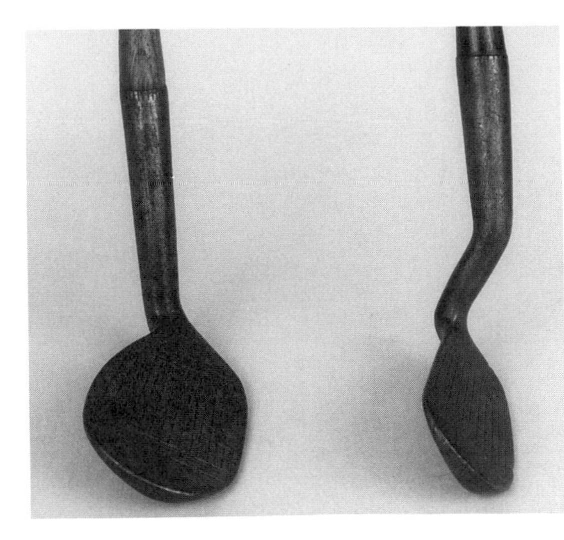

6-71 *Shanking, socketing or whatever cursed name golfers call that dreadful lateral shot has been part of the game for ages. Clubmakers first attempted to cure this malady in the 1890s by eliminating the socket area of the hosel. The two most significant designs were the Fairlie patent (left) that positioned the leading edge of the club way ahead of the shaft and the Smith patent (right) that had a double bend in the hosel. Produced for several decades, both models are readily obtainable and make wonderful conversation pieces.*

6-72 *Thomas Carruthers' concept of a thru-bore hosel, with the shaft extending through the bottom of the club, was patented in 1891. A century later, Wilson Sporting Goods and other manufacturers are still touting the advantages of the design.*

NIBLICKS

6-73 *The niblick, the traditional lofted short iron that eventually approximated the 9-iron, grew to enormous proportions in the 20th century. Cochrane's "mammoth" niblick (left) measured 6 inches from heel to toe, while a "giant" Cardinal niblick (center) measured 4 1/2 inches. The conventional sand iron (right) is from the 1930s. The clubs were a short-lived fad, since the novelty soon wore off when the average golfer realized how unwieldy the clubs were.*

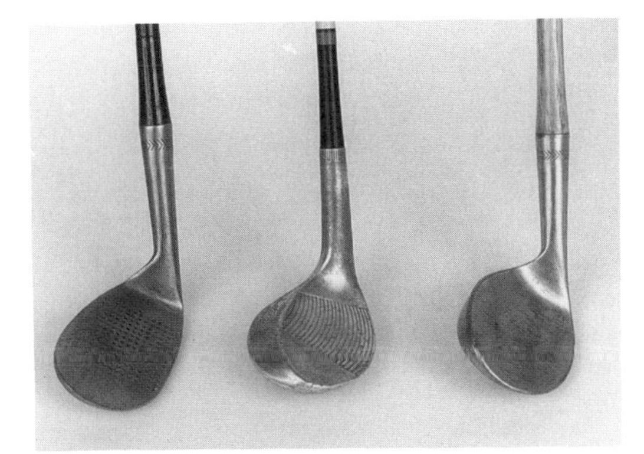

6-74 *The L.A. Young Company of Detroit manufactured the Walter Hagen line of golf clubs prior to its acquisition by Wilson Sporting Goods. Their most noteworthy clubs were their sand wedges: from left, the Iron Man, the round-bottomed Sandy Andy and the concave wedge with its huge flange. The patented concave wedge, introduced in 1929 and used by Bobby Jones, was outlawed in 1931 after it was determined that the club was likely to contact the ball more than once during a shot.*

PATENT PUTTERS

Rather than improve their putting skills by practicing, many golfers chose to invent new putters. Some of the putter designs were a combination of imagination and frustration, while others utilized common sense. Interestingly, two features commonly seen on contemporary putters were so unusual nearly a century ago, they qualified for patent protection.

The majority of putters sold today feature offset or gooseneck — hosels that aid in properly positioning the golfer's hands ahead of the clubface. This concept is attributed to two-time British Open champion Willie Park, Jr., who single-handedly developed and popularized the idea. Park's Wry Necked Putter, patented in 1894, was a simple steel blade-style putter with a bend in the hosel (see photo 6-78).

Park's putter was a novelty at a time when many golfers were still using old-fashioned, scared-head wooden putters. *Golf Illustrated* provided support for the club in 1899, when it reported that the "unorthodox appearance soon vanishes after a few waggles."

Another feature, so unassuming that few would think its design was once protected by a patent, is the attachment of the shaft to the head at a point away from the heel of the club — the center-shafted putter. A modern example of this concept is the Bulls-eye putter, one of the all-time, best-selling clubs.

6-75 *A Mills cross-head, or mallet, aluminum putter.*

It's difficult to imagine, but in 1910, the R & A initiated a ban on center-shafted clubs that lasted for nearly half a century. Many golf history books report that the rules change was precipitated by the winning of the 1904 British Amateur Championship by Walter Travis, an American. But it was not until 1908 that the R & A seriously contemplated outlawing the popular American club design.

6-76 *Although most adjustable clubs were made as all-in-one irons, some putters also were produced. Dating from the early-20thcentury, the Boye patent (left) featured a lie adjustment, while the ball-and-socket design of the Sprague patent (right) afforded adjustments in both lie and loft.*

6-77 *Some of the unconventional putters were the Dalrymple patent of 1892, with an additional lofted face for chipping and a center-shafted disc type model.*

6-78 *The 1894 patent awarded to Willie Park, Jr. for his wry-neck putter has been the most significant putter patent in golf history. The majority of putters made today employ this simple feature that helps the golfer to position his hands. Although the club is marked "Willie Park's Original Bent Neck Putter" (left), it is not an original, but rather one of the numerous models made after the turn-of-the-century. The initial clubs were stamped with Park's regular name stamp (right). They frequently are worn thin from years of use and polishing.*

6-79 *Although the unusual Hackbarth putter was not invented by golf pro Otto Hackbarth, he made and sold the forked putters in the early 20th century. He was not a touring pro, but played well enough to win the 1940 PGA Seniors' Championship. He held club jobs in St. Louis, Chicago and later in Cincinnati, where this photo was taken in 1934 — when he was using a mallet-type putter!*

6-80 *Croquet-style putting — where the golfer faces the hole and swings the putter between his legs — has been both legal and illegal during the 20th century. Easily recognized by its perfectly upright shaft, this Pendulum patent putter dates to the turn-of-the-century. Sam Snead was the most notable player to putt astride the ball, but he did so by separating his hands on a conventional putter. When the method was finally barred in 1967, the persistent Snead compromised with his own "side-saddle" style.*

6-81 *Mallet-style putters were shafted either in the middle or heel of the clubhead. The large wooden club (left) was designed by Frenchman Jean Gassiat, a dominant player on the Continent and longtime professional at Chantilly Golf Club in the early 20th century. The McDougal patent (right) was an aluminum club from the 1920s that had a T-square alignment feature.*

6-82 *George Bussey and Co. of London, made a line of clubs that featured a brass head welded to a steel hosel. When new, Bussey patent putters and irons had a one-piece leather grip with a long, sewn seam. Since the bi-metal heads often tarnish and discolor, it is usually the grip that tips the astute collector off to this collectible patent.*

6-83 *This aluminum putter had a built-in cavity so that the golfer could pick up a ball without bending over.*

6-84 *The Terwhit putter, with its convex face and hollow back, probably was designed to minimize the con-tact area between the clubface and ball. Perhaps the concept seemed ideal on paper, but in actual use, an imprecise stroke likely would result in a topped or even double-hit putt.*

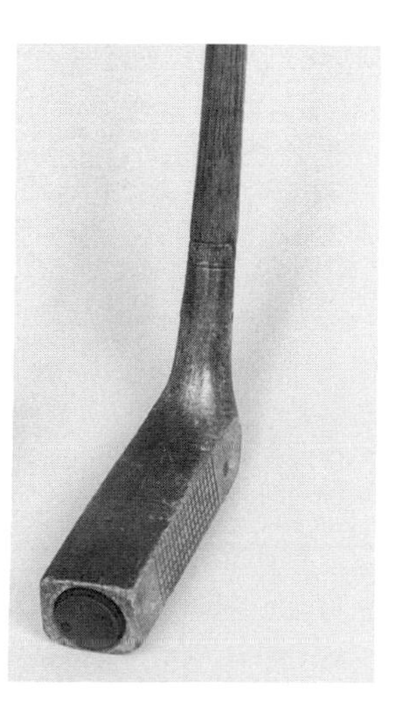

6-85 *The Daniel putter could be used right- or left-handed. Its patented characteristic was a cavity that held an adjustable weight. A removable brass screw afforded access to the weights.*

6-86 *Most offset, or wry-neck, putters were constructed of metal. This unique beech scared-head example was made by Brand of Carnoustie, circa 1900.*

THE CONTROVERSIAL SCHENECTADY PUTTER

6-87 *The Schenectady center-shafted, mallet-style putter, was patented in 1903 by Arthur Knight from, where else but Schenectady, New York. Hard-to-find early examples were made prior to the patent award (far left). The "patented" designation (left) is the marking commonly seen today.*

6-88 *The controversy over clubs like the Schenectady was played out in the golf magazines from 1908 to 1910. This cartoon summarizes the plight of the golf professional when the clubs were banned in Great Britain.*

IMPORTANT NOTICE—to Golfers using Centre Shafted and ***SCHENECTADY*** Putters, the only Clubs to take their place are the

"BRAID-MILLS" Putters.

To be had from all Professionals and Sports Outfitters, and

The Sole Manufacturers, THE STANDARD GOLF CO., SUNDERLAND.

6-90 *The Standard Golf Company was more than willing to sell conforming clubs to former Schenectady users.*

6-89 *After Walter Travis putted brilliantly with a Schenectady to win the 1904 British Amateur, several clubmakers began advertising the new club. Spalding, Standard Golf and Lillywhites all claimed to be selling the same model that Travis used.*

6-91 *William Howard Taft, an avid golfer, was president of the United States when the R & A modified their rules in 1910 to prohibit center-shafted putters. Like most American golfers, he must have been pleased when the USGA chose to maintain the status quo in 1911. Otherwise he would have had to abandon his trusty putter, shown here.*

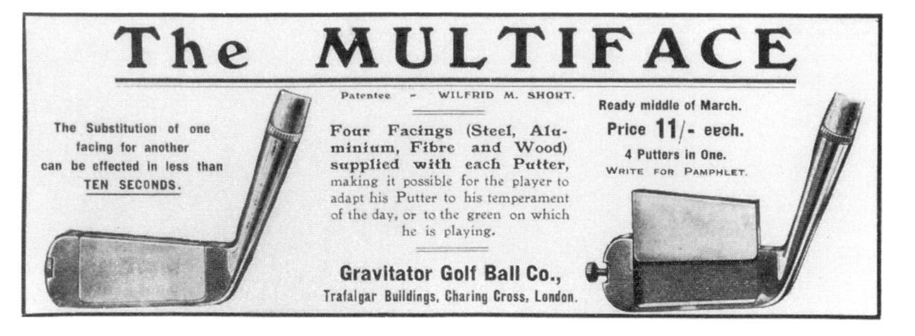

6-92 *Patented by Wilfrid Short in 1906, the Multiface putter had removable inserts of varying hardness so that the golfer could change the feel of the club as necessary.*

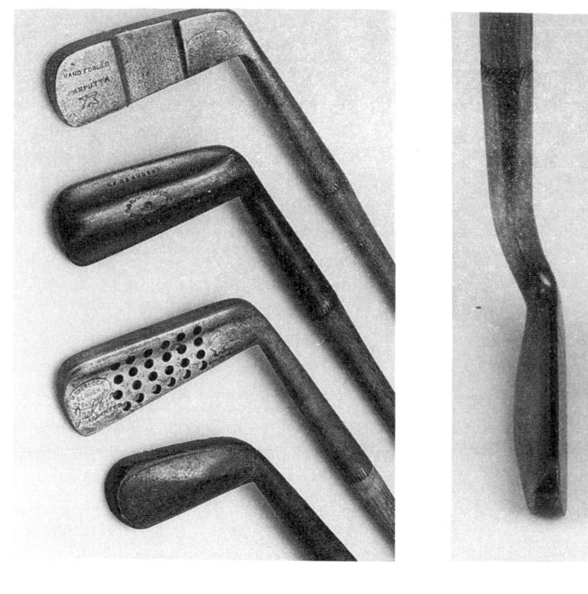

6-93 *For the last 100 years, clubmakers have toyed with the weighting of putters. Some place extra weight behind the center of the putter blade, while others concentrate the weight around the perimeter.*

6-94 *Most offset putters position the shaft ahead of the blade to help the golfer keep his hands in a desirable forward position. This putter, however, had a reverse offset.*

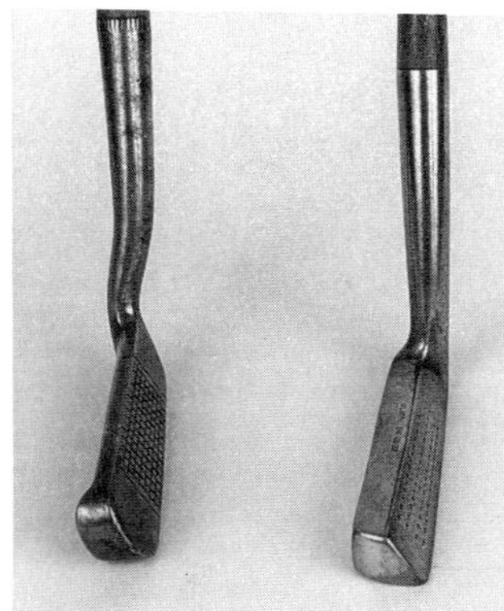

6-95 *Some clubs were made for long approach putts from on or off the green. Two such specialty clubs were the "Semi-putter" by MacGregor (left) and "The Scuffler" by the Stadium Golf Company of London (right).*

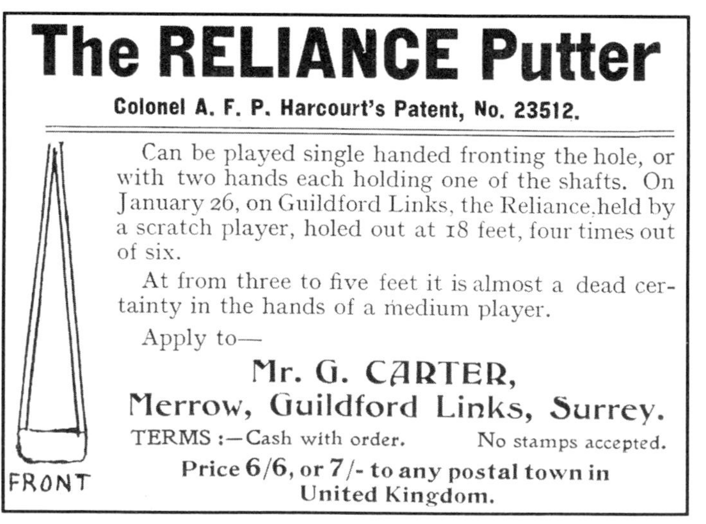

6-96 *Although this 1908 ad for the Reliance double-shaft putter claims that "from three to five feet it is almost a dead certainty..." the golfing public apparently did not agree. Probably only a few prototypes were produced as the authors have yet to see one.*

BOBBY JONES CLUBS

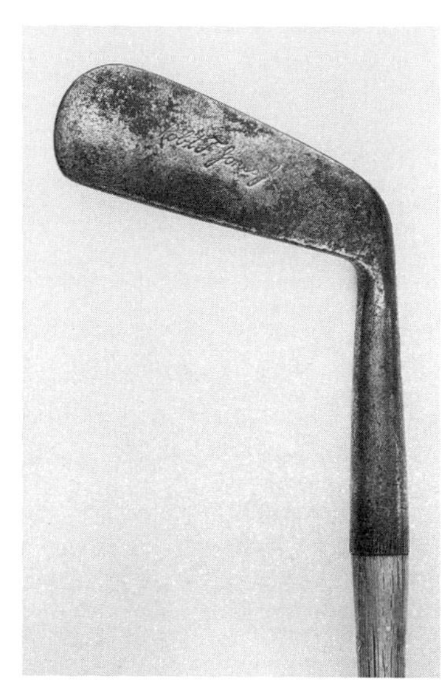

6-97 *The original Calamity Jane putter used by Bobby Jones was a simple offset blade putter, forged by Condie and sold by William Winton. It was nearly 20 years old and already had been nicknamed when it was given to Jones in 1920. According to a 1960 letter from Jones, he replaced the putter with a duplicate in 1926. Made by Spalding and known as Calamity Jane II, this putter helped Jones win the last 10 of his major championships. He later gave it to the USGA Museum, where it is now on public display. Calamity Jane I is at the Augusta National Golf Club.*

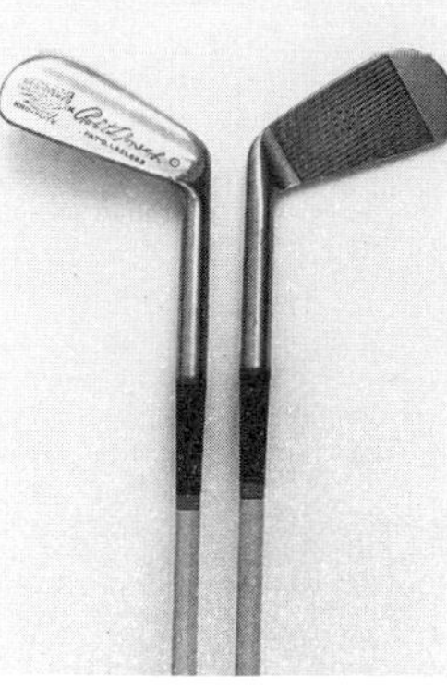

6-98 *Jones retired from competition after winning the Grand Slam in 1930 and became a consultant to Spalding, the clubmaking giant. (Although they liberally used his name to promote golf products, Jones never turned professional. He considered himself a "non-amateur.") The Bobby Jones line of clubs sold by the millions, making them one of the all-time top sellers. The clubs were introduced in 1932 in both steel and hickory versions, but after one year the hickory line was discontinued. Because the metal shafts had a wood-grain finish, many people mistake them for the rare wooden ones.*

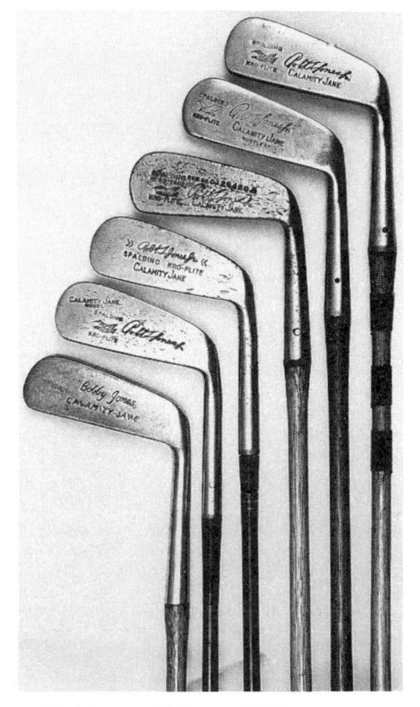

6-99 *From 1932 to 1973, Spalding made dozens of Calamity Jane models with both hickory and steel shafts. Some of the hickory-shafted models had three bands of whipping on the shaft, similar to Jones' original.*

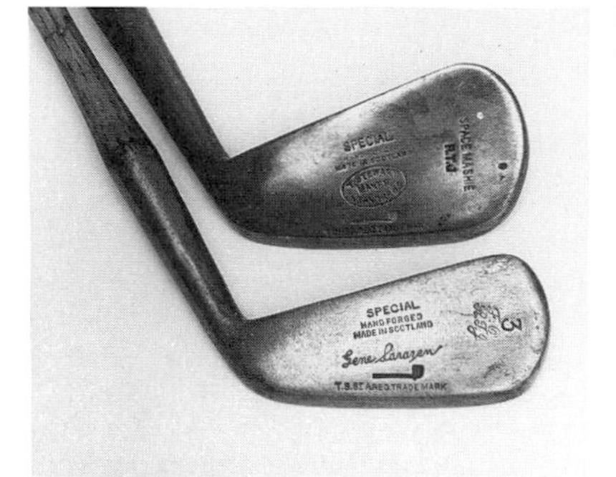

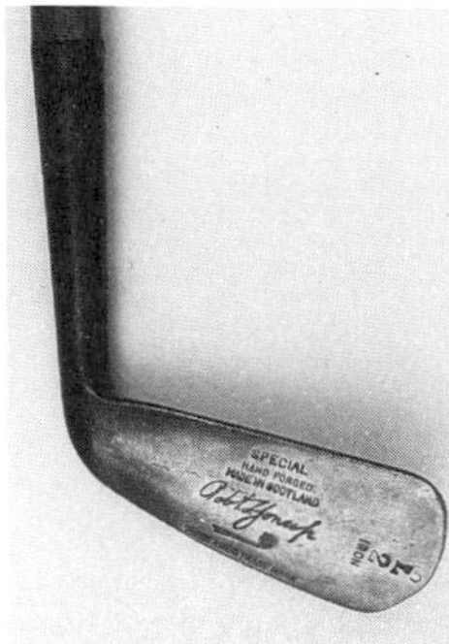

6-100 *Clubmaker Tom Stewart of St. Andrews took advantage of his relationship with Bobby Jones. After making some clubs for the great amateur in the late 1920s, Stewart sold a limited number of similar clubs to the public, stamped with the initials of Jones and also ones which had both Jones' initials and those of Francis Ouimet, another noted amateur (left). He also made a small number of clubs with Jones' signature (right).*

Shafts And Grips

While many enthusiasts focus their attention on the head of a club, it is important to consider the club as a whole. And that includes the shaft and grip.

The wooden shafts prior to 1800, usually were made of ash. The 19th-century clubmakers experimented with various woods (see photo 6-102), and in the 1850s, found imported American hickory to be the best material.

Hickory — durable and flexible — prevailed for nearly a century until steel took over. Although the first steel shaft was patented in 1894, it wasn't until the 1920s that golfers found the new material was capable of living up to the claims of superior accuracy, distance and feel. The metal-shafted clubs were so revolutionary that they weren't approved for use until 1925 by the USGA and until 1929 by the R & A.

The conversion from leather to rubber grips took much longer. (Jack Nicklaus and others still swear by leather grips.) But leather wasn't even the first type of grip. Clubs made prior to the mid-18th century usually had no grips at all. Then cloth strips — called listing — were wrapped around the club handle, and by the 19th century, sheepskin and other leathers were used.

Beginning in the 1890s, rubber and similar materials were wrapped, braided, slipped on and smeared on to shafts in an effort to make a more water-resistant grip. Finally by the 1950s, quality slip-on rubber grips became a popular choice of golfers.

6-101 *The most collectible early steel shaft is the Lard patent, nicknamed the "Whistler" because of the noise created during use as the air races through its intricate perforations.*

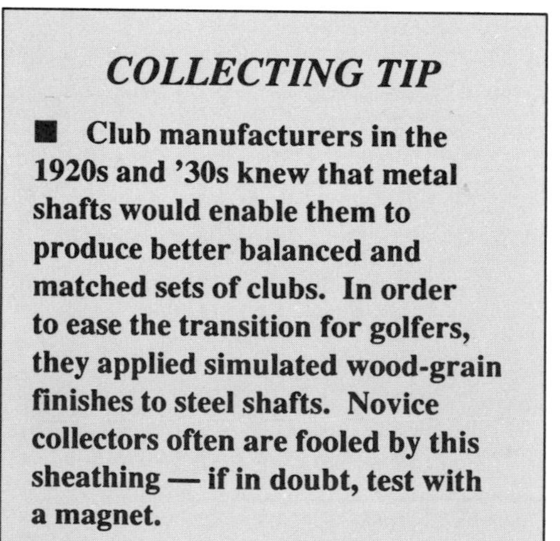

COLLECTING TIP

■ **Club manufacturers in the 1920s and '30s knew that metal shafts would enable them to produce better balanced and matched sets of clubs. In order to ease the transition for golfers, they applied simulated wood-grain finishes to steel shafts. Novice collectors often are fooled by this sheathing — if in doubt, test with a magnet.**

6-102 *In the 1890s clubmakers had a wide variety of woods to chose from for making shafts. Hickory, imported to Britain from the United States for use as tool handles as early as the 1820s, had become the preferred material by the middle of the century.*

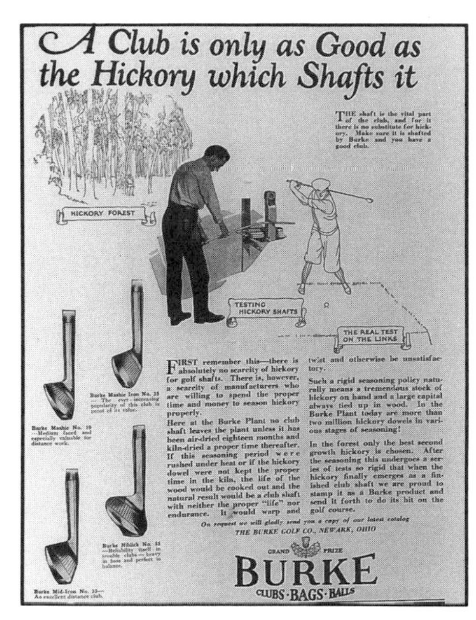

6-103 *In 1925, after about six years of serious experimentation, steel-shafted clubs were declared legal for use in the United States. These full-page magazine ads illustrate the steel versus hickory controversy that continued into the 1930s.*

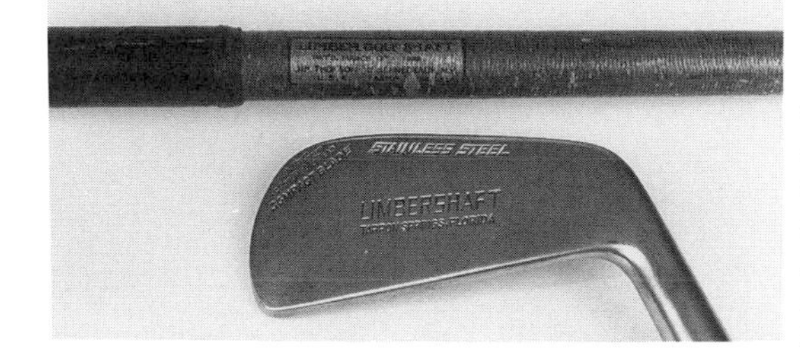

6-104 *The Limbershaft was a composition shaft made in the 1920s and offered by the Walter Hagen Company of Tarpon Springs, Florida. The Florida company was a financial disaster for Hagen. By the end of the decade, Hagen closed the factory and became affiliated with the L.A. Young Company of Detroit.*

6-105 *Some out-of-the-ordinary grips: from left, a silk damask listing, circa 1725, and an early 19th-century leather grip over a wool listing over-wrapped with leather; the Ashford, or Bussey, patent leather grip with a sewn seam, from the 1890s; wrapped rubber and braided rubber grips from the 1920s; and a wooden paddle grip called Little Poison.*

REPRODUCTIONS

Numerous non-authentic golf clubs have been made over the years. They range from counterfeit Philp long-nose woods crafted by unscrupulous clubmakers 130 years ago to recently-made replicas of famous clubs, such as the Calamity Jane putter used by Bobby Jones or the MacGregor clubs used by Jack Nicklaus.

Reproductions, fakes, forgeries, replicas — they're known by different names, for various reasons. The legitimate reason is to provide enthusiasts with an imitation of a rare club for a fraction of the cost of the original, which often is one-of-a-kind. The illegitimate reason is for monetary gain.

With the rapid growth of golf collecting in the past decade, it was inevitable that unscrupulous individuals would produce fakes and alter clubs to deceive collectors. Some examples are so authentic looking they can fool the experts. Sometimes, unfortunately, it is a greedy expert, who, because of his intimate knowledge of antique clubs, is able to perpetrate a fraud.

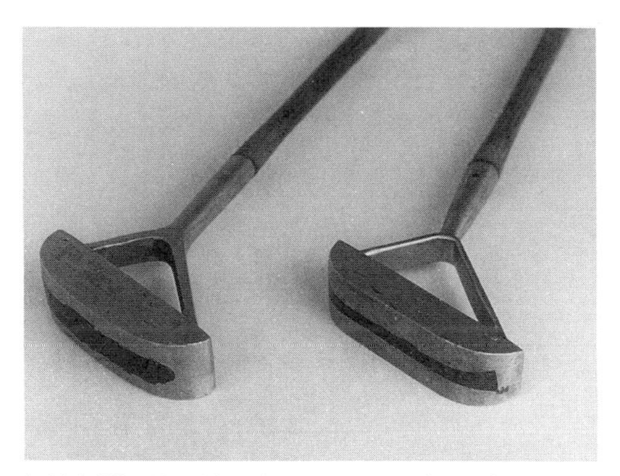

6-106 *The Hackbarth putter (see photo 6-79) is one of several patent clubs that have been reproduced. The poorly made copy (left) can be distinguished by its non-dovetailed lead insert and the lack of loft. The original putter (right) has noticeable loft on both striking faces.*

The best protection against buying a fake is to deal with reputable sources who will unconditionally guarantee the authenticity of the goods they sell. As for reproductions, don't buy shoddy imitations — they're an insult to the skilled clubmakers of yesteryear.

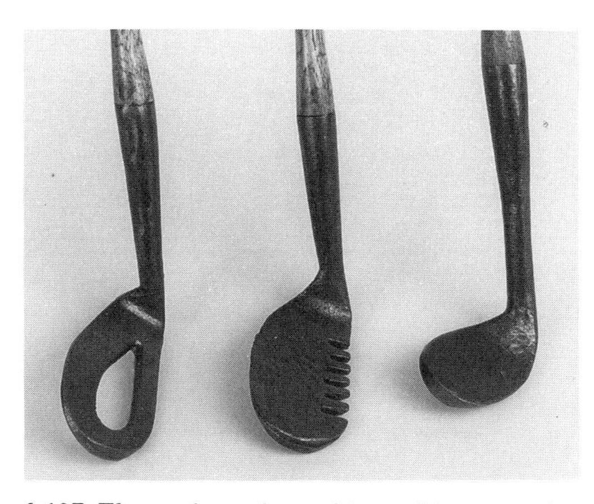

6-107 *The crude workmanship on this group of replica irons is apparent. New shafts and grips, along with rough casting marks and lack of knurling at the top of the hosel are the giveaways.*

6-108 *What at first glance appears to be a long-nose putter really is a copy made with a socket joint rather than the traditional splice. Stamped "John Doe," the ram's horn on the sole is secured with screws instead of the proper wood pegs. It was made in the early 20th century, probably for an older golfer who had fond memories of the old-style clubs.*

6-109 *The most convincing forgeries are the Winton giant niblicks, thought to have been made in the 1960s. These clubs have fooled reputable dealers and knowledgeable collectors. They look so real, that is, until you place two of them together and discover that they were identically cast from the same mold. Variances in grinding makes them vary slightly, but measurements of the name stampings reveal that the clubs are identical — authentic stamps would have been struck individually and would not appear on two clubs in the same identical position.*

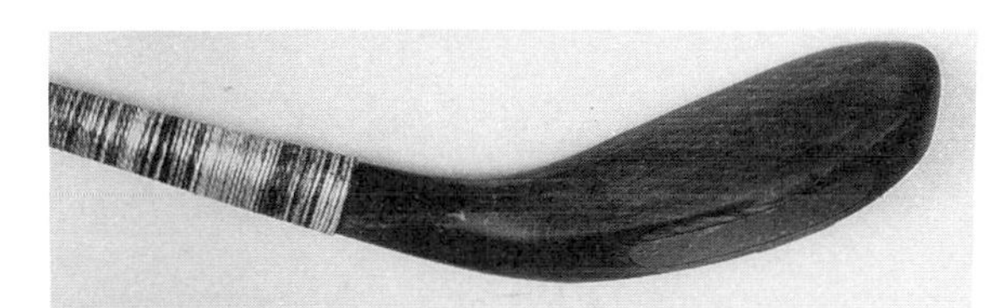

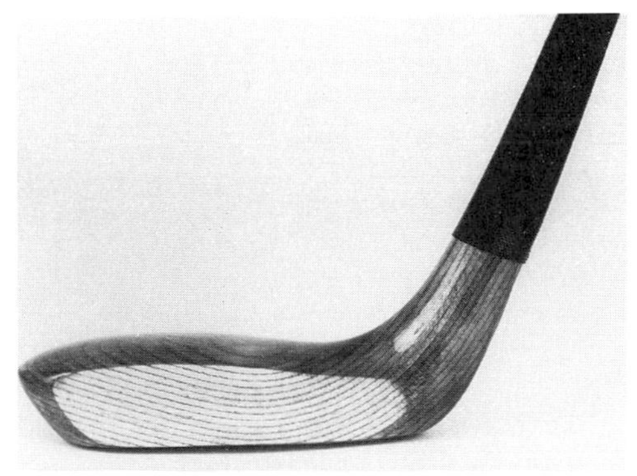

6-110 *Some replica long-nose woods are far from being authentic. Fresh-looking whipping — sometimes even colored monofilament is used — and perfectly smooth lead backweights do not accurately represent 19th-century clubs. The biggest sin, however, is making old-style heads out of modern, laminated maple (right) rather than solid blocks of wood.*

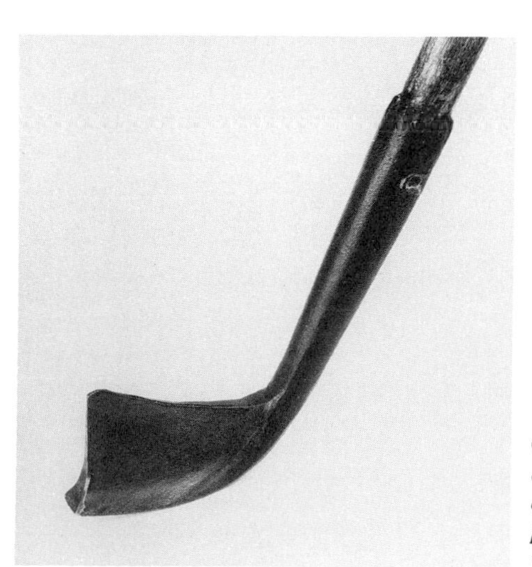

6-111 *A well-made copy of one of the historic 18th-century Troon clubs (see photo 6-4), this iron was authentically hand forged by a blacksmith. The probability of a collector finding an authentic club of this vintage is slim, since only a couple are known to exist.*

NON-GOLF CLUBS

Over the centuries, there have been several golf-related games. Evidence suggests that the Dutch game of "colf," played from the 14th to 18th centuries, may have been the forerunner to golf (see page 144). Clubs from these and similar "stick-and-ball" sports have influenced golf club design.

Other items that might be mistaken for golf clubs are toy clubs and walking sticks fashioned after golf clubs.

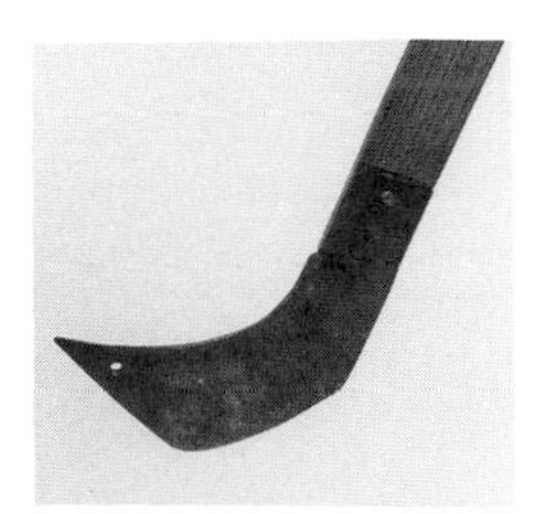

6-112 *Resembling an ax, this club is used to play kolf, a Dutch game which began in the early 18th century. It is still played today on small indoor courts resembling curling rinks. The clubs, with thick, rectangular wooden shafts, are difficult to date.*

6-113 *A brass-headed chole club with multiple striking faces of various lofts. Chole was played in limited areas of France and Belgium. Similar clubs still are used to play the game of crosse.*

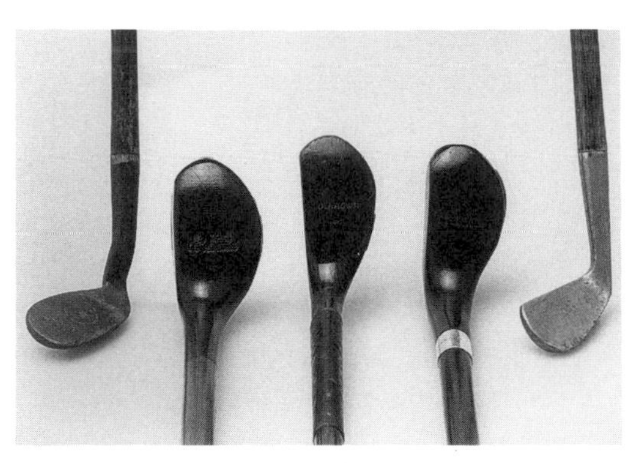

6-114 *In the 1890s, it was common for a golfer's walking stick to be fashioned after a golf club. At first glance, they resemble small-headed golf clubs. But a walking stick differs from a real club in that the shaft has a reverse taper — that is, it comes to a point at the grip end. These stylish canes are sometimes called Sunday clubs, because in the days when golf courses were closed on the Sabbath, a golfer could take a few practice shots while strolling.*

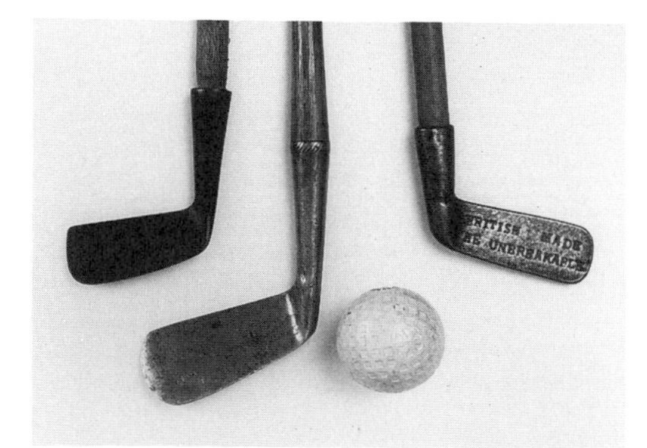

6-115 *These three clubs appear to be juvenile-sized irons. The center club was crafted by a clubmaker, but the other two are toys. Note the hosel area and the crude manner in which the shafts are fitted.*

6-116 *Mallet-headed clubs were used with wooden balls to play a game known as* jeu de mail *in France and pall mall (or pell mell) in England. Several turn-of-the-century golf club designs were influenced by this head shape.*

CHAPTER 7

BALLS

A study of the evolution of golf reveals that the significant changes in the game over the centuries have resulted from advances in equipment. Nowhere is this more apparent than when the ancient feather-stuffed leather ball was replaced by the molded gutta percha ball in the 1850s. Or when the rubber-core ball became the standard in the early 1900s.

In both instances, balls became livelier and more durable. As a result, clubs had to be sturdier, the golf swing in turn became more aggressive, and eventually, golf courses had to be lengthened and to make them more difficult — all because of improvements to the golf ball. Although today's ball manufacturers inundate golfers with new designs and claims of superior distance, tight standards established by the U.S. Golf Association and the Royal & Ancient Golf Club (R & A) render most top-of-the-line modern balls relatively similar in performance. This wasn't always the case. Prior to 1921, there were no regulations regarding golf ball design, so hundreds of different balls — many with preposterous claims — flooded the marketplace. These unusual balls now are a source of amusement to anyone who plays golf.

The three major categories of collectible golf balls are the feather ball, used from at least the 16th century until the 1850s; the gutta percha (or gutty) ball, popular from the late 1840s until about 1908; and the rubber-core ball, which got its start in 1898 and after many refinements, is still in use today. (Although solid and two piece balls have become popular during the last 25 years, their collectibility is limited.)

FEATHER BALLS

Although the leather-covered golf ball was in use for more than 400 years, it remains one of the most prized golf relics today. Known as a feather ball — or feathery — for its core of tightly packed feathers, these balls were produced as far back as the 16th century, according to ballmaker references in trade directories and census rolls.

Ballmaking was an intricate procedure practiced by skilled craftsmen, whose production averaged only three or four per day. The following first-hand account of the lengthy process appeared in *Reminiscences of Golf and Golfers,* a booklet written by H. Thomas Peter in 1890. (Peter was an avid Scottish golfer who first visited St. Andrews in 1837 and developed friendships with noted craftsmen and golfers of the period.) "The making of first-class feather balls was almost a science," Peter wrote. ". . . The leather was of untanned bull's hide, two round pieces for the ends and a strip for the middle were cut to suit the weight wanted. These were properly shaped, after being sufficiently softened, firmly sewn together [with a waxed linen thread] — a small hole being of course left, through which the feathers might be afterwards inserted. But, before stuffing, it was through this little hole that the leather itself had to be turned outside in, so that the seams should be inside.

"The skin was then placed in a cup-shaped stand, the worker having the feathers [from the breast of a goose or chicken] in an apron in front of him, and the actual stuffing done with a crutch-handled steel rod [known as a brogue], which the maker placed under his arm. And very hard work, I may add, it was. Thereafter the aperture was closed and firmly sewed up: and this outside seam was the only one visible."

7-1 *A feathery, showing wear from use and the barely visible stamp of Thomas Stewart, a ballmaker from Musselburgh.*

Peter neglected to relate the most intriguing aspects of creating these special balls. The quantity of feathers — traditionally an amount required to fill a top hat — first were softened by boiling in water. The soggy feathers were then tightly stuffed into the leather shell, which was first wetted with a solution of alum and water. As the drying took place, the feathers naturally expanded, while the leather cover contracted. The result was a surprisingly hard ball that could be driven a distance of 150-200 yards.

The balls were painted white for increased visibility and, at least during the 19th century, stamped with the maker's name. Some balls also were painted red, apparently for increased visibility in the snow — a hazardous environment since moisture was the arch enemy of a feather ball. Another thing that often shortened the already limited life of the ball was a poorly executed iron shot. Fortunately, most strokes were made in a sweeping fashion with the long-nose wooden clubs of the era, while irons were used sparingly, usually from difficult lies.

The diameters of the featheries varied slightly, but were comparable in size and weight to a modern ball. In addition to being stamped with the maker's name, they usually were numbered by hand with their weight in drams. (One dram equals 1/16 oz).

Although most balls were made in the 25 to 32 range, the numbers quickly lost their purpose when the balls became water-laden on a rainy day.

Most of the feather balls still in existence were produced in Scotland during the first half of the 19th century. The most famous maker was Allan Robertson (1815-1859) of St. Andrews, who was reputed to be the best golfer of his time. Although most ballmakers had a metal stamp containing their first initial and last name that they inked and imprinted onto the ball, Robertson was so well known that he merely marked his golf balls "ALLAN."

Other notable makers were Old Tom Morris, who apprenticed under Robertson at St. Andrews and worked for himself in St. Andrews and Prestwick, and brothers John and William Gourlay of Bruntsfield and later Musselburgh. If no name is visible on a ball, it either was worn off from use or the ball dates prior to 1820, when stamping was not widely practiced.

Much of the allure surrounding feather balls is their scarcity and the fact that their fragility is so unlike the rugged, surlyn-covered modern balls, which remain

COLLECTING TIP

■ **Prior to the 1820s, ballmakers did not stamp their names on feather balls. The following 19th-century makers are known to have marked their balls. Those marked with an asterisk were the most prolific makers.**

T. Alexander *
Wm. Gourlay *
W & J Gourlay *
J. Gourlay *
D. Gressick
S. Pirie
ALLAN (Allan Robertson) *
Wm. Robertson
J. Sharp
T. Stewart
J. Ramsay
T. Morris *
D. Marshall

7-2 *A mint condition Allan Robertson feather ball (top) with its unique first-name stamp. The "29" indicates the ball's weight in drams when new. Robertson, a top-notch match player, never had the opportunity to prove himself in stroke play competition because he died in 1859 — the year before the first Open Championship.*

playable indefinitely. Although thousands of featheries were made — in 1838 alone, more than 10,000 were made in St. Andrews — less than 400-500 remain today.

As a rule, stamped balls and those by some of the more obscure makers, such as Gressick, Alexander and Sharp, are in greater demand by ardent ball collectors.

HOW TO AUTHENTICATE A FEATHER BALL

Every golf collector dreams of acquiring a feather ball from an unknowing soul for a bargain price. The chances of this happening are virtually nil, since most remaining featheries have been located. What does happen, from time to time, however, is that people vaguely familiar with golf balls find what they think is a feather ball.

Most golf-ball-sized spheres with leather covers found today were made for games other than golf. The major difference evident with most non-golf balls is that the stitches appear on the outside, whereas the cover of a golf ball has the seams hidden on the inside.

A frequently mistaken ball is the one used to play "fives," a British version of handball. It's easy to distinguish because the sections of leather are assembled similar to the way wedges are cut from a lemon, rather than the two circles and center strip used on a golf ball. Other pretenders have a two-piece cover like a baseball.

Reproduction feather balls usually are easy to distinguish. Some are marked as replicas, while others have loose seams or are soft when squeezed. Authentic feather balls are as hard as a modern golf ball, a characteristic few replica makers or forgers can reproduce. When in doubt, consult an expert.

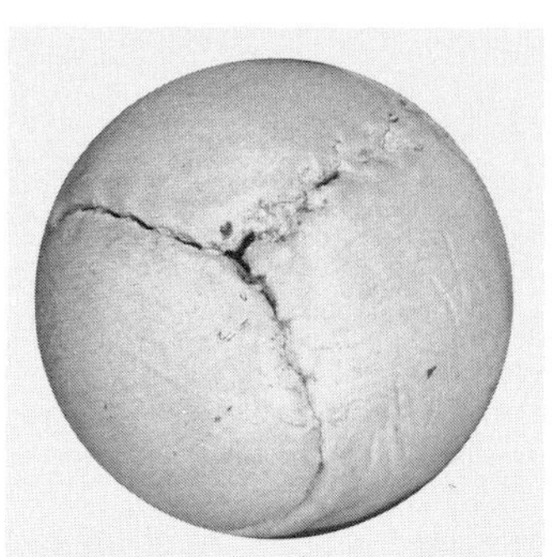

7-3
Reproduction feather balls usually look new, not 150 years old. They also have a tendency to be too soft to the touch.

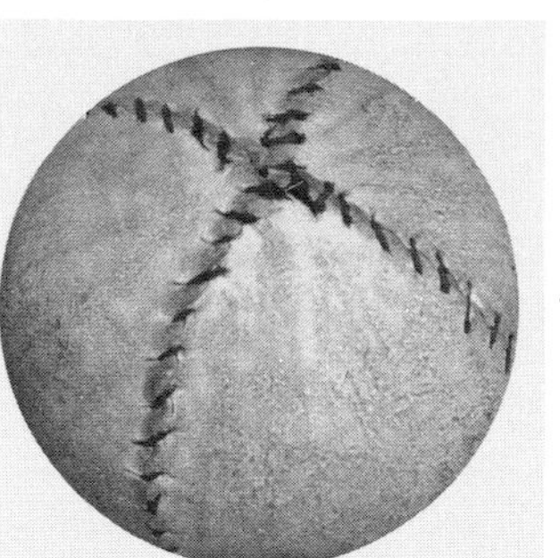

7-4
A "fives" ball. Note the external stitches and four-piece cover.

Gutta Percha Golf Balls

As the Industrial Revolution progressed in Great Britain during the mid-19th century, it was only a matter of time before creativity and inventive genius would make an impact on the game of golf. Because of the fragility and high cost of the feather ball, it was inevitable that someone would develop alternative methods for making golf balls.

Rubber had been used since the late 18th century to waterproof objects and to make balls for other games, but it was too soft for golf balls. However, a material called gutta percha — similar to rubber, but harder and less elastic — proved to be ideal.

Gutta percha is the milky liquid obtained from the Palaquium genus of trees native to Malaysia, India, and Ceylon. When harvested, it is dried into thin sheets or ropelike strands. It was introduced to Europe in the early 1840s, when manufacturers discovered it became soft and pliable when heated, then hard and resilient when cooled. These properties made gutta percha perfectly suited for tool handles, packing material, shoe soles, even ideal for dental repairs and orthopedic devices.

AFFORDABILITY

Because the gutty ball, as it was called, could be made for a tenth of the price of a feather ball, golf became a more affordable game during the second half of the 19th century. Not only were gutties less expensive, they easily could be remolded if damaged. No longer was golf a pastime of the wealthy. The economy of the new ball led to increased participation in golf by the working class, often referred to as artisans, who formed their own clubs and built their own courses.

INVENTOR UNKNOWN

No one knows for sure who developed the first gutta percha golf ball. Although 1848 is generally acknowledged as the year the new ball was accepted as an alternative to the traditional feathery, it was not until the early 1900s that the matter of its inventor became an issue.

Articles appearing in *Golf Illustrated* magazine from 1900 until 1902 argued the origination of the gutty ball. The field of inventors was reduced to two: Robert Paterson, a 16-year-old from St. Andrews, who in 1845 experimented with gutta percha that had been packed around a Hindu statue shipped from Singapore or William Smith, a clockmaker and inventor from Musselburgh, who formed golf balls made of gutta percha in a wooden mold in 1846 or '47.

7-5 *Rare hand-nicked gutty balls from the 1850s — made by Allan Robertson, Tom Morris, Sr. and Willie Dunn, Sr. — former feather ballmakers who also were among the finest players of the mid-19th century.*

7-6 *Legend has it that the Rev. Dr. Robert Paterson (far left) pioneered the use of gutta percha for golf balls as a teenager in 1845. Paterson's New Composite ball (left) was produced by his brother John, who lived near St. Andrews, circa 1850. Smooth gutties are the ultimate collectible golf ball. Only made for a few years, few remain today since most were hand-hammered to improve playing characteristics.*

It is interesting that no references can be found about either claim until the publication of the magazine articles — more than 50 years after the fact. Evidently, neither individual thought he had done anything extraordinary until golf writers J.G. McPherson and W. Dalrymple began a campaign to establish Paterson as the inventor.

Although it is likely that we will never know who first developed the gutty ball, the Paterson legend has received the most coverage in golf history books. This can be attributed to the fact that many authors were unaware of the turn-of-the-century *Golf Illustrated* articles. Surprisingly, Robert Browning, in his highly respected 1956 *A History of Golf*, does not mention Paterson or Smith. He surmises that perhaps a company such as Henley's Telegraph Works, a maker of insulated cable (and a golf ballmaker in the 1890s) may have pioneered gutta percha golf balls.

FABRICATION

Although William Smith claimed to have used a wooden mold in the 1840s, most of the early gutty balls were formed by softening a chunk of gutta percha in boiling water and then rolling it into a sphere between the hands. Before long, ballmakers began using two-piece brass or steel molds

7-7 *By the late 1890s, U.S. golfers became less dependent on the British for their golf equipment. The first American golf balls were handmade by transplanted Scottish professionals. Early manufacturers were the B.F. Goodrich Company and the Whitman & Barnes Mfg. Co., which made the patriotic Stars and Stripes gutty (left) for Willie Dunn, Jr. Dunn, a member of a famous golfing family, was a noted player and golf architect.*

(see photo 7-15). By compressing the mold in a vise or press, a consistent shape could be obtained.

The first gutties had smooth surfaces and were painted white or their natural color of black or brown. In the early 1850s, when golfers discovered that balls flew much better after they had been nicked from use, the ballmakers began to purposely disfigure the balls prior to sale. This was accomplished by making knife cuts or hammering with the a chisel-shaped end of a cross-peen hammer. This intentional notching was initially done in a random manner, until Robert Forgan initiated a cross-nicking pattern around 1860.

In the 1870s, patterned molds replaced the smooth molds and eliminated the need for hand-hammering. Popular designs included a gridlike mesh and a bramble pattern, so-called for its bumpy texture resembling a raspberry. Until the 1880s, gutty balls were marked with weights of 26 to 30 drams, similar to feather balls. Thereafter, the pennyweight (1/20 oz.) was the standard measurement, with an average ball weighing about 32.

In addition to the improved aerodynamics of the marked ball, it was discovered that older balls performed better than fresh ones. In order to properly "season" balls, makers stored them for as long as a year before they were painted and sold. Gutty ball boxes usually were marked with the date of manufacture so that purchasers could determine how long the balls had aged.

Towards the end of the 19th century, many gutties contained ground cork, leather, metal shavings and other materials that supposedly enhanced their performance.

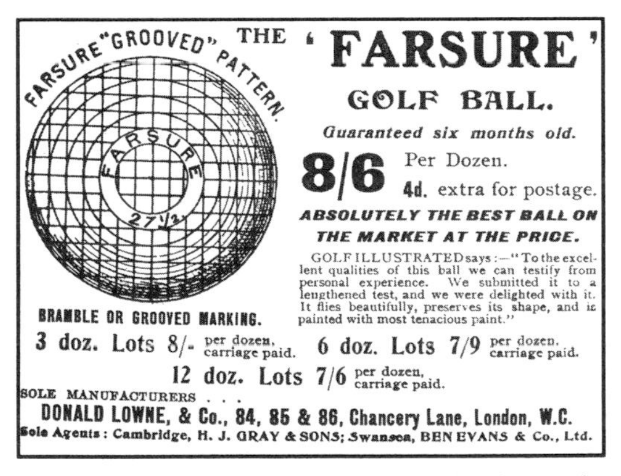

7-8 *The Farsure ball was guaranteed to be aged six months before sale.*

7-9 *The concept of selling golf balls by the dozen is a century old. Ball boxes from the gutty era are prized by collectors, regardless of condition.*

7-10 *Until ballmaking technology improved in the early 20th century, the paint did not adhere to the ball's surface very well. The best method for repainting was messy; it required the golfer to place a small amount of paint in a cupped hand and then roll the ball between his palms. This small can measures only 2 inches high, but once contained enough paint to last an entire season.*

GUTTY BALLMAKERS

When golfers started using gutties in the late 1840s, it only was natural that skilled makers of feather balls would resent the use of the easily molded ball. Allan Robertson of St. Andrews, the premier ballmaker whose family had been making feather balls for more than a century, was so opposed to the new ball that he reportedly bought as many as he could and burned them. In 1850 Robertson got so enraged at Tom Morris, his assistant, for playing with a gutty that the two severed their relationship. Morris went into business for himself and left St. Andrews for a 14-year stint in Prestwick.

Morris, Willie Dunn and James Gourlay were among the veteran feather ballmakers who foresaw the demise of the feathery and switched to gutty making. And before his death in 1859, Allan Robertson even succumbed to the demands of golfers and began molding balls from gutta percha.

By the end of the 19th century, individual ballmakers were replaced by factories that could produce hundreds of thousands of gutties. Major British producers included

7-11 *The Vardon Flyer was the last great gutty ball. It was introduced the 1899, the same year the Haskell rubber-core ball went into production. Harry Vardon, the first professional athlete to endorse commercial products, toured the United States in 1900 to promote the new ball and other Spalding equipment. While on tour, the greatest player of his time proved the merits of the ball, using it to win the U.S. Open at Chicago Golf Club.*

COLLECTING TIPS

■ **Although feather balls are sought for their rarity and mystique, they are not as scarce as some of the early gutty balls. Whereas feather balls were made for several hundred years, the smooth gutties and those with hammered markings were made for less than 20 years. This limited production, combined with the fact that many of the balls were later remolded, makes early gutties the rarest collectible golf ball.**

■ **Many hammered or smooth gutty balls do not bear a maker's stamp. Names likely to be marked on an early gutty are:**

G.D. Brown
J. Dunn
Wm. Dunn
R. Forgan
J. Gourlay
McEwan
T. Morris
W. Park
Paterson
ALLAN (Allan Robertson)

7-12 *One wonders what Willie Park, Jr. had in mind when he produced the Royal, circa 1896. The hexagonal facets could not have been conducive to accurate putting.*

7-13 *The Henley, sporting a cover resembling the British flag, was made in the mid-1890s by Henley's Telegraphic Works, a London-based manufacturer of insulated electrical cable.*

7-14 *The Faroid gutty had to be struck at a certain angle so that the benefits of its concentric ridges could be realized. The opposite side of the ball was stamped with the instructions: "this side up."*

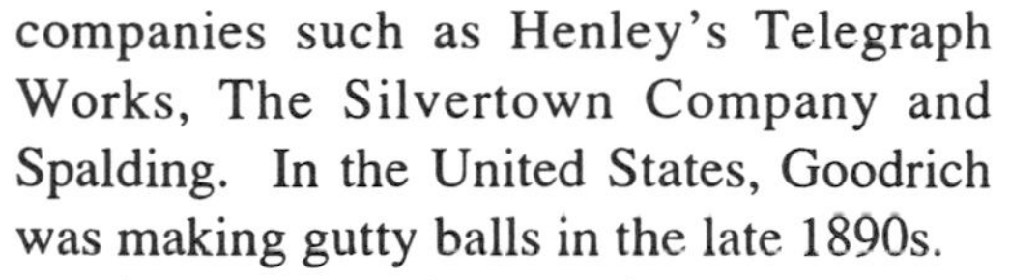

companies such as Henley's Telegraph Works, The Silvertown Company and Spalding. In the United States, Goodrich was making gutty balls in the late 1890s.

At the same time, golf pros and small ballmaking concerns switched their efforts to the recycling of old, damaged gutties. They advertised for used balls, which were remolded and sold for about 40% less than the cost of a new ball. Remakes were offered with all of the popular surface patterns. Slightly worn balls usually were heated and pressed in a smaller mold, so a size 30 would end up a size 28. Cracked or severely damaged balls also were reprocessed.

CLUB DESIGNS MODIFIED

As golfers adopted the gutty in the 1850s, they discovered that long-nose wooden clubs designed for the feather ball lacked the durability to withstand the impact of the harder ball. To keep clubs from breaking, some players had leather inserts fitted to clubfaces to soften the blow. But the eventual solution was to construct clubheads with thicker necks (see page 50).

Since the gutty could withstand the off-center hits that destroyed feather balls, golfers adopted a more aggressive style of play. In particular, the use of niblicks and other iron-headed clubs increased dramatically.

7-15 *Steel and brass molds were used to form gutty balls from the late 1850s until they went out of vogue by 1910. The early molds produced smooth balls, but by the 1870s machinists were able to incorporate grooved and bramble surfaces into the molds. Although most remolding was done by ballmakers and golf professional, the home press (right) was perfect for the do-it-yourselfer.*

RUBBER-CORE BALLS

At the end of the 19th century, a major change in the game took place. The economical one-piece gutty ball that had enjoyed a half-century of unrivaled popularity faced a challenge from the newfangled rubber-core ball. And to add insult to injury, the idea for the new ball came from the United States, where golf had been widely played for less than a decade. No wonder the British were so opposed to the invention — they had controlled the progress of the game for more than 400 years!

THE HASKELL BALL

The rubber-core golf ball was the brainchild of Coburn Haskell and Bertram Work. Haskell, a wealthy sportsman, combined forces in 1898 with his friend Bertram Work of the B.F. Goodrich Company in Akron, Ohio, to develop a golf ball containing a center of rubber thread wound under tension. Their intention was to produce a ball with a liveliness not attainable with the hard gutta percha ball in use at the time. Because Goodrich was making gutty balls in addition to other rubber-related products, the company was eager to develop a better golf ball to increase profits.

After submitting their invention to the U.S. Patent Office in 1898, the two were granted a patent the following year. The early Haskell balls — as they were known — were hand wound, then covered with a shell of gutta percha. When they applied for a patent, the two men were not sure how

7-16 *The Goodyear Tire & Rubber Company, built its empire by making tires capable of holding air. They carried this concept over to golf ball manufacturing when they announced the Pneumatic ball (above) in 1905. With a center of compressed air, the ball was highly advertised and was used to win several championships. However, its tendency to unexpectedly explode in hot weather eventually made the ball unpopular and Goodyear ceased production.*

7-17 *Unusual line-marked balls from the early 20th century: the Bruce Core (top), featuring a spider insignia and spider web pattern; Wanamaker's Defender (bottom left), with a swirl pattern; and a concentric circled example (bottom right).*

THE HASKELL BALL

7-18 *The original Haskell ball, patented in 1899, was made by B.F. Goodrich with a mesh cover (right). When it was discovered that a bramble cover offered superior performance, the company redesigned its molds and began making the Haskell Bramble (far right).*

NOTICE!

The sale or use in this country of foreign-made Golf Balls, having centers made of rubber under tension, is an infringement of the Haskell United States patent.

Dealers and players handling or using such balls render themselves liable to legal proceedings : : : : :

The only balls licensed under the Haskell U. S. patent are those made in this country by

THE B. F. GOODRICH COMPANY,
A. G. SPALDING & BROS.,
THE KEMPSHALL MFG. CO.,
and
THE WORTHINGTON BALL CO.

The HASKELL GOLF BALL CO.

7-19 *Early rubber-core balls were prone to splitting (right). Therefore, manufacturers were forced to offer guarantees and provisions for remaking damaged balls (above ads).*

7-20 *After an involved court case in 1905, the Haskell ball patent was ruled invalid in Great Britain. The company subsequently went to great means to prevent any of the "black market" balls from entering the United States.*

COLLECTING TIPS

■ How does one distinguish a rubber-core ball from a gutty without cutting it open? Any ball with dimples is a rubber-core, while a mesh- or bramble-patterned one may be either. The best method is to consult the extensive lists in *The Encyclopedia of Golf Collectibles* or talk to an expert who might have seen the ball advertised.

■ Early rubber-cores were covered with gutta percha. By the 1920s, balata, the rubberlike material still used to cover golf balls, became the preferred covering. When bounced on tabletop, a balata-covered ball will have a softer sound than one made of gutta percha. This test will help ascertain a ball's exterior, but cannot verify the inside composition.

they would make their new ball in large quantities. They gave John Gammeter, an engineer at Goodrich, the responsibility of designing a ball-winding machine. Finally in 1900, when Gammeter received a patent for his thread-winding device, the company had the ability to produce balls by the thousands.

Although the first Haskell balls were far from a success on the golf course, golfers were amused by their novelty and purchased them out of curiosity. The balls were so lively that they were nicknamed "Bounding Billies." In fact, golfers were astounded at the great distances that a topped shot would travel. But they also had a tendency to "duck and dart" out of control and their covers were prone to splitting.

Goodrich was determined to solve these problems since they were becoming the laughing stock of the golf industry. Fortunately, one of their customers came to the rescue. The original balls had a mesh-patterned cover like many of the gutty balls of the period and could easily be mistaken for one. James Foulis, professional at the

7-21 *One of the most unique golf balls ever produced — the rare Map of the World Ball. Note the intricate detail of the continents, oceans and north pole. Since an elaborate die undoubtedly was fabricated to form the markings, it remains a mystery as to why only a few examples exist.*

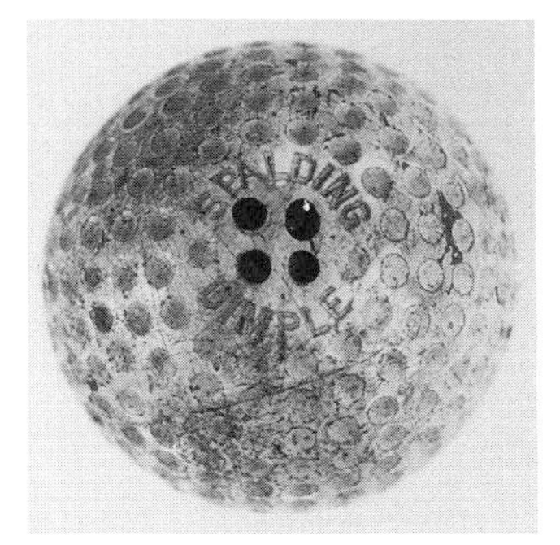

7-22 *Spalding was the first golf ball manufacturer to make dimpled golf balls. After the patent was awarded in 1905, they made several styles, including the Spalding Dimple.*

7-23 *The most successful center developed for a wound golf ball is a small liquid-filled sac. One of the first examples was the St. Mungo Water-Core, made at the beginning of the 20th century.*

UNUSUAL GOLF BALLS

Prior to the 1920s, many ballmakers were preoccupied with cosmetics rather than aerodynamics. This resulted in the production of a plethora of unusual designs that are treasured by collectors and museums.

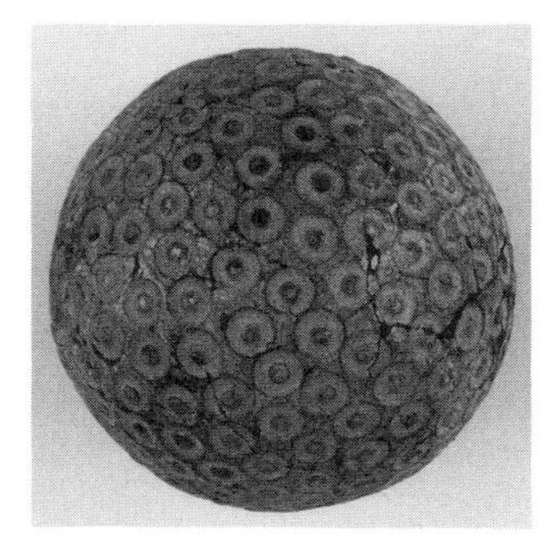

7-24 *Non-Skid*

7-25 *Wonder Ball*

7-26 *Waffle pattern*

7-27 *Crescent Colonel*

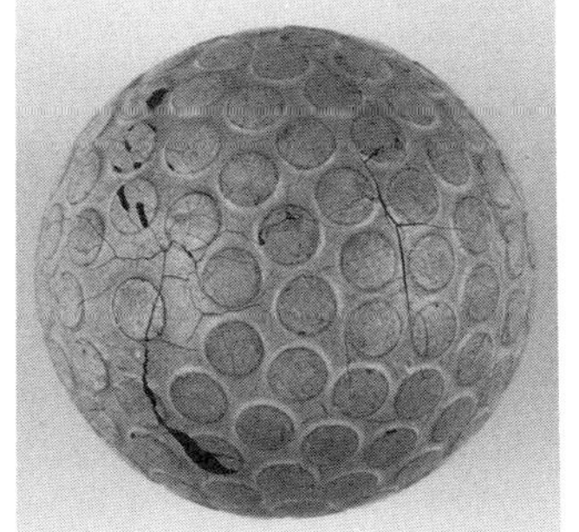

7-28 *Ocobo*

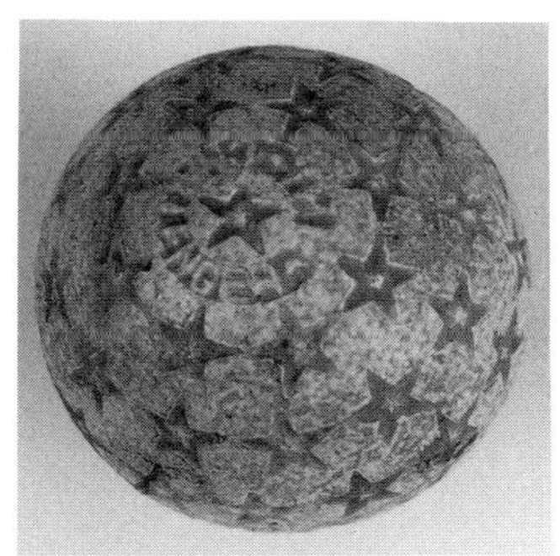

7-29 *Star Challenger*

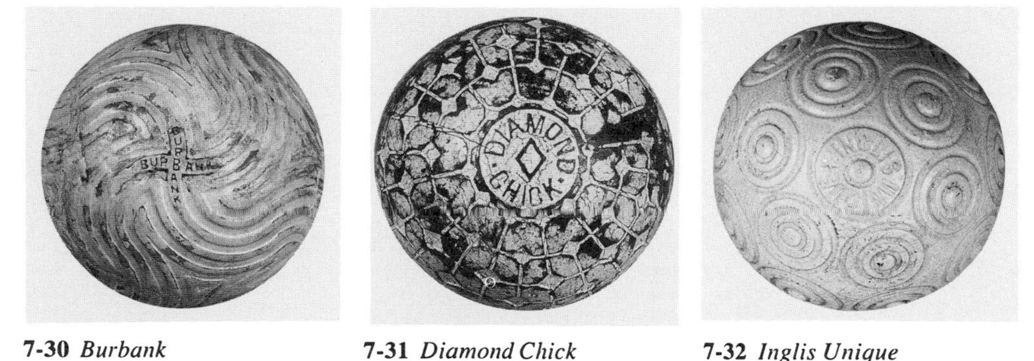

7-30 *Burbank*

7-31 *Diamond Chick*

7-32 *Inglis Unique*

Chicago Golf Club, thinking he was remolding a gutty ball, molded a Haskell with a bramble pattern one day. When Foulis played with this remade Haskell, he was astonished by his ability to control the ball and was so intrigued that he cut it open for inspection. To his surprise, he discovered he had been playing with a Haskell ball. Goodrich responded by abandoning the mesh pattern and within

7-33 *The Wizard, introduced in 1903, was redesigned in 1904 to offer more of a "click" sound associated with the old gutty. But when the redesigned ball lacked durability, Spalding went back to the original design and golfers became accustomed to the quieter sound of 20th-century golf balls.*

a few years, the rubber-core ball became the preferred type of golf ball over the gutty.

Goodrich subsequently formed a subsidiary called the Haskell Golf Ball Company and allowed other ballmakers to manufacture rubber-core balls under a licensing agreement. The first licensees in the early 1900s were A.G. Spalding & Bros., Kempshall Manufacturing Company, Worthington Ball Company and St. Mungo Manufacturing Company of Glasgow, Scotland. Balls made under the Haskell patent began to appear in Great Britain in 1901, but were scorned by skeptics who thought they would make the game too easy. In 1902, Sandy Herd became the first to win the British Open with a Haskell ball, using the same ball for the entire 72 holes. His ball was so tattered that the elastic threads showed through the cover for the final nine holes. Although it was reported that he was the only player in the field to use the new ball, his victory was sufficient to cause the new ball to be accepted by the British golfers.

COLLECTING TIPS

■ **A ball collection should emphasize variety and quality rather than quantity. Look for balls with unusual markings or interesting names. See how many different varieties of Spalding Dots or Titleists you can find. Be a specialist, or you'll end up with 10,000 golf balls that you can't enjoy.**

■ **Egg cartons are perfect for organizing and storing a ball collection. For display, consider buying or making an attractive case similar to the one shown on page 23.**

THE GREAT GOLF BALL LAWSUIT

Even though American and British patents were issued for the Haskell ball, several British companies began to manufacture their own versions of the

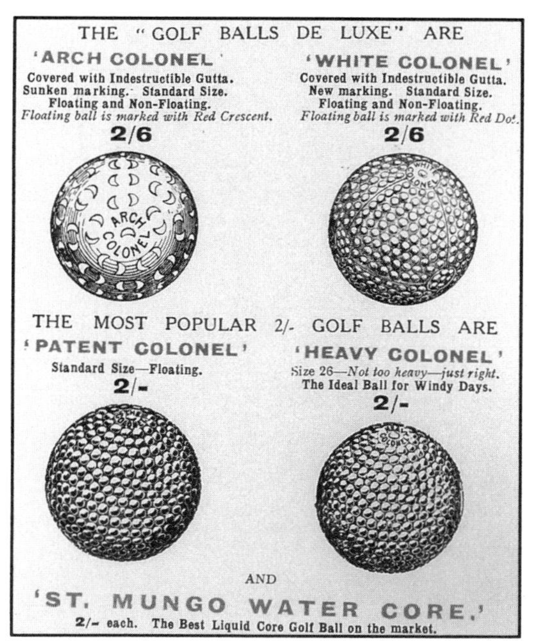

7-34 *The Colonel range of balls for 1913, made by the St. Mungo Manufacturing Co. of Glasgow. Note the options regarding size and weight. Large, lightweight balls were called "floaters" because they actually floated on water.*

7-35 *The dimple pattern is the only one of the three predominant golf ball markings in the 1930s that has survived to this day. The mesh (far left) and bramble (left) were not as aerodynamically sound.*

rubber-core ball. In 1905, the Haskell Golf Ball Company filed a patent in- fringement suit against Hutchison, Main & Company of Glasgow to put an end to the unauthorized use of their patent. In a well-publicized week-long trial, complete with courtroom experiments, the Haskell patent was declared void in Great Britain on the grounds that it was not a novel idea. Witnesses for the defense testified that there had been similarly wound toy balls in the 1860s and '70s as well as earlier golf balls with an elastic center. The decision was appealed in 1906 and was upheld after another lengthy trial.

As a result of the decision, many companies began to produce rubber-core balls in Great Britain, while the American balls were still subject to the Haskell patent. Although attempts were made to sell the British-made balls in the United States, where the patent was still in effect, Haskell Golf Ball Company was effective in thwarting the efforts (see photo 7-20).

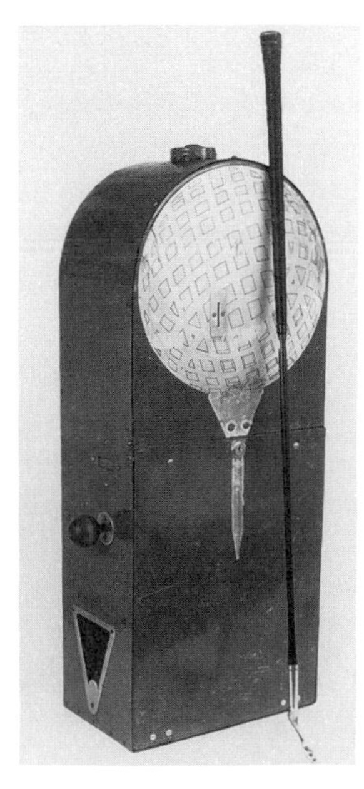

7-36 *A golf ball vending machine, probably from the late 1930s. Other coin-operated ball dispensers included slot machines that paid off in golf balls (see page 43).*

FURTHER IMPROVEMENTS

By 1910, the rubber-core ball established itself as the ball of choice. Although the basic concept has carried forth to modern-day balls, numerous improvements have been made. In 1905, William Taylor, an Englishman, patented the dimple method of golf ball marking, claiming a better flying ball. Spalding bought the American rights to the patent and began to make the dimpled balls in 1909. Until Taylor's patent expired in the 1920s, there were many types of ball markings, including geometric shapes, facets and even a map of the world (see photo 7-21). However, the dimple pattern performed far superior to others and by 1930, it was the industry standard. The small ballmakers eventually dropped out of the marketplace as large companies like St. Mungo and Spalding dominated the industry. In 1935, St. Mungo was making 32 different styles of balls and was shipping 900 dozen balls every day!

The other significant improvement was the incorporation of an uncompressible liquid into the center of the ball. In America,

Eleazer Kempshall had experimented with water-filled capsules as early as 1902, and, as a result of his patents, received royalties for all liquid-core balls sold from 1902 to 1919. There were later patents such as the 1905 one by Frank Mingay of Scotland which were based on Kempshall's idea.

Other improvements were developed and hundreds of patents were granted, but the dimpled cover combined with a liquid center became the mainstay of the industry until the one-piece rubber ball was developed in the mid 1960s.

STANDARDIZATION

Prior to 1921, there was no standard size for the golf ball. From the days of the feathery, balls were made in varying combinations of size and weight. Many of the large, lightweight balls actually floated in water and appropriately were called "floaters." It was not unusual for a golfer to select a ball based on the wind, temperature, and the course which he was playing.

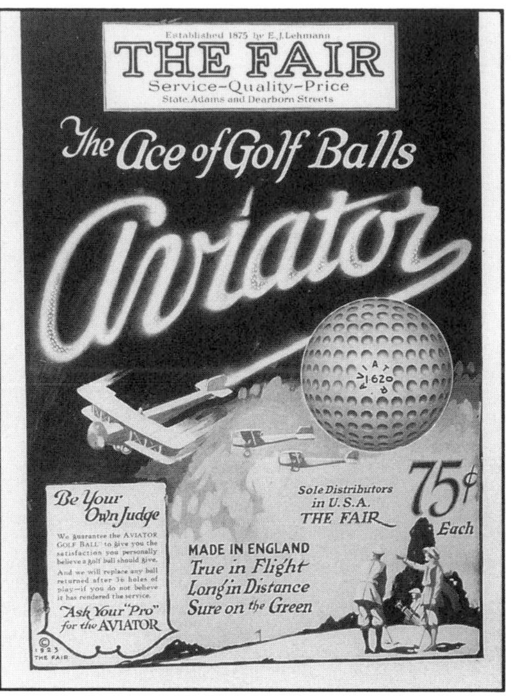

7-37 *A dramatic advertisement for the 1923 Aviator golf ball.*

After 10 years of toying with varying ball sizes, the USGA established criteria in 1932 that are still adhered to: weight not greater than 1.62 ounces and diameter not less than 1.68 inches. The R & A, which administers the rules of golf outside the United States maintained use of the "small" ball, which although it weighed the same as the American ball, could be as small as 1.62 inches in diameter.

The small ball performed much better in the wind, but in the 1960s the British players decided that they must master the large ball if they were to equal the superior play demonstrated by American professionals (who at the time were unquestionably the top players in the world).

First the British PGA experimented with the larger American ball in 1968. Then in

7-38 *The 1924 Silver Kings were the first to have identification numbers. The popular English golf balls were distributed in the United States by Wanamaker's.*

1974, instead of being at the player's option, the large ball became mandatory for the British Open Championship. When the R & A finally sanctioned the large ball for all competitions in January, 1983, it became, with few exceptions, the universal ball used throughout the golfing world.

MODERN BALLS

Many golfers collect logo balls — those that are imprinted with names, logos and even photographs to publicize companies, products, golf courses and other events. During the last several decades, tens of thousands of different customized balls were produced for use as gifts and advertising. Since collecting possibilities are limitless, collectors should concentrate on a particular area of interest, such as famous golf courses, Fortune 500 companies or balls bearing the names of famous players.

7-39 *Since most post-World War II golf balls have identical dimpled exteriors, the attribute that makes them collectible are their names. As shown (right), you can find virtually any name from "Aaron to Zarley."*

7-40 *Compared to the colorful seals and facsimile signatures featured on recent presidential golf balls, these two examples are likely to pass by unnoticed. These balls belonged to Warren G. Harding (far left) and Dwight D. Eisenhower (left).*

7-41 *Presidential golf balls have been a favorite White House souvenir for years. Usually given away in individual boxes (above), they are not purchased at government expense. The avid golfing presidents have been: Harding, Wilson, Taft (see page 79), Eisenhower, Kennedy, Nixon, Ford and Bush. Carter and Reagan, while not enthusiastic about the game, nevertheless had golf balls made to give as souvenirs.*

GOLF BALL PACKAGING

7-42 *Of the early 20th-century golf ball manufacturers that primarily were in the tire business — Goodrich, Goodyear and Dunlop — only the Dunlop name has survived. Innovative packaging may account for their longevity: colorful box depicting the R & A clubhouse in St. Andrews (above left), a plastic snowman and screw-top metal container (above center), and tin countertop case picturing the famous Dunlop Man character (right, also see page 184).*

7-44 *The endorsement of a championship golfer can help golf ball sales immensely. But the naming of a ball after a famous player limits the chance that sales will be enhanced because of its use by top professionals. After all, why would a competitor of Harry Vardon or Tommy Armour want to chance winning an event with a ball displaying an archrival's name. That's why brand names like Titleist, Maxfli and Top Flite have remained popular for decades.*

7-43 *Wright & Ditson, a subsidiary of Spalding, divided its box of Bullet balls into two six-packs. When these balls were made in the 1920s, the printing of identification numbers on balls was not universally practiced. The Bullet came with red, green, black and blue colored name imprints. (See photo 7-38)*

7-45 *Golf ball manufacturers have employed various advertising tactics over the years. St. Mungo had their popular Colonel models, complete with a fictitious character. Spalding, who dominated the ball market for the first three decades of this century, could sell balls on their name alone, as shown on this plain two-ball Honor box. The Burnet-50 and other less-popular models often resorted to giveaways, such as free tees, to break into the marketplace.*

CHAPTER 8

TEES

An entire chapter devoted to golf tees? Sure. Although tees now are taken for granted as a generic essential of the game, golfers once purchased them by brand name and style. From the 1890s through the 1930s, hundreds of tee styles were produced. And top players such as Gene Sarazen and Walter Hagen were paid for their endorsements of specific brands.

For hundreds of years, golfers started each hole by driving a ball which had been placed on a small mound of sand. The golfer or his caddy took a pinch of soil from the bottom of the hole just completed and shaped it into a little hill with their fingers. Until the adoption of separate areas for teeing off in the 1880s, golfers started each hole within a prescribed distance from the hole — from one to 12 club lengths, depending on the rules in effect. Since the holes had no liners and got deeper with play, caddies often were required to carry a supply of moistened sand.

With the immense growth of golf at the end of the 19th century came a flood of tee designs. Several styles of tee molds came into use. These were conical-shaped devices, usually made of metal or wood, that performed like a cookie-cutter to create uniform sand tees without dirtying the hands. As golf courses became more crowded, greenkeepers provided a sand supply at each teeing area. (This is where the term "tee box" originated.) Often, a bucket of water was furnished so that the sand could be mixed to the right consistency (see page 241).

The first artificial tees were produced in the late 1880s, and in 1889 a patent was awarded to Messrs. Bloxsom and Douglas of Scotland for a tee consisting of a rubber platform with protruding fingers to support the ball. Various styles of these surface-mounted tees were used into the 1900s. The inserted, or peg-type, tee we are most familiar with today was available in the 1890s, but it wasn't until the Reddy Tee came on the market in 1920s that the style became popular and replaced the sand tee.

SURFACE TEE TYPES

SAND MOLD

Used to shape a moist pile of sand into a conically-shaped mound. An improvement on the traditional hand-shaped pinch of sand.

8-1 *As recently as the mid 1920s, tee molds still were being advertised in golf magazines. By the end of the decade, however, all but the diehard traditional golfers had switched to inserted tees.*

8-2 *Tethered surface tees had a piece of yarn, a weight or other anchor to keep them from traveling too far after a drive.*

TETHERED SURFACE

Units wherein the working part of the tee was fastened with string, yarn or chain to another portion that was anchored into the ground or weighted to keep the tee from traveling too far after a shot was played.

PAPER

Strips of heavy paper that were formed into three-dimensional stand-up circles, squares and other shapes sturdy enough to support the weight of a ball. They were produced in flat strips or booklets that allowed the golfer to tear one off as needed.

WEIGHTED

Heavy, little platforms, usually made of molded rubber and sometimes weighted with lead.

TRUNCATED CONE

Small volcano-like shapes that rest on top of the ground.

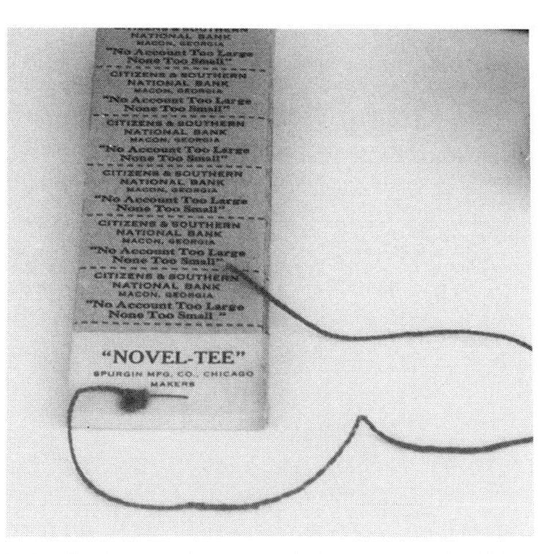

8-3 *The Novel-Tee certainly was novel. The perforated strips of paper that unfolded to form a tee came in a booklet that could be tied to the golfer's bag. Imprinted with an advertisement, 1,000 booklets sold for $35.*

8-4 *Directional tees were made in surface and inserted styles. Some assisted with alignment only, while others were designed to correct the flight of the ball. Tees of this nature are illegal according to the Rules of Golf.*

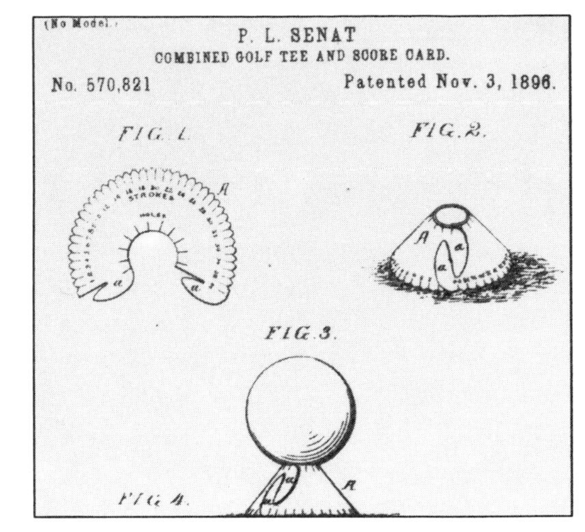

8-5 *The first U.S. patent for a golf tee was granted to Prosper L. Senat, of Philadelphia, in 1896. His paper tee doubled as a scorecard.*

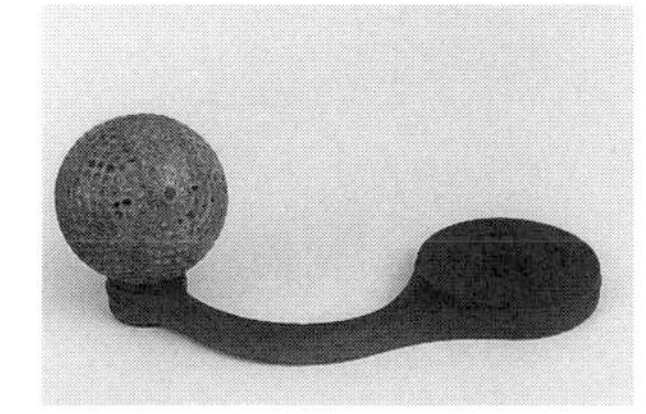

8-6 *A surface tee cast from a metal alloy that features a high and low position. It is marked with the inventor's name: "Otto Eick."*

8-7 *The O-Katy was made in 1928 by the Acushnet Process Company. A few years later, the Massachusetts company started producing another golf product, which since has become legendary. . . the Titleist golf ball.*

COLLECTING TIP

■ The names of tees often are as interesting as the tees themselves. Usually tees are not labeledwith their brand name, so old ads are the best means of identification. Some amusing brand names from the more than 1,000 tees styles that have been manufactured to date are: *Always Ready, Angle, Daintee, Dodo, Exact-a-tee, Formatee, Go-Tee, Holdfast, Infinitee, Launching Pad, Magic, Mightee Flightee, Never Lose, No Looz, Novel-Tee, O-Katy, Par Buster, Par-Tee, Pencil, Perfec Tee, Perfectum, Perma-Tee, Rev-Tee, Rex, Rite, Rite-Hite, Site-tee, Stay Put, Strip-Tees, Tip Top, Tip Not Tee, Tip, Triple, Tripod, Tru-Drive* and *Wright-Way.*

INSERTED TEES

COMMON SHAPES

These pegs were the most widely used tees in the 1920s and '30s. Most tees were under $1^1/_2$ inches in length, whereas most tees today are about 2 inches long.

Carrot: A cone shape, resembling a carrot, with no distinct head and stem.

Classic: A popular style in the 1920s, characterized by a short, tapered stem and compact, flared head.

Funnel: Conical head quickly tapering to a thin, constant diameter stem.

Goblet: Goblet-shaped top with a thin, constant diameter stem.

Trumpet: The modern tee, with a pointed stem that flares into the head.

INSERTED TETHERED

Peg-type tee with an auxiliary tee or weight attached by string or chain, designed to reduce the chance of loss.

CONSTANT HEIGHT

Has some sort of stop or barrier that limits the depth of insertion into the ground.

VARIABLE HEIGHT

Single tee that provides various fixed heights, depending on how it is inserted.

LEANER

A peg-type design that leans toward the golfer's target while still supporting the ball. They are supposed to aid in alignment and reduce clubhead interference.

METAL

Unusual metal tees not conforming to any other classification, such as ones made of bent wire and sheet metal.

SWIVELS

Designed to reduce the interference of the tee with the clubhead by allowing the ball supporting portion of the tee to swivel out of the way upon impact.

NOVELTY

Not intended for serious use, but rather for advertising, entertainment or shock value. Includes nude figurines and liquor bottle shapes.

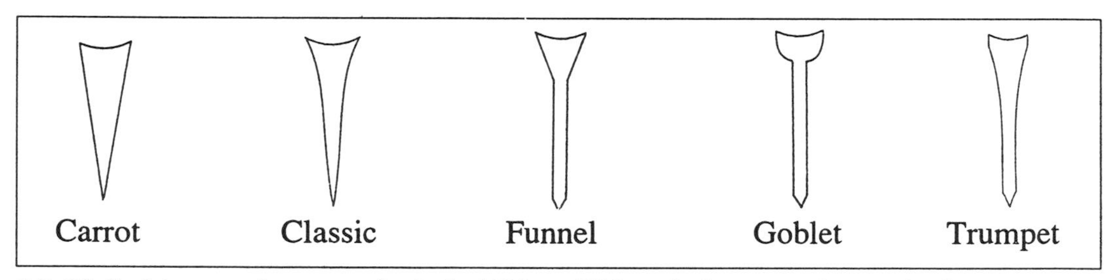

8-8 *Of all of these tee shapes popular in the 1920s and '30s, only the trumpet has survived. An estimated 600 million of these plain wooden tees are produced annually.*

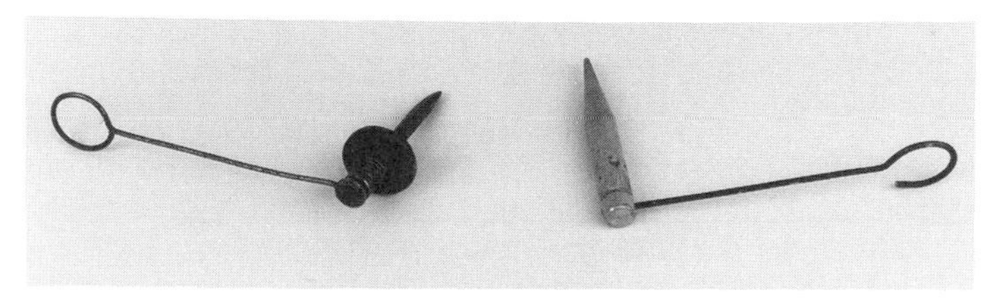

8-9 *Two versions of swivel tees. The ball was placed on the wire support, which was designed to swivel out of the way on impact. Theoretically, the tee should have remained in place after the shot, but in reality the unit often would be dislodged from the ground.*

8-10 *The Reddy Tee, a funnel-shaped wooden tee manufactured by The Nieblo Manufacturing Company, was the most popular tee during the 1920s. William Lowell, a dentist from New Jersey, applied for a patent for his idea in 1922 and received it in 1924. Because of broad claims of the patent and challenges from other manufacturers, the company spent much of their profits on legal fees. Although the Reddy Tee — named for its red color and readiness — prospered for a decade, it eventually went out of production when the company went bankrupt in the early 1930s. (Although Dr. Lowell was influential in converting millions of golfers to the wooden tee, he often is erroneously credited in golf publications with the invention of golf tees in general. He did, however, forsee the future when he suggested that his tees could be made from a vegetable material that would decompose and act as fertilizer. Ecology minded tees are just now entering the marketplace.)*

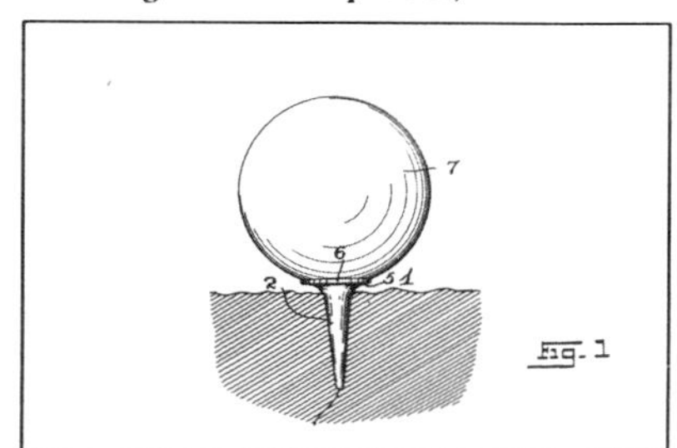

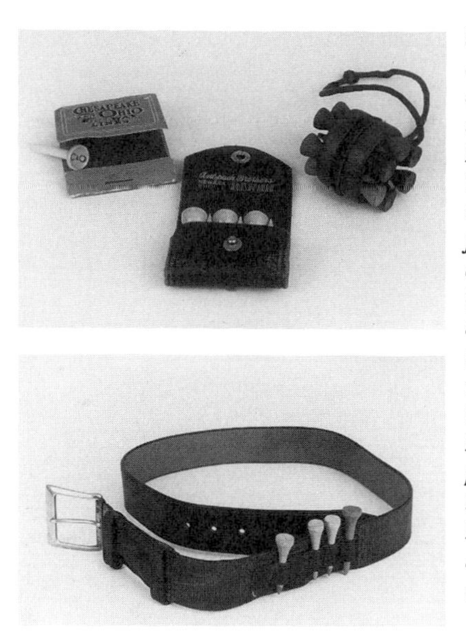

8-11 *Tee holders could be worn, carried in a pocket or tied to a golf bag. Matchbook-style holders, made of cardboard, frequently carried advertisements (top) and were disposable, whereas the leather and wooden ones lasted longer. The Tee Belt (bottom) was patented in 1915 by the Linney Belt Company and provided a convenient holster.*

8-12 *There was much competition among tee manufacturers in the 1920s and '30s, so it was crucial to have packaging that would catch the golfer's eye and encourage a purchase. (Also see color photo page 41)*

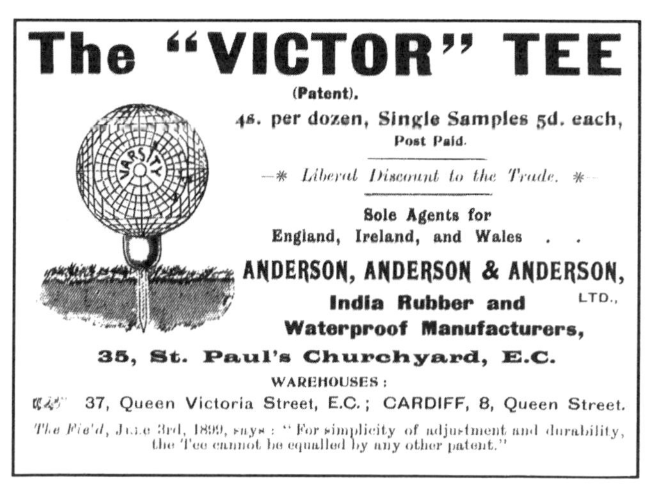

8-13 *The Victor goblet-shaped tee was produced at the end of the 19th century, about 20 years ahead of its time.*

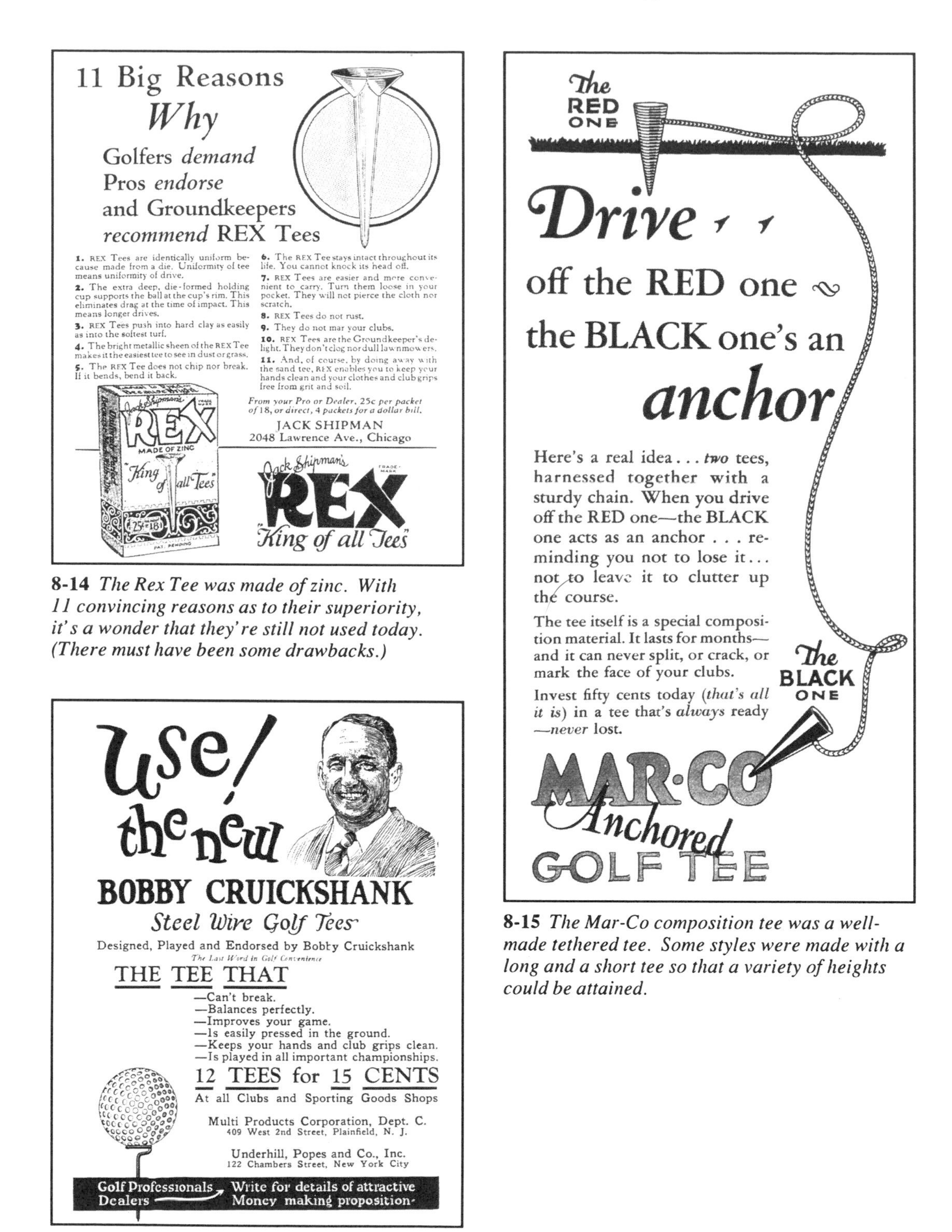

8-14 *The Rex Tee was made of zinc. With 11 convincing reasons as to their superiority, it's a wonder that they're still not used today. (There must have been some drawbacks.)*

8-15 *The Mar-Co composition tee was a well-made tethered tee. Some styles were made with a long and a short tee so that a variety of heights could be attained.*

8-16 *Bobby Cruickshank was one of many touring professionals who endorsed golf tees. Wire tees were fine for teeing the ball, but were impractical: the thin points poked through pockets (and skin) and steel ones left rust stains.*

CHAPTER 9

INSTRUCTIONAL AIDS & PRACTICE ITEMS

Did you ever know a golfer who was 100% satisfied with his or her game? Probably not. Perhaps that's what makes golf so enticing: the ever-present chance for improvement.

Expert advice, special practice methods and all sorts of unusual gadgets have been thrust upon golfers for more than a century. And that's in addition to the perennial promises of improved play from the club and ball manufacturers.

Currently, instructional video tapes are the rage. But years ago, before there were video recorders and televised golf tips by Ken Venturi and Peter Alliss, golfers turned to phonograph records, stereoscopes and film strips for high-tech nurturing of their games. The most significant vintage audio-visual instruction was a series of film shorts made by Bobby Jones 60 years ago. Now available on video tape, this classic instruction is valued by both students of the golf swing and sports history.

Collectibles that go hand in hand with the instructional aids are the old-fashioned practice devices. Most were designed for home use, for indoor putting — once known as parlor putting or for outdoor activity on the lawn. (Items primarily marketed for their entertainment value rather than their ability to improve golf technique are discussed in Chapter 15 - Toys and Games.) Although many of these contraptions had short production lives due to poor design or lack of consumer appeal, they now are sought after by collectors. The unusual ones make fantastic conversation pieces that are sure to elicit a chuckle from golfers who can relate to the woes of their forefathers.

INSTRUCTIONAL AIDS

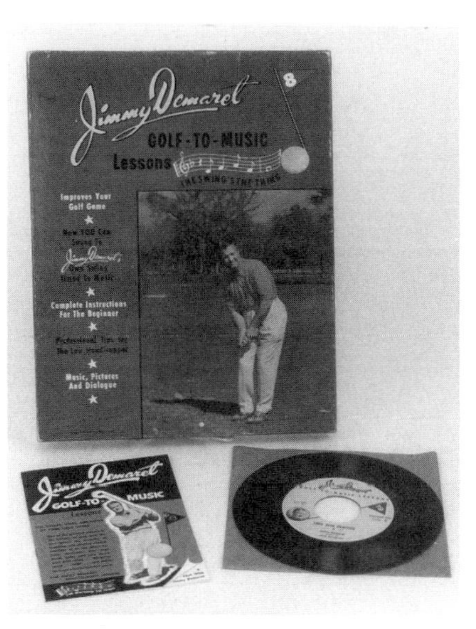

9-1 *Jimmy Demaret's background as a nightclub entertainer proved helpful in the creation of this musical approach to hitting a golf ball. The boxed set of six 45 rpm records included illustrated booklets. Produced in 1959, these were far from being the first golf records —Chick Evans gave recorded golf lessons in the late 1920s. (Since Evans was an amateur, he used the proceeds from his records to establish the Evans' Scholarship Fund to provide college scholarships for caddies.)*

9-2 *After listening to 32-year-old Arnold Palmer discuss the mechanics of the swing with sportscaster Chris Schenkel on this 1962 record, you'll be convinced that a picture is worth a thousand words.*

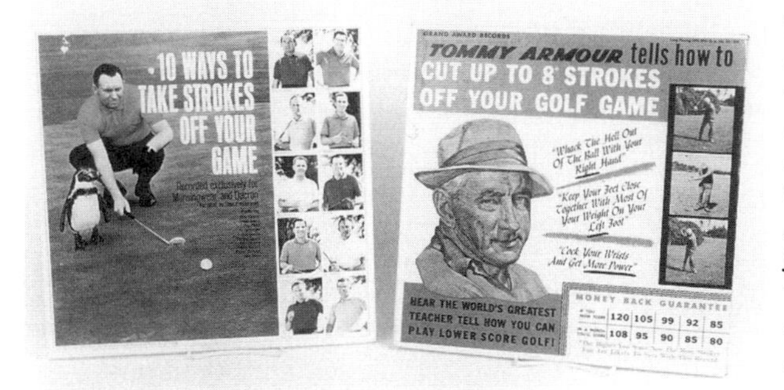

9-3 *These records preached stroke-saving methods. The promotional record (left) was issued by the Munsingwear sportswear company in 1967. Narrated by Dow Finsterwald, it featured tips from Billy Casper (seen on the jacket showing a penguin how to line up a putt) and other famous pros who wore shirts emblazoned with the likeness of Casper's friend. Tommy Armour's record offered a money-back guarantee that scores would improve by a certain amount within a month.*

9-4 *When a specially created pair of photographs is placed in a stereoscope (above), a single three-dimensional image can be seen through the viewfinder. Stereo optical cards were a popular diversion at the beginning of the century and often showed tourist sites and famous personalities. Several of the top golfers were photographed, including the Triumvirate of J.H. Taylor, Harry Vardon and James Braid (right).*

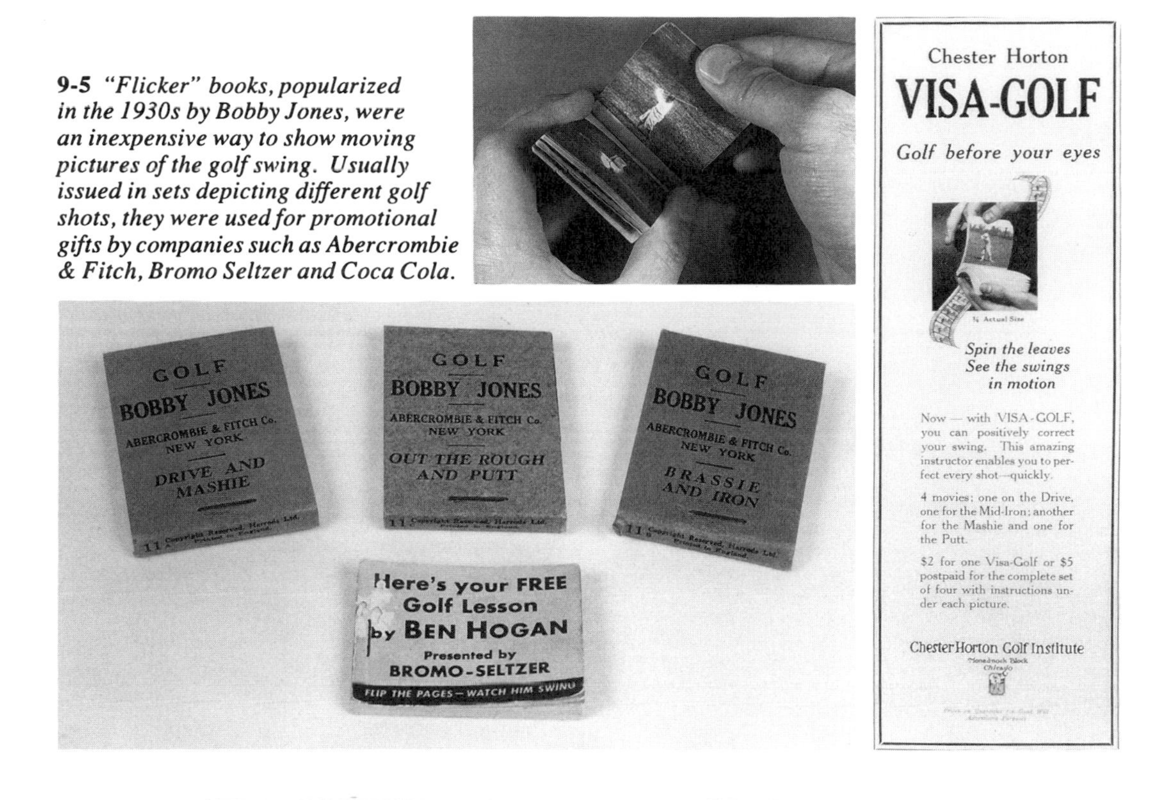

***9-5** "Flicker" books, popularized in the 1930s by Bobby Jones, were an inexpensive way to show moving pictures of the golf swing. Usually issued in sets depicting different golf shots, they were used for promotional gifts by companies such as Abercrombie & Fitch, Bromo Seltzer and Coca Cola.*

***9-6** Bobby Jones starred in a series of 18 film shorts, produced by Warner Brothers from 1931 to 1933. In addition to explaining his swing in remarkable slow motion sequences, the champion takes part in golf scenes with Hollywood celebrities. The stars include W.C. Fields, Joe E. Brown and Douglas Fairbanks, Jr. These amusing films were reissued as a video cassette package in 1987 by Sybervision Systems.*

***9-7** The Tru-Vu company issued a series of Bobby Jones swing sequences for exclusive use with their viewer.*

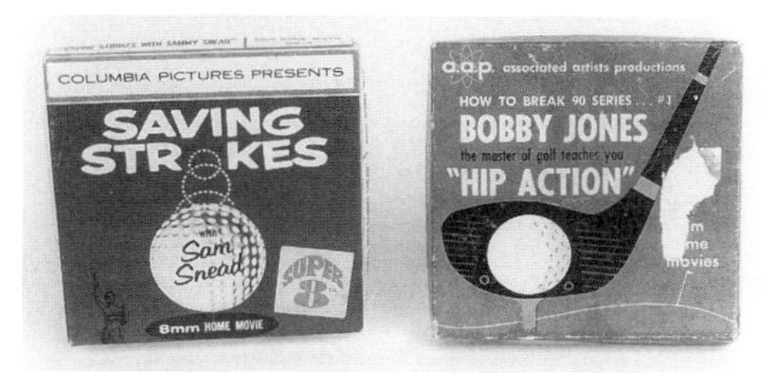

***9-8** Before video cassettes, 8mm and Super 8 films were the rage in home movie viewing. These films featured Sam Snead and Bobby Jones.*

PRACTICE ITEMS

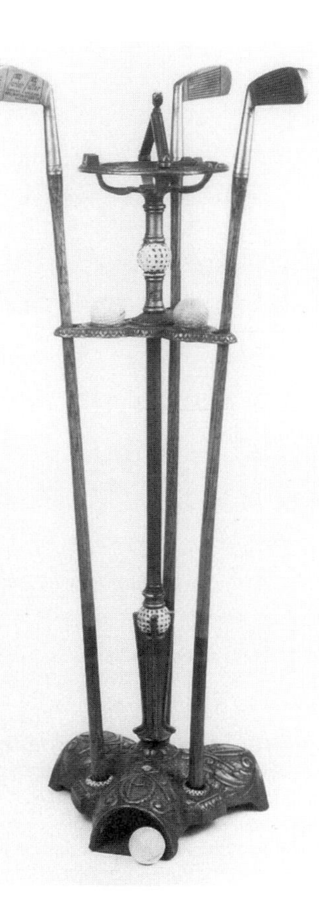

9-9 *The most collectible antique indoor putting device is the Parlor Putter. Cast in iron or brass in several styles, they feature elaborate embellishments and varying paint schemes. They are especially desirable when accompanied by the original "Parlor" brand putters. (Replica models have been produced in recent years.)*

9-10 *The benefits of off-season exercises for golfers were being preached back in 1914 by Gil Nicholls, a noted professional.*

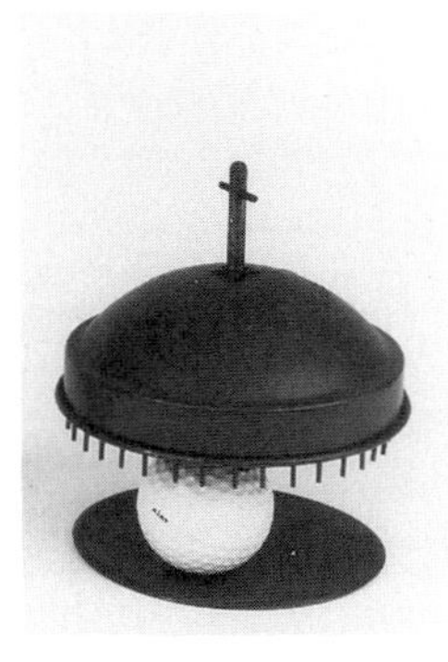

9-11 *Bobby's Portable Golf Hole is an indoor (or outdoor) putting target that places a premium on speed. Suspended metal "fingers" capture a ball traveling at just the right speed.*

What fitter gift for the golfer than this?—

A KUMBAK, regularly used, will improve any golfer's putting. With it, he—or she—can get all-year-'round practice; the KUMBAK can be used in any ordinary-sized room. And it returns the ball to the player after *every* stroke.

Walter Hagen and many other leading players highly recommend the KUMBAK as the most practical device of its kind. Designed by a golfer, it duplicates playing conditions. See it and try it at your dealer's. The price is $3.50 ($3.75 in Far West).

FOX MFG. CO., 4704 N. 18th St., Philadelphia

9-12 *In 1929, indoor putting "greens" varied from the one-hole Kumbak (far left) to the nine-hole Perfection (left).*

9-13 *J.B. Halley was a golf ball manufacturer at the turn-of-the-century, so it was only natural that they offer a practice aid. Their captive ball was tethered to a steel pin that could be inserted into the ground or screwed to a large fixed object. It is not known whether the heavy spring actually limited the rebound of the ball or encouraged it.*

9-14 *This practice ball was attached to a weighted wooden anchor, or "bottle," that was supposed to limit the flight of the ball. Undoubtedly, more time was spent retrieving the ball than practicing.*

9-15 *Patented in 1926, practice balls knitted from wool or cotton were promoted for indoor and outdoor practice sessions.*

9-16 *The 20th Tee and Chip Shot utilized regular golf balls and required airborne shots — indoors! Marketed in the late 1920s, they featured a scoring system to make practice more enjoyable.*

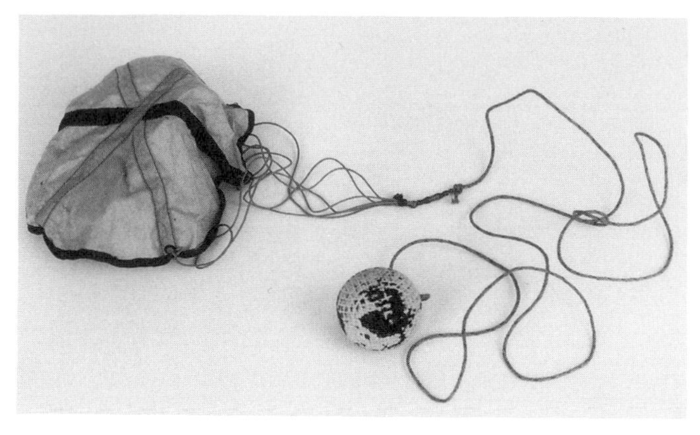

9-17 *One of the earliest, and most novel, practice aids was the Parachute Golf Ball. It was developed in the early 1890s and is one of the few practice gimmicks to incorporate the 19th century gutty ball.*

THE
PARACHUTE
GOLF BALL.

For restricting the flight of the Ball, and enabling Golfers to practise in confined spaces.

Every player should possess one.

THE
PARACHUTE
GOLF BALL.

PRICES:
Complete with Compo. Ball, 1s. 6d.
Ditto with Patent Tee and best Gutta Ball, 2s.
Postage 3d.

Illustrated Golf List and Full Sports Catalogue, Free by Post.

SOLE AGENTS FOR THE INVENTORS,
J. JAQUES & SONS, Manufacturers of all Sports & Games, HATTON GARDEN, LONDON, E.C.

9-18 *The Biffit tethered ball, patented in 1933, had a remote anchor designed to return the ball to the golfer without hitting him. Note the condition of the tattered ball inside the box.*

CHAPTER 10

ACCESSORIES

Golf accessories consist of items which are not essential to the game, but are intended to enhance the golfer's enjoyment and comfort. Some equipment now taken for granted — golf bags and spiked shoes, for example — was once regarded as a luxury. Up until a century ago, golfers wore plain-soled shoes and caddies carried clubs bunched under their arms.

As golf became popular in the 1890s, ingenuity prevailed. In addition to golf bags and carriers, golfers were introduced to club and ball cleaning devices, mechanical scorekeepers, special golf clothing, ball imprinting tools and other conveniences. Several types of accessories, such as tees, instructional aids and practice devices, were produced so extensively that they warrant their own chapters in this book.

Various categories of ancillary equipment are illustrated on the following pages. While most collectors attempt to obtain representative examples for an overall display of golf antiques, there now is a growing trend of specialization. Vintage golf clothing specialists, for instance, will create files of old photographs and advertisements so that they will recognize items at secondhand shops or antiques shows that were designed as golfwear.

Old accessories, such as high-top golf shoes or early club carriers, make wonderful conversation pieces and add diversity to a collection of clubs or books.

Clubs Carriers And Golf Bags

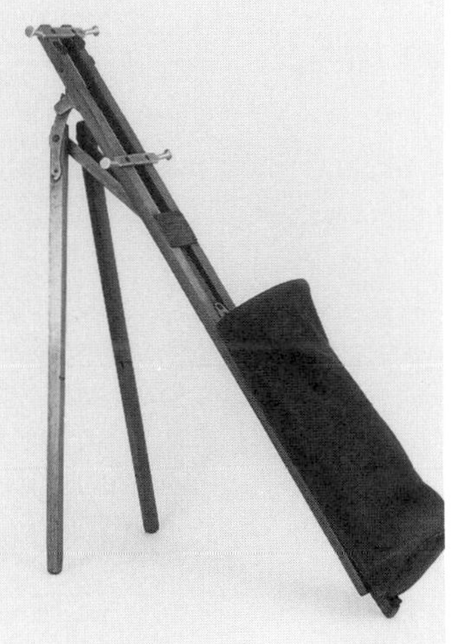

10-1 *George Bussey & Co. made a full line of golf equipment. Their "stand-up" caddy, popular during the 1890s with golfers, is now sought by collectors to showcase old clubs.*

10-2 *Osmond's "Automaton," patented in 1893, made club carrying an easy task. These fold-up club carriers were sold primarily in Great Britain around the turn of the century. However, bag attachments using the same principle are enjoying a renewed popularity with golfers today.*

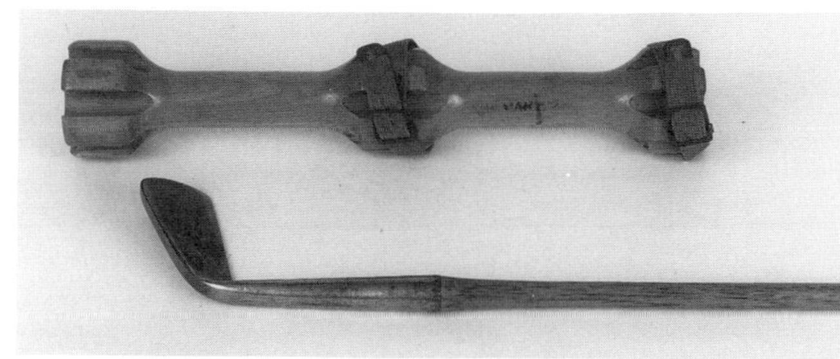

10-3 *Designed to keep wooden club shafts from warping, this device was similar in function to the screw-down presses used for storing tennis racquets (back when they were constructed of wood).*

10-4 *Nesser golf bags were a nicely detailed product of the 1920s.*

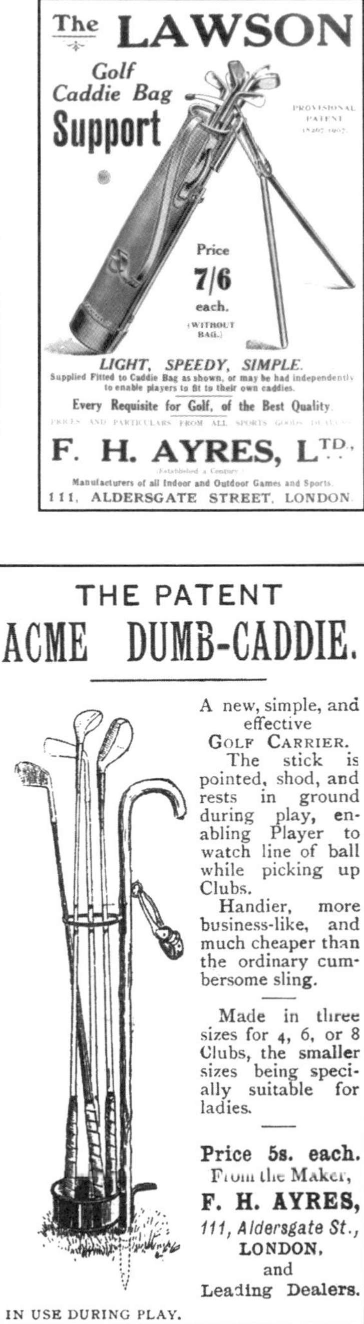

10-5 *The Lawson bag stand (left) of 1907 was an improvement over the Osmond and Bussey models because it could be affixed to and removed from any type of golf bag. Notice how the term "caddie" was used to describe the bag and not the person who carried it.*

10-6 *Most of the classic small diameter golf bags from the 1890s through the 1930s were made of canvas or leather (see page 38). A variation was the lightweight wicker bag, with compartment for balls and tees.*

10-7 *The name of this club carrier was not intended to be derogatory. "Dumb-caddie" is merely the golf equivalent of the dumbwaiter. This cane-type carrier was invented in the early 1890s.*

10-8 *Joe Kirkwood, noted pro golfer and trick shot artist, offered his endorsement of this pull-cart (or trolley) in 1926.*

CLOTHING

10-9 *Burberrys, the famed English clothiers, offered stylish golf clothing at the turn of the century.*

10-10 *Four-piece golf suits — with jacket, vest, knickers and trousers — were sold by Robinson's in Los Angeles during the Roaring Twenties.*

10-11 *Longer drives and more accurate putts? Truth-in-advertising must have been unheard-of in 1926.*

10-12 *These patented knickers did away with the traditional buckles, straps and buttons that held the cuffs in place. Gene Sarazen — the golfer who made knickers his lifelong trademark — has carried the no-buckle concept even further. His tailors now utilize Velcro-type tabs for a positive fit.*

10-13 *Although golf gloves didn't enjoy widespread use until the 1960s, they were available in the late 1890s.*

SHOES

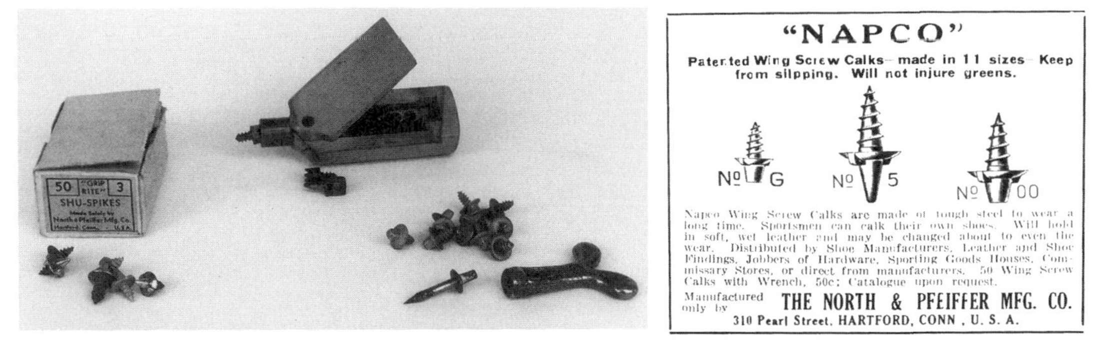

10-14 *From the late 19th century until about 1920, golfers and shoemakers converted street shoes and boots into studded golf shoes. Special applicators and storage containers (left) permitted golfers to make simple repairs. Spikes, also called calks (right), came in several sizes.*

10-15 *Fashionable women's golf boots, circa 1900, were sold by outfitters such as Abercrombie & Fitch.*

10-16 *Scafe's patent from 1891 was one of the first for golf footwear.*

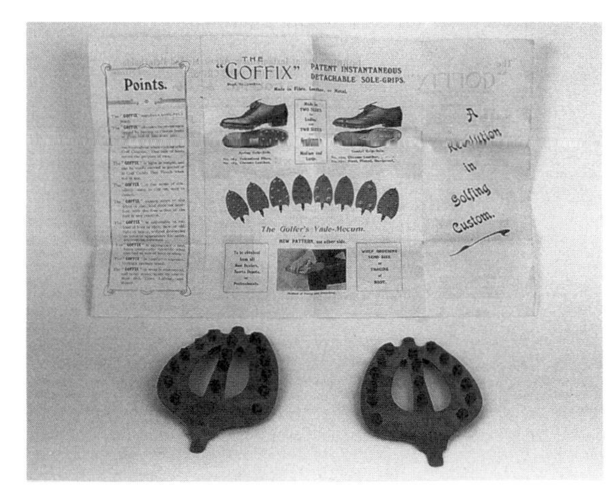

10-17 *Easily detachable spikes were made under the Goffix patent, shown here in mint condition with the original instructions.*

10-18 *Harry Vardon, one of the first professional athletes to endorse commercial products, had his own brand of shoes in 1914.*

SCOREKEEPERS

10-19 *Pocket scorekeepers (above and right) were made of metal, celluloid, paper and plastic. They used wheels, dials, balls and other methods to indicate the score. Although paper scorecards were in use as early as the mid-19th century, these items primarily were sold as novelty or gift items.*

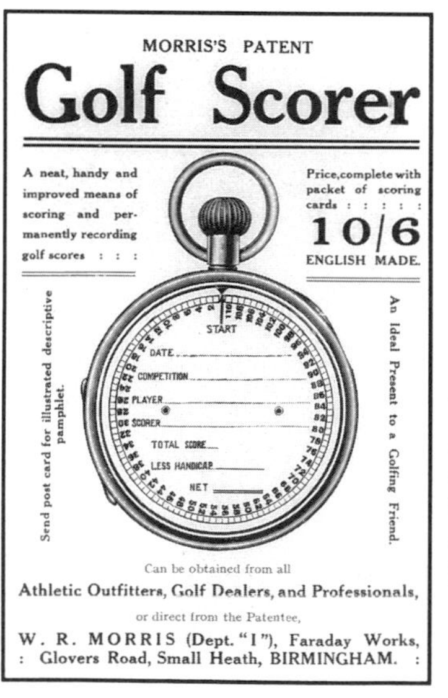

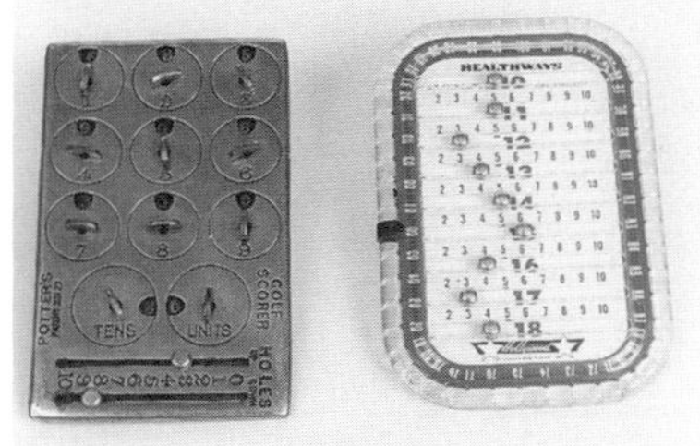

10-20 *Scorekeepers resembling watches usually kept a cumulative score for the round rather than a hole-by-hole account. The Morris Golf Scorer (left) recorded a score on paper, giving the player a permanent record.*

10-21 *For the golfer of 1926 who had everything: a first-rate mechanical pencil that conveniently stored in the end of a putter grip.*

MISCELLANEOUS ACCESSORIES

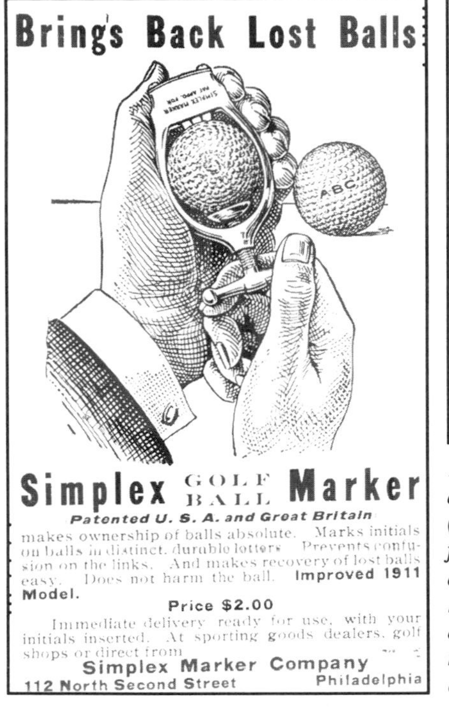

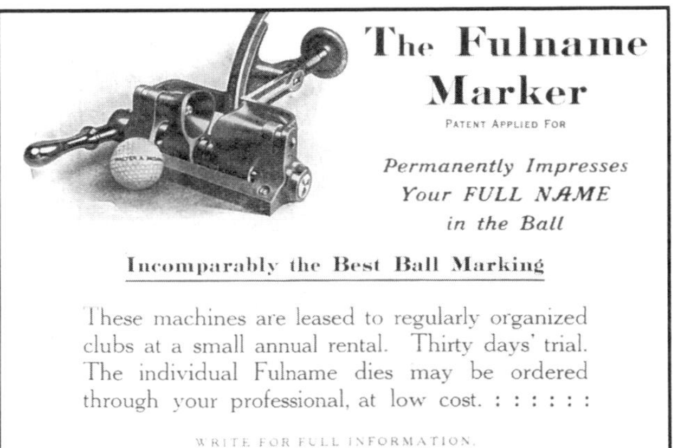

10-22 *The two most popular golf ball marking devices developed in the early 20th century were the Fulname (above), designed for pro shop use and the Simplex (left), for personal use. After furnishing a golf professional with a marking machine, the Fulname Company supplied dies for individual golfers. Thereafter, the pro imprinted the balls as a service to his members. Fulname boasted of thousands of machines in use during the 1920s — some of which were still operational in the 1960s.*

10-23 *A dampened sponge was the preferred ball cleaner a century ago. Sponge containers, constructed of brass, tin or rubber, were attached to the golf bag or stored in a pocket.*

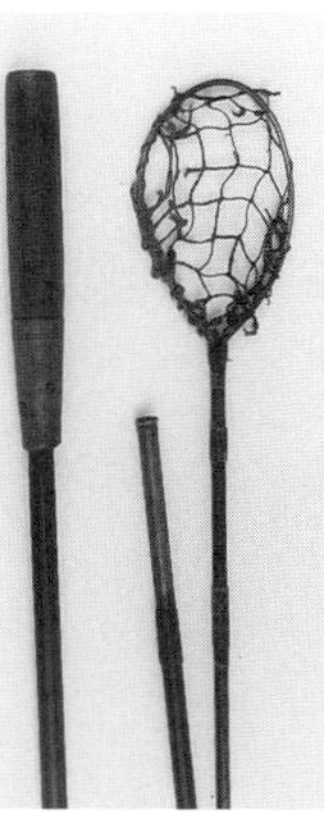

10-24 *This three-piece ball retriever (left) is similar to the one used in a 1906 illustration (above) for an article about the enormous, undulating putting course at St. Andrews, known as the "Himalayas." The story tells how the 15th hole was cut so close to the Swilcan Burn that a great number of balls were entering the water hazard.*

COLLECTING TIP

■ One of the unique aspects of collecting golf artifacts is that many items can be put to their original use. It's not unusual for a collector to have a set of 60-year-old, hickory-shafted clubs that he plays with, as a occasional lark or in an organized "hickory hacker" tournament. And what better way to play a round of old-time golf than by wearing old-time golf attire. Plus four knickers for men and long skirts for women can be found in vintage clothing shops. Try it . . . There aren't many sports that let you return to the "good old days."

10-25 *Golfers didn't think much about protecting their wood-headed clubs until well into the 20th century. These leather headcovers date to the early 1950s.*

10-26 *The far-fetched claim that this rubber shaft tip actually "adds yards to your shots" is equally as outrageous as the guarantees stated in the jock strap ad in photo 10-11.*

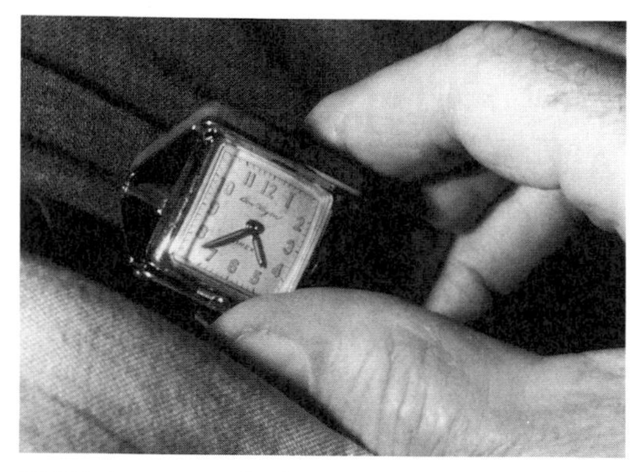

10-27 *A compromise between a wristwatch and a pocket watch is a belt-mounted timepiece. This one was made by Timex, circa 1953, and featured a "Ben Hogan" signature on the dial. The normally closed case automatically opens upon depressing a release button.*

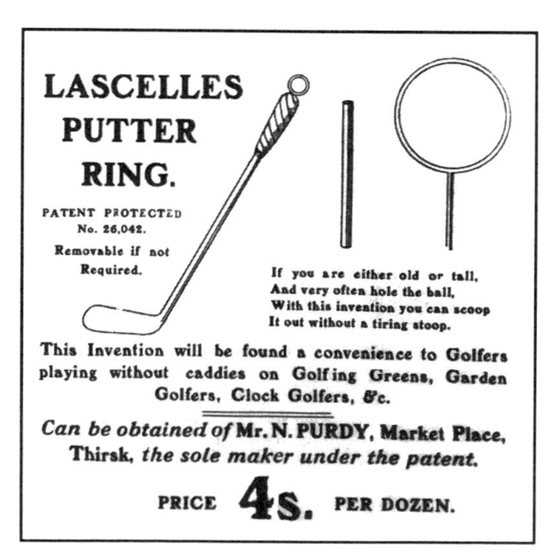

10-28 *Modern golfers with back problems employ a grip-mounted rubber suction cup to remove the ball from the hole. Eighty-six years ago, the Lascelles Putter Ring did the same job.*

CHAPTER 11

PRINTS & PAINTINGS

Paintings of golfers first became popular in Scotland and England in the late 18th century when golfing societies began to honor their officers by having their portraits painted. When it became evident that other golfers might want copies of the portraits, engravers created plates so that prints could be produced. The first such print — a black-and-white mezzotint showing William Innes, captain of the Royal Blackheath Golf Club — was published in 1790.

Often referred to as "The Blackheath Golfer," the representation of Innes, resplendent in red golfing jacket and white breeches and accompanied by his caddy, has been reproduced countless times in publications to typify the image of an early golfer. The portrait also has the distinction of being reproduced more than any other piece of golf art.

By 1812, prints of three other golf portraits had been published. In the decades that followed, several more significant portraits of well-to-do British golfers were painted and Thomas Hodge and Francis Powell Hopkins created hundreds of watercolors of golfers and scenes, but the only print published prior to the golf boom of the 1890s was "The Golfers" in 1850, by Charles Lees.

The 1890s brought forth many golf paintings, and the demand for prints — some of which were in color — increased dramatically. Even in America, where golf was just becoming popular, golfers fell in love with the art of the game. Refinements in the printing of books, magazines and artwork around the turn of the century paved the way for a new breed of artist — the illustrator. Before long, thousands of golf drawings and paintings were created by the likes of Cecil Aldin, William Heath Robinson, Charles Dana Gibson and A.B. Frost.

The publishing of golf prints virtually ceased in the 1930s, but when interest in golf memorabilia developed in the 1970s, there was a resurgence in the art market. Now there are so many golf prints produced that the supply appears to be exceeding the demand.

ORIGINAL ART

NOTE: When *The Encyclopedia of Golf Collectibles* was assembled in 1985, nearly every known golf print and famous painting was documented. To repeat that task now would result in a huge catalog dominated by contemporary prints. Instead, this chapter is devoted to a discussion of significant older examples of golf art, which have been separated into three categories: portraits, scenes and illustrations.

Although many original works of golf art are available, most of the well-known paintings are owned by the R & A, Honourable Company of Edinburgh Golfers (at Muirfield Golf Club), Royal Blackheath Golf Club and the USGA. Other noteworthy works are in museums, such as the National Portrait Gallery of Scotland and the British Museum in London. (To see some of the masterpieces can be a thrill. First-time viewers usually are startled by the immense size of the oil paintings, many of which are life-size, full-length portraits.)

Some of the vintage paintings, however, are owned privately, and rarely come up for sale. Most were done in the late 19th and early 20th centuries — it's unusual to come across any dated before 1850. Collectors have a better chance of buying a watercolor or sketch by Thomas Hodge, Francis Powell Hopkins (Major S) or Harry Furniss — all prolific, yet highly regarded, British illustrators of the 19th century.

***11-1** CARLO MARINI-RIGHI*
Painting of a period scene, done in oil on copper in the style of A.B Frost. These contemporary works are being represented (perhaps unknowingly) by some dealers as antique. Produced in quantity in the 1980s in Italy, they have been signed C.M. Righi, C.M. and M. Righi.

***11-2** J. MICHAEL BROWN*
Described in a 1991 auction catalog as a pencil and chalk sketch by an anonymous artist, this piece is actually an unsigned study done by Brown for his large painting of the 1901 British Ladies' Amateur Championship. (The finished work was published as a photo-gravure in 1902.) Molly Graham (right) putts while runner-up Rhona Adair observes.

Perhaps the most desirable paintings are those which have been reproduced as prints or bookplates. Those that have sold in recent years include several of the *Vanity Fair* watercolors by "SPY" (Sir Leslie Ward), a series of three scenes by Charles Edmund Brock, and some of the Harry Rountree watercolors used to illustrate *The Golf Courses of the British Isles*. The most significant sale of this sort was a study in oil done by Sir Francis Grant preparatory to executing his famous portrait of John Whyte-Melville (see photo 11-13). The 28-inch high painting sold at auction for more than $270,000.

An often overlooked genre of artist is the engraver. For in order to reproduce a picture prior to the development of photomechanical printing methods in the late 19th century, it was necessary for an engraver to meticulously create printing plates so that the image could be transferred onto paper. Engravers noted for their golf works include: Valentine Green, G. Dawe, J. Jones and William Ward for their mezzotints of the first four golf prints; Walter A. Cox and Will Henderson for their early 20th-century color mezzotints of the classic portraits; James Dobie for his engravings of the Sadler and Brock paintings; John Barclay for his stylish etchings and Lawrence Josset, who worked during this century.

***11-3** FRITH*
Silhouette, dated 1843, showing George (left) and William Condie, members of an illustrious family of golfers from Perth, Scotland. The Frith family was well known for their silhouettes, which were often embellished with brushwork. The art form declined in popularity after the development of photography.

***11-4** GEORGE AIKMAN (1830-1905)*
Even though the back side of the old frame on this oil painting carried the notation "Tom Morris," it is doubtful that the famous golfer is the subject. The painting is dated 1869 and historians believe that the likelihood of having a famous artist paint a professional golfer — even Tom Morris — at that point in time is remote. Photographic research indicates that the golfer is probably John Blyth, a prominent 19th-century amateur golfer from North Berwick, who had the financial resources to commission the painting. The lesson to be learned here is that sometimes written information cannot be taken for face value. Although the notation on the picture frame may have been old, it easily could have been an assumption made by an unknowing dealer decades after the work was painted.

TYPES OF PRINTS

Many collectors of golf memorabilia consider a print to be just another "pretty picture." That is, until they decide to acquire one and are faced with determining what price to pay. Therefore, it is helpful to be acquainted with the various types of prints.

Prints range from ones meticulously printed from hand-prepared plates to those run off of high-speed multicolor presses. Old-fashioned prints are not necessarily better than modern ones. They're just different. There is no question that the reproductive quality of a modern offset color lithograph is superior to a 100-year-old lithograph made off a limestone slab. But to an art connoisseur, that means little. An old stone lithograph with its "softer appearance" is considered a work of art because it was prepared by an artist, who either created his own original image onto the stone or produced his interpretation of a painting. The same applies to the engraver or etcher who may spend months transferring an image onto a metal plate.

It is this craftsmanship that makes old prints inherently more valuable than their modern counterparts. Print runs in earlier times were short — sometimes only 50 or 100 copies due to wear of the soft copper printing plates. In a modern printing job, on the other hand, the difference between a press run of 200 and 400 prints is merely a matter of minutes.

Because the older prints were laboriously produced in limited quantities and since many have been lost or destroyed, it's easy to see how they can be valued in the thousands of dollars. Collectors, however, often have the choice of purchasing a less-expensive reproduction of an old golf subject, usually in the form of an offset lithograph.

COMMON PRINTING METHODS

Although there are dozens of printing techniques, only a few have been used to produce the majority of golf prints. The following three antiquated methods usually were printed with black or sepia inks. The varying tones result from the spacing and thickness of thousands of tiny lines or scratches. Some prints were later hand-colored with watercolors.

Mezzotint was the process employed in producing all of the early golf portraits. The engraver began by raising a "burr" on a copper plate, which was then smoothed in varying degrees to create the desired tones. It was possible to print in color by brushing colored inks onto the plate before pressing it to the paper; the term for this elaborate process is "à la poupée."

Line engravings and **dry-point etchings** are similar — their metal plates have been scratched and gouged with special tools to create grooves for holding ink. Engravings usually can be distinguished by their deeper, more linear grooves. The durability of engraving plates made them preferable for creating illustrations for books and magazines, about a century ago.

Most prints that relate the exact textures and brush strokes of their original paintings have been reproduced by a photomechanical method. Printed in color or black and white, these scenes are probably **photogravures** or **lithographs**. The lithograph — modern ones are printed by the improved offset method — can be distinguished under magnification by its grid pattern of tiny dots,

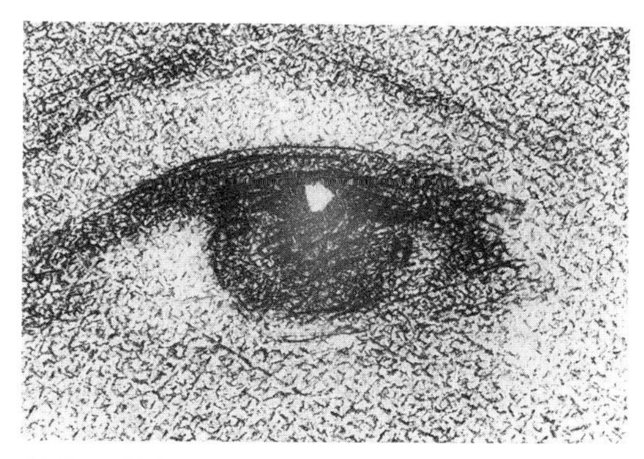

11-5 *MEZZOTINT CLOSE-UP*
Note the characteristic grain caused by the mechanically roughened metal printing plate. This is the eye of James Balfour (see photo 11-12).

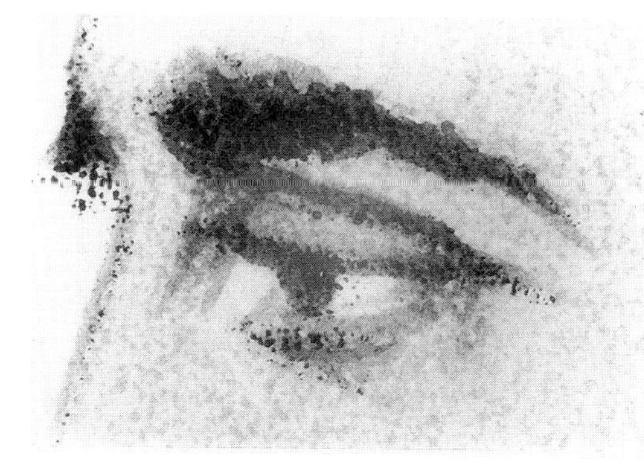

11-6 *STONE LITHOGRAPH CLOSE-UP*
The eye of Horace Hutchinson on a Vanity Fair *print shows the smooth distribution of ink associated with a print made from a limestone slab. (See photo 11-49 for the entire image.)*

while the photogravure has a finer grain resembling the continuous tones of a photograph.

There are also two other fine-grained types of old prints. **Stone lithographs** and **aquatints** have soft, pleasing colors, frequently seen on humorous golf prints. Since both the heavy stone slabs and metal aquatint plates were inked by hand, the images are not always crisp and colors sometimes overlap. Under magnification, the aquatint exhibits a characteristic lacelike pattern, whereas the stone lithograph has a smoother, continuous texture.

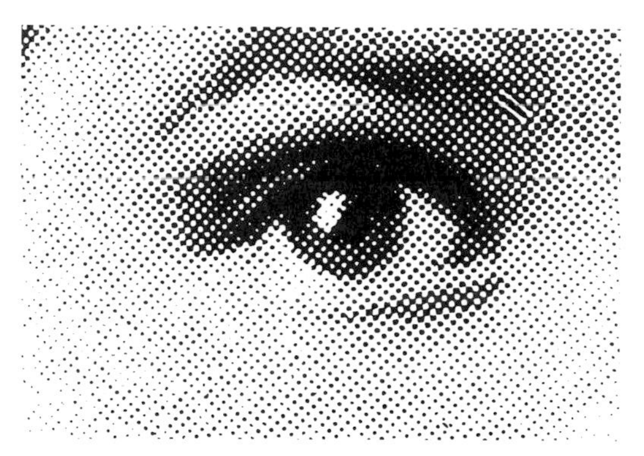

11-7 *OFFSET LITHOGRAPH CLOSE-UP*
The regular dot pattern makes this the easiest type of print to identify. Most color printing utilizes dots of four different colors. However the number of colors can vary. This is the eye of William Innes (see photo 11-11), taken from a reproduction print.

COLLECTING TIPS

- **Buy a good magnifier, or loupe, to assist with identification of prints. Available from stamp and coin dealers, magnification power from 8x to 16x should be adequate.**
- **A comprehensive reference book for the serious print collector is *How to Identify Prints* by Bamber Gascoigne (New York: Thames & Hudson, 1986).**

EVALUATING A PRINT

When buying a print from an art or golf memorabilia dealer, try to obtain a written description of the piece. If the dealer is reputable and stands behind his representations about its age and originality, you should have no qualms about its authenticity.

Oftentimes, however, prints may be improperly described or are sold "as is" because the seller is unfamiliar with the item. When this situation occurs, you need to do some investigating, or consult an expert. The most common error in buying golf prints is overpaying for a reproduction. And yes, forgeries do exist, so buyers need to be careful.

Most conscientiously reproduced golf prints are imprinted with the new publisher's name or other marking, or are done in a different size than the original. Unfortunately, a reproduction can look awfully real, especially behind glass in an old frame.

If you are considering purchasing an expensive framed print, ask the owner to remove it from the frame so you can examine the paper. (If he refuses, you'll have to decide if his reason is sincere or if he is trying to hide something.) If you can handle the print, examine both sides. Old paper usually looks old and new paper new. (The exceptions being old paper that has been cleaned by a professional conservator and new paper stained to look old.)

An easy examination, that even can be done on a framed print, is to look at various areas of the subject through a magnifying glass. If you see the dots associated with lithography and collecting guides describe the original as an engraving, you know you are looking at a reproduction.

Don't be fooled by color on a print that you know was originally printed in black and white. Many old pieces have been tinted with watercolors. The telltale black ink will show through the translucent colors. Keep in mind, however, that hand-colored engravings still are being produced, often

11-8
LAWRENCE JOSSET "St. Andrews, 1800." A recently published print incorporating centuries-old techniques. Josset engraved this scene from one originally done by Frank Paton in 1894. The prints then were colored with a watercolor wash. Because of the date in the caption, heavy paper and the engraved image, this print is sometimes mistaken for old.

from the original plates. (Because of the personal touch involved, these restrikes are more desirable than a reproduction lithograph.)

Prints signed by the artist and/or engraver usually are more desirable than an unsigned one. The exception is a rare form of engraving with no title or other lettering, known as a "proof before letters." These proofs were pulled prior to completion of the plate so that the engraver could evaluate his work. At the other end of the spectrum is a print containing a printed signature, referred to as being "signed in the plate." These signatures are usually darker and denser, although it is possible to produce a good imitation of a pencil signature with screen tints or gray ink.

The consecutive numbering of prints with a notation such as "51/300" indicates that the print is the 51st out of a limited edition of 300. This designation predominantly appears on 20th-century prints — earlier ones were not numbered. Traditionally, when prints were made from handmade plates, the first ones were of better quality, since plate wear often became apparent after a few dozen prints.

Modern printing presses, however, are capable of producing thousands of exact images. Therefore, when buying a modern lithograph, your prime concern should be with the second number and not the first. Since a limited edition of more than 1,000 prints is hardly exclusive, you should take this into account when making a purchase. In addition to the stated size of the edition, a dozen or so extra prints are often designated as artist's proofs and given to the artist or used for promotional purposes.

A special feature sometimes found on a print is a remarque, a small original pencil or watercolor sketch of a golfer or other related topic placed in the lower margin by the artist. If authentic — some are printed along with the main subject — they greatly enhance the value of the print.

The last bit of advice is to look for a continuous impression around the perimeter of the image, known as a plate mark. This may or may not have a bearing on the age or type of print. When a mezzotint or other engraving is printed, the plate is pressed against the paper with great force and the paper, being larger than the plate, ends up with an indentation from the edge of the plate. However, sometimes an old print may have been trimmed down, so no plate mark will show. Other times, especially with prints issued during the last 20 years, a false plate mark has been applied with a blank die to make a print look more distinctive.

COLLECTING TIP

■ Don't always assume that a date or printing description is accurate. Many old prints have been reproduced in their entirety, so a print with the notation "mezzotint 1790" could easily be a reproduction printed in 1970. Remember that there are many more reproductions of famous vintage golf pitures than there are originals.

Portraits

As previously mentioned, oil portraits were the predominant type of golf art produced during the 18th and 19th centuries. Although portraits had been painted decades earlier, a group of four paintings by Henry Raeburn and Lemuel Francis Abbott, done between 1790 and 1812, became noteworthy since they were the first to be reproduced as prints. They are now referred to by historians as "The First Four."

Most portraits featured respected members of society in formal poses until the 1890s when the socioeconomic makeup of the British golfing community changed. During this period, when mass production of golf equipment made the game affordable to the general population, the artwork of the game also experienced a change. As the game became less stuffy, the artwork became less formal. In 1890 *Vanity Fair* magazine began to publish prints of the famous caricatures painted by "SPY" that featured noted amateur players, such as Horace Hutchinson and John Ball.

***11-10** SIR GEORGE CHALMERS (1720-1791) Perhaps the first known golfer to be professionally painted, "William St. Clair of Roslin" — as he is described in history books — posed for Chalmers in 1771. St. Clair, a captain of the Honourable Company, was also a noted archer.*

Even professional golfers, long regarded as lower class citizens, became worthy of having their portraits done in oil. Allan Robertson, Willie Park, Sr. and Old Tom Morris were all subjects of outstanding portraits, now in the possession of the R & A. (Morris and others previously had been featured in informal sketches by Thomas Hodge.) The first prints depicting groups of noted professionals were done from paintings by J. Michael Brown and W.G. Stevenson in the early 1890s. However, it wasn't until 1897 that a portrait of a professional was published. That honor went to a photogravure of Old Tom Morris done from a painting by H.J. Brooks.

***11-9** FREDERICK REYNOLDS Mezzotint in color of "James Ashton, Golfer" published in the United States in 1924 by a New York art gallery.*

In 1913, Clement Flower produced his famous life-size portrait of The Triumvirate:

J.H. Taylor, James Braid and Harry Vardon. (Taylor and Braid had been portrayed in *Vanity Fair* a few years earlier, but they never featured Vardon, regarded as the best player of the three.)

The next distinguished golfer to be honored by portraiture and subsequent editions of prints — was Bobby Jones, whose phenomenal play during the 1920s and Grand Slam of 1930 made him a deserving subject.

Another significant group of prints was done in the 1980s from paintings by noted golf course artist Arthur Weaver. His work consisted of four separate full-body portraits of the only two father-son teams to win a major golf championship: British Open winners Tom Morris, Sr. and Jr. and Willie Park, Sr. and Jr.

***11-11** LEMUEL FRANCIS ABBOTT (1760-1803)*
William Innes was captain of the Society of Golfers at Blackheath, now known as Royal Blackheath. Painted by Abbott, then produced as a mezzotint in 1790, it was the first golf print to be published.

"Blackheath Golfer" Print

The print of William Innes, "The Blackheath Golfer," has been published so many times that it can be difficult to distinguish between the issues. This dilemma can be alleviated using the following guidelines:

1. The original print was a black-and-white mezzotint by Valentine Green, printed in 1790. The image measures 17 by 23 3/4 inches and may have been hand-tinted at a later date. Less than 15 are known to exist.

2. In 1893, a black-and-white print was made in platinotype — a photographic rather than printed image. The next print was a black-and-white photogravure, published in Edinburgh, circa 1901.

3. Between 1914 and 1917, a mezzotint by Will Henderson was published in color. The print was signed and was issued along with prints of two other golf subjects: John Taylor and Henry Callender.

4. In 1926, Walter A. Cox produced a set of mezzotints in color, similar to Henderson. They also were signed in pencil.

5. All other prints of Innes are reproductions of the above prints, since the original painting was reportedly destroyed in the mid-19th century. The many reproductions — almost all are in color — have been done as lithographs, gravures and by other methods in varying sizes and quality. Most reproductions have the inscription: "Engraving by V. Green Mezzotinto." This phrase was copied from the original print and is not relevant.

11-12 *HENRY RAEBURN (1756-1823)*
A distinguished member of the Royal Academy, Raeburn was one of the premier portrait artists of his time. His paintings of James Balfour (left) and John Gray (right) do not appear to be golf related. However, the captions on the mezzotints refer to both as being office holders of "The Edinburgh Company of Golfers" (now known as The Honourable Company of Edinburgh Golfers). In the picture of Balfour — known as "Singing Jamie" for his jovial personality — are two books related to his duties as secretary and treasurer of the golfing society. The books are "Record of Gentlemen Golfers" and "Bet Book." The Balfour print was published in 1796, the one of Gray in 1806. Neither has been reproduced, except as book illustrations.

11-13 *SIR FRANCIS GRANT (1803-1878)*
Most of the classic golf portraits of the 19th century — such as John Whyte-Melville, shown here — were done life-size. This striking portrait hangs in the Big Room at the R & A, where Whyte-Melville held the office of captain in 1823. He was re-elected in 1883, but died prior to entering office, thus leaving a blank space in the record books for that year. Grant also produced a smaller version of this portrait — probably a preliminary study — which sold for more than $270,000 at a 1991 auction.

11-14 *LEMUEL FRANCIS ABBOTT (1760-1803)*
Henry Callender was a captain of the Society of Golfers at Blackheath. This Abbot painting was produced as a mezzotint in 1812.

11-15 *CLEMENT FLOWER*
One wonders whether Flower realized that his 1913 painting of champion golfers J.H. Taylor, James Braid and Harry Vardon — known as "The Triumvirate" — would become one of the most recognized golf pictures of the 20th century. It has been reproduced as a print several times and has appeared on the cover of national periodicals. Plans to publish prints in 1914 fell through, but a few of the proofs survived and were used as the basis for most of the reproductions, which were first printed in 1978. The imposing painting is owned by the R & A.

11-16 *SIR JOHN WATSON GORDON (1788-1864)*
John Taylor, subject of this painting, was captain of the Honourable Company of Edinburgh Golfers several times between 1807 and 1825. Although Henry Raeburn is sometimes credited with the painting, he probably did no more that start it. The early prints were mezzotints done by Will Henderson in 1914 and W.A. Cox in 1926.

11-17 *Painting by DAVID ALLAN (1744-1796)*
Print by LAWRENCE JOSSET
Allan's classic portrait of William Inglis, Captain of the Honourable Company of Edinburgh Golfers from 1782 to 1784. One of the first significant golf paintings, it was not produced as a print until Josset produced it as a colored mezzotint in 1954. The scene is of particular interest because the historic "procession of the silver club" is illustrated in the background. *(See drawing, page 172)*

OLD TOM MORRIS

Tom Morris, Sr. (1821-1908) was the Grand Old Man of Golf. He was known as a proficient ballmaker, clubmaker, professional and greenkeeper in St. Andrews, and for a short while in Prestwick. Old Tom was the British Open Champion in 1861, '62, '64 and '67. (See color portrait on page 37)

11-18 *Old Tom and Young Tom Morris shown in an original 19th-century pencil sketch.*

11-20 *H. J. BROOKS (1865-)*
The first print to be published of a professional golfer, a photogravure from 1897.

11-19 *SIR GEORGE REID (1841-1913)*
Painted circa 1899, this photogravure of Morris was issued in 1903. Many were autographed. The original painting hangs in the Big Room of the R & A.

11-21 *ARTHUR WEAVER (1918-)*
Weaver's depiction, taken from an old photograph, shows Old Tom near the sands (beach) of St. Andrews.

ROBERT TYRE JONES, JR.

Perhaps the greatest golfer of all time, Bobby Jones has a record as a amateur that will never be equaled: five U.S. Amateur titles, four U.S. Open titles, three British Open titles and one British Amateur title — all between 1923 and 1930. And to top it off, he was unsurpassed as a sportsman and gentleman.

11-22 THOMAS E. STEPHENS
This portrait is the focal point of the Bobby Jones Room at the USGA's Golf House. It was reproduced in an edition of 1,000 lithographs in 1952. The USGA recently issued its own edition of the painting.

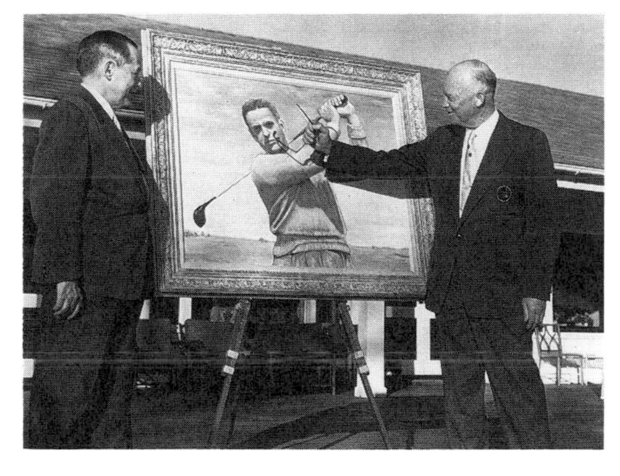

11-23 DWIGHT D. EISENHOWER (1890-1969)
In addition to painting Bobby Jones (photo 11-22), Thomas Stephens painted two dozen portraits of President Eisenhower. During one of the presidential sittings, the artist gave Eisenhower some tips on painting techniques. Before long, the president became an avid hobbyist and copied Stephens' portrait of Jones. Eisenhower completed his masterpiece in 1954 and is shown presenting it to Jones for display at Augusta National Country Club.

11-24 WILLIAM STEENE (1888-)
Steene is best known for his courthouse murals and portraits of Southern public officials. This portrait of a popular Southerner titled "Bobby Jones Concentration" — was published in print form in the 1970s.

11-25 W. DOUGLAS MACLEOD
Originally etched by Macleod in the 1930s, this print is enjoying renewed popularity as re-strikes are being done from the original plate. The originals bear the artist's signature.

SCENES

Golf scenes usually consist of golf course views or large groups of golfers. The first noteworthy depiction was an oil painting completed in 1847 by Charles Lees, a member of the Royal Scottish Academy. The 7-foot-long painting portrays a famous match at St. Andrews and includes many notable golfers in the gallery (see photo 11-27). Lees' magnificent work was first reproduced in 1850. Other momentous scenes that have been offered as prints were painted by J. Michael Brown.

Views of famous golf courses are fashionable now that television and exotic golf travel have made the great courses of the world more visible. The first published views appeared in the early 1890s, when Charles Edmund Brock and Douglas Adams each created a series of three scenes and George Aikman engraved the paintings of John Smart for a bound folio titled *A Round of the Links: A View of the Golf Greens of Scotland.*

***11-26** CHARLES EDMUND BROCK (1870-1938) Painted by Brock, "The Drive" was engraved by Frank Paton in 1894. Also done at the same time were "The Putt" and "The Bunker." The originals were printed in black-and-white. However, some have been hand-colored.*

In 1910, Harry Rountree's highly regarded watercolors appeared in the classic *Golf Courses of the British Isles* written by Bernard Darwin. Due to the poor color reproduction, the views are far from flattering. However, Darwin's vivid descriptions compensate for the pressman's shortcomings.

Probably the most significant golf course scenes to be published in color are the six Cecil Aldin lithographs from the 1920s. Known as "Famous Golf Links," the precise, but mellow, views are especially nice when embellished with Aldin's characteristic signature.

Few serious golf scenes were done until Englishman Arthur Weaver began to take commissions in the late 1950s. With more than 100 golf paintings completed, Weaver still is in demand. Almost 30 of his works have been published, and he is currently working on a St. Andrews sketchbook — a collection of views and portraits of golf and historical significance. Other contemporary golf artists who enjoy popularity include Britons Kenneth Reed and Bill Waugh and Americans Linda Hartough and Donald Voorhees.

Not to be ignored are the Dutch scenes, painted between the 13th and 17th centuries, that show people playing "colf" — sometimes referred to as "Dutch golf." Some historians feel that the club-and-ball game was a forerunner to Scottish golf, but since it often was played on frozen rivers over long distances rather than to a series of holes, the Dutch game is generally classified as "golf-related." Furthermore, no direct link between the two games has been established.

11-27 CHARLES LEES (1800-1880)
A noted British artist, Lees painted "The Golfers," a famous match in St. Andrews, in 1847. Three years later, an engraving was done by Charles Wegstaffe. The original black-and-white prints are rare. However, several reproductions are available, as well as a key identifying all of the subjects. Prior to executing his 7-foot-long masterpiece, Lees painted small portraits in oil, some of which appear in A History of the Royal and Ancient Golf Club *by H.S.C. Everard and are now privately owned. The painting is owned by a descendant of one of the subjects.* *(Also see color illustration on page 37)*

11-28 *J. MICHAEL BROWN*
Brown is best known for his detailed paintings incorporated in the calendars issued by the Life Association of Scotland from 1895 to 1916. However, this scene, "The Open Championship - St. Andrews 1895," was first offered circa 1900 as a photogravure in sepia and more recently as a colored lithograph. J.H. Taylor, the winner, is shown addressing the ball.

11-29 *ALLAN STEWART (1865-)*
Printed in 1908, "The Stymie" is one of several paintings of Stewart's which have been reproduced. His other notable golf work is "The First International Foursome," a scene depicting a famous match played at Leith Links in 1682, which is owned by the USGA and has been issued several times as a print.

11-30 *W. DENDY SADLER (1854-1923)*
One of a series of five scenes painted by Sadler, "The Stymie" illustrates the now-obsolete putting predicament. As with most of Sadler's works, the golf prints were engraved by James Dobie. They have been issued numerous times, including the originals done between 1914 and 1917, a 1926 edition offered by Dewars Whiskey, a 1972 reproduction in a larger size and recent restrikes from the original plates. They can be found in black-and-white, hand-colored and offset printed formats.

11-31 *W.G. STEVENSON (1849-1919)*
Engraved by Clive Murray in 1892, this untitled print shows 1883 British Open Champion Willie Fernie driving (left), while two-time champion Willie Park, Jr. putts (right). In the background are several famous players, including: Horace Hutchinson, John Laidlay, brothers Andrew and Hugh Kirkaldy, John Ball, Tom Morris and Bob Ferguson.

11-32 *DOUGLAS ADAMS (1853-1920)*
First printed as black-and-white photogravures in the early 1890s, the popular golf course views painted by Adams are very popular. Hand-colored restrikes and reproductions lithographs abound, but beware. Some were poorly done. The three scenes are "A Difficult Bunker" (left), "The Drive" and "The Putting Green."

11-33 *JOHN CHARLES DOLLMAN (1851-1934)*
"The Sabbath Breakers" shows an interpretation of the famous story of two golfers who, in 1608, violated an edict passed in 1593 that prohibited the playing golf on a holy day. The painting was first engraved in 1896 and has been reproduced numerous times.

11-34 *CECIL ALDIN (1870-1935)*
The 17th at Walton Heath (left) and the 4th at Sunningdale (right) are two of the six golf course views portrayed by Aldin. The scenes were done by the popular British illustrator in the 1920s. Although not numbered, only a limited quantity were done and a complete set is difficult to assemble. These prints are atypical of the coach scenes, old buildings and dogs commonly associated with Aldin. His life's work is detailed in Cecil Aldin –The Story of a Sporting Artist *written by Roy Heron (Exeter, England: Webb & Bower, 1981).*

11-35 *JOHN SMART (1838-1899)*
Smart painted scenes of Carnoustie (left) and other golf courses for a bound folio titled A Round of the Links: Views of the Golf Greens of Scotland. *George Aikman produced engravings for the book, which was originally published as a limited edition of 100 copies in 1893 and later offered in a facsimile edition in 1980. There were no known overruns, so it is assumed that loose any prints were taken from the 1893 book.*

11-36 *EVERETT HENRY (1893-1961)*
A depiction of "The First Amateur Championship Held in America" not the U.S. Amateur, but a match played at the historic St. Andrew's Golf Club in Yonkers, N.Y. in 1894. First published by E. Currier in 1931 as the fourth of a series of golf scenes, it was recently reproduced by the USGA.

11-37
HARRY ROUNTREE (1880-1950)
Watercolor of the sixth green at Romford Golf Club, near London, once the home course of the famous James Braid. A color plate of this painting appears in The Golf Courses of the British Isles, *written by Bernard Darwin in 1910. Because of his illustrations for Darwin's epic work, Rountree's watercolors and oils are highly desirable. He also illustrated for several British magazines.*

CONTEMPORARY SCENES

11-38 *ARTHUR WEAVER (1918-)*
The eleventh green of the Old Course at St. Andrews is one the recent golf course views painted by Englishman Arthur Weaver. He has been heralded as the one of the premier golf artists since the late 1950s. His limited edition prints — often personalized with handsome remarques — and paintings are highly collectible.

11-39 *LINDA HARTOUGH and KENNETH REED*
Two highly regarded painters of golf course scenes. Their lithographs of well-known courses are produced as signed and numbered lithographs. The 16th hole at Hazeltine National Golf Club (left) was done by Hartough as part of a series showing holes on U.S. Open courses. The seventh hole at Pebble Beach (right) is a popular example of Reed's work.

DUTCH GOLF SCENES

11-40
REMBRANDT HARMENSZ van RIJN (1606-1669)
While almost universally referred to as the "Kolf Player" or "Golf Player," this Rembrandt etching done in 1654 actually depicts neither. According to Steven J.H. van Hengel, the authority on early Dutch golf, the game depicted is called Beugelen.

11-41 *AERT van der NEER (1603-1677)*
Dutch scene engraved by Jacques Phillipe Le Bas (1707-1783), showing various winter activities on a frozen river. Several people can be seen playing the golf-related game of colf.

11-42
ADRIAEN van de VELDE (1635-1672)
This illustration shows "Amusemens de L'Hiver," a black-and-white engraving of the original oil painting, titled "Winter Landscape," done by van de Velde in 1668. When Jacques Aliamet (1726-1788) produced the engraving, he neglected to reverse his image on the plate to enable the printed version to resemble the original painting. A color lithograph of the painting was included in A Golfer's Gallery by Old Masters, *a portfolio published circa 1920.*

ILLUSTRATIONS

As golf periodicals and highly illustrated books came into being about 1890, the number of artists with a flair for golf emerged. The works of these illustrators were created primarily to enhance the text. However, they also were used for magazine covers, in advertisements, on postcards and on ceramics. Many illustrations also were offered as prints for framing.

Some of the often-published British illustrators were Charles Crombie, noted for his humorous *Rules of Golf* and cartoons in *Golf Illustrated*; Thomas Hodge and Harry Furniss, who both contributed classic illustrations to *Golf: The Badminton Library*; Francis Powell Hopkins who wrote about and illustrated golf topics for *The Field* magazine; John Hassall, who produced a folio titled *The Seven Ages of Golf* in 1899. Others British favorites include: Cecil Aldin, Henry Mayo Bateman, Tom Browne, Lionel Edwards and Victor Venner.

When golf became popular in America just before the turn of the century, A.B. Frost

***11-43* JOHN HASSALL (1868-1948)** *A prolific English illustrator, Hassall included this print in* The Seven Ages of Golf, *published in 1899. Many of his colorful prints have been reproduced, including a series of four carefully reproduced scenes that have been sold to unsuspecting collectors as originals.*

***11-44* ARTHUR BURDETT FROST (1851-1928)** *One of America's favorite illustrators, A.B. Frost frequently worked for* Harper's Weekly. *A plethora of his golf prints have been published in black-and-white, color and hand-colored styles.*

— the extremely popular and prolific illustrator — became the foremost illustrator of American golf scenes. Prints and reproductions of his often humorous watercolors are readily attainable and accurately reflect the golfing styles of his time.

Other American golf drawings and watercolors were done by many of the famous illustrators, including Howard Chandler Christy, Harrison Fisher, James Montgomery Flagg, Norman Rockwell, Charles Dana Gibson and even the incomparable Dr. Suess, noted author and illustrator of children's books.

Cartoonists on both sides of the Atlantic had a fondness for golf. Included in this group are: Clare Briggs, who illustrated his own *Golf: The Book of a Thousand Chuckles* and other golf books; Fontaine Fox of "Toonerville Trolley" fame; Charles Schulz, creator of Snoopy and Charlie Brown of "Peanuts"; and William Heath Robinson, the master of humorous golf contraptions and predicaments.

THOMAS HODGE (1827-1907)

Hodge was more than just an illustrator with an interest in golf. He was a schoolmaster in St. Andrews and a distinguished member of the Royal & Ancient Golf Club, where he won four important golf medals during the 1860s and where many of his paintings are displayed. His watercolor portraits appeared in numerous golf publications, including *The Badminton Library — Golf.* His work is significant since he personally knew and painted virtually every notable St. Andrews golfer of the 19th century.

Although Hodge painted several hundred golf subjects, his works were not offered in print form until the 1980s. More than 70 original watercolors were sold at a Sotheby's sale in 1988. Some of his works are unsigned, but most carry his characteristic "T.H." signature along with the year of completion. (See color illustration on page 37)

***11-45** THOMAS HODGE (1827-1907)*
Hodge knew and painted hundreds of golfers who frequented St. Andrews, such as a pair of unidentified women golfers called "The Ladies' Links" (left) in 1885 and golf writer and noted amateur Horace Hutchinson (above right) in 1890.

FRANCIS POWELL HOPKINS (1830-1913)

***11-46** FRANCIS POWELL HOPKINS, F. P. HOPKINS, MAJOR SHORTSPOON, MAJOR S, (1830-1913)*
All of these names refer to the same prolific illustrator of British golf scenes. Many of his watercolors were done on a blue tinted paper, such as this special one-of-a-kind bound volume of watercolors done in 1876, probably as a gift to one of his golfing friends. His golf works were published in Shortspoon (see page 255).

VANITY FAIR

Vanity Fair was a weekly English magazine that flourished from 1869 until 1914. A popular feature was the "Men of the Day" caricature that was accompanied by a short biography. These lithographs — the early ones were done from stone — came with each issue and were also available loose from the publisher. Eight noted golfers were depicted — seven were painted by "SPY" (Sir Leslie Ward) and one by "LIB" (Liberio Prosperi). SPY also painted Prime Minister H. Lloyd George in a similar style for *The World* magazine in 1910. (Two other *Vanity Fair* portraits — Marshall Roberts and George Rowe — mention golf in their biographies. However, neither have any indication of golf in the picture.)

Reproduction offset lithographs of varying quality recently have become available. Behind glass, the new ones may appear authentic. A close look will disclose whether or not the paper is new.

***11-47** LIB*
John Ball, Jr., the only Vanity Fair *golfer not painted by SPY. Published in 1892.*

***11-48** SPY*
Harold Hilton, with the caption reading "Hoylake," his home golf course. Published in 1903.

***11-49** SPY*
Horace Hutchinson, fine amateur golfer and prolific golf author. Published in 1890.

VANITY FAIR AND "SPY" GOLF SUBJECTS

Horace G. Hutchinson, 1890
John Ball, Jr., 1892
Harold H. Hilton (Hoylake), 1903
Samuel Mure Fergusson (Muir), 1906
John H. Taylor (John Henry), 1906
Robert Maxwell (North Berwick), 1906
George Rowe (A Celebrated Oarsman), 1906
H. Mallaby-Deeley (The Prince of Princes), 1906
James Braid (Jimmy), 1907
H. Lloyd George, 1910
Marshall Roberts (Easton Hall), 1911

THE AMERICAN GIRL

HOWARD CHANDLER CHRISTY (1873-1952)

CHARLES DANA GIBSON (1867-1944)

HARRISON FISHER (1875-1934)

11-50 *The idealized woman that was a symbol of American pulchritude was popularized in sketch form by Charles Dana Gibson (above) in the late 19th-century. His character was known worldwide as the "Gibson Girl." Similar beauties were created by Howard Chandler Christy (top) and Harrison Fisher (left). Examples of all three illustrators can be found in the form of mass-produced prints, cartoons, postcards and magazine covers. Many of the illustrations have been clipped from periodicals and hand-colored and matted for framing.*

OTHER ILLUSTRATIONS

11-51 N. ARTHUR LORRAINE
A chromolithograph, circa 1901, depicting a mixed foursome.

11-52 LEALAND GUSTAVSON (1899-1976)
A series of six paintings produced by Gustavson depict the history of golf in America. The originals hang in the PGA/World Golf Hall of Fame and the lithographs — done in 1967 — are popular decorations. Shown above is the original clubhouse at Shinnecock Hills Golf Club, "The First Clubhouse in America — 1892."

11-53 Print of a young golfer was done in relief by an unknown artist as part of a hardware store promotion. It was printed in St. Louis, circa 1904.

***11-54** CHARLES CROMBIE (1885-1967)*
The Rules of Golf, *a bound portfolio containing humorous depictions of golf rules, was done by Charles Crombie in 1905. The 24 stone lithographs were part of a promotion organized by the Perrier water company, which included similar books by Crombie on the rules of the road (*Motoritis*) and on cricket. Although Crombie produced numerous golf subjects, including cartoons for the British* Golf Illustrated *magazine, his golf rules are classics. There were two original printings (which carry a Perrier ad on the back of each print) and several modern printings (which were done by offset lithography and do not have the ads). It is becoming increasingly difficult to find either portfolio intact, since the plates usually are removed and framed for display.*

***11-56** MAUDE HUMPHREY (c1845-1940)*
Original and reproduction prints of Maude Humphrey's work exist. Primarily an illustrator of children's books, was the mother of actor Humphrey Bogart.

***11-55** F.T. RICHARDS (1864-1921)*
One of six hand colored prints of golfers in period costume, published in a 1901 folio. Later editions, smaller in size, were printed in color.

***11-57** VICTOR VENNER*
"Attempting to Drive Off," shown here, was one of two comical scenes published in 1903. The companion print was titled "Looking for the Ball." Venner's scenes also appear on ceramic plates (see page 164).

11-58 *HENRY MAYO BATEMAN (1887-1970)*
Bateman's cartoon figures are noted for their odd expressions. His illustrations frequented Punch *magazine and Royal Doulton ceramics.*

11-59 *Travel posters, mostly from the 1920s and 1930s, often featured golf destinations in England, Scotland, France and Germany. They are usually printed on paper and mounted on canvas and can be as large as 3 by 5 feet. Reproductions of various posters now are being published.*

11-61
J. GILES
The unusual shape of this original water-color makes it particularly interesting. It is dated 1907 and was done with a companion tennis player.

11-60
SIR WILLIAM NICHOLSON (1872-1949)
In 1898, Nicholson illustrated An Almanac of Twelve Sports, *a calendar with verse written by Rudyard Kipling. The October illustration featured golf. Both original and reproduction prints can be found.*

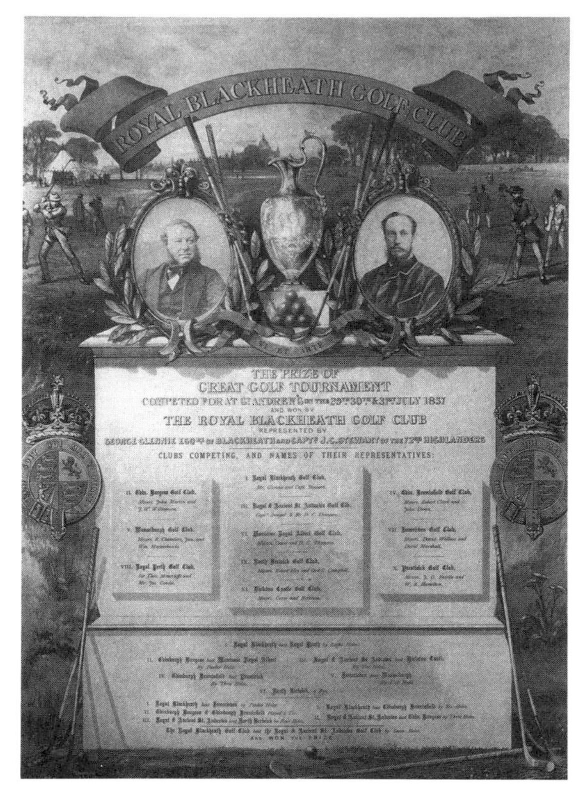

11-62 ANONYMOUS
This lithograph from 1857 acknowledges the clubs that participated in a "Great Golf Tournament," held that year at St. Andrews. The winning team was from Royal Blackheath Golf Club.

***11-63** TOM BROWNE (1872-1910)*
This original watercolor and pastel painting is typical of Browne's style, often seen in English publications and on postcards.

***11-64** HARRY ROUNTREE (1880-1950)*
Rountree, an avid golfer, displays his form in 1912 (right), when he was captain of the London Press Golfing Society. His familiarity with the game is evident in his paintings of golf courses and humorous cartoons.

CHAPTER 12

CERAMICS

Most collectible ceramics decorated with golf motifs were produced between 1890 and 1935, although Delft tiles depicting Dutch games similar to golf were made as early as the 17th century. Since dining and social gatherings were primary forms of entertainment years ago, it was natural for ardent golfers to amuse their guests with decorative golf objects. Desirable articles included plates, mugs, bowls, pitchers and other ceramics — many of which were awarded as tournament prizes.

The most noted manufacturers of golf ceramics were Royal Doulton and Copeland Spode of England and Lenox of the United States. Other firms were located in Germany, France, Spain and Japan. The early examples usually were hand painted in limited quantities. The later pieces, many of which were produced in larger quantities, had preprinted decorations which were applied by the transfer method — similar to a decal.

Shortly after the turn-of-the-century, most of the firms ceased production of their golf designs, with the exception of Royal Doulton, which took advantage of the wide-open market. They offered such a huge variety of golf items that more than half of the antique golf ceramics in existence were made by Doulton.

By World War II, the production of golf ceramics had ceased. Since the war, many ceramics have been produced, but few can equal the quality of the early hand-painted examples. Most modern pieces are souvenirs or promotional items, such as Jim Beam whiskey decanters.

Golf collectors acquire ceramics for various reasons. Some are serious collectors, while others have only a few pieces for decorative purposes. Methods of collecting can include specializing in one manufacturer or in a single object, such as mugs or plates. (See page 41 for examples in color.)

MAKERS OF GOLF CERAMICS

The following companies have produced golf-themed ceramics and glassware:

Amphora
Arcadian
Beleek
Bridgewood
Cambridge Glass
Carleton Ware
Copeland Spode
Crown Staffordshire
Dartmouth
Foley
Gerz
Goss
Grimwades
Handel
Hauber & Reuther
T.G. Hawkes
Heisey
Lenox
Limoges
Minton
Noritake
O'Hara Dial
Richardson
Robinson
Rookwood
Royal Bonn
Royal Doulton
Sleepy Eye
Teplitz
Taylor Tunnecliffe
Warwick
Wedgwood
Weller
Willow Art
Arthur Wood
Worcester Porcelain

12-1 *Ceramics with golf motifs were made in countless styles and shapes, beginning in the mid-1890s.*

Royal Doulton

The largest producer of ceramics with golf themes was the British firm of Royal Doulton (which prior to 1902 was known simply as Doulton). Most of these pieces were produced in the late-19th and early-20th century in the company's primary styles: Doulton Lambeth, Morrissian Ware, Kingsware, Burslem and Series Ware. They also made one-of-a-kind trophies, custom-designed advertising items, and in recent years, character jugs.

12-2 *Royal Doulton did not receive its "Royal" appointment as a preferred supplier to the reigning family until 1902 (center). Most of the Lambeth, Burslem and other early golf pieces were not marked Royal.*

DOULTON LAMBETH

Articles marked "Lambeth" are stoneware that were produced in the Lambeth borough of London. Although Doulton was in business in Lambeth in 1815, it didn't make the distinctive tan-colored golf pottery until around 1900.

Most of the Lambeth examples have scenes done in relief, formed by the application of several layers of watery clay, known as slip. Three different scenes — "Lost Ball," "Driving" and "Putting" — are off-white in color and often enhanced with brown or blue borders.

12-3 *Royal Doulton made many advertising items, such as this stoneware jug for Colonel Bogey Whisky.*

12-4 *Doulton Lambeth featured colorful floral borders that enhanced the cream-colored relief figures. Shown are two flared mugs and a silver-rimmed beaker.*

MORRISIAN WARE

Morrisian Ware, with its characteristic detailed borders and festively attired golfers, was made in limited quantities at Doulton's Burslem works from 1900 until 1924. The figures were painted in the style of American illustrator Will Bradley. Some pieces were not marked "Morrisian," but still are classified as such. The backgrounds are usually red or muted yellow.

12-5 *Morrissian Ware was the most elegant of the Doulton ceramics. This 7-inch-high jug was embellished with gold. Other shapes include vases, jardinieres and fern stands.*

KINGSWARE

Kingsware mugs and jugs are easily recognized by their relief scenes patterned after the work of Charles Crombie (see page 150). Rather than painting figures on blank pieces of pottery, a factory artist applied scenes onto the interior of a two-piece plaster mold which contained impressions of the desired design. After the mold was put together, dark brown or pale yellow slip was poured which fused with the painted design. A transparent glaze was then applied to enhance the tones.

Kingsware, which was produced for most of the first half of this century, should not be confused with Queensware, which was similarly made from a light-colored clay or a later Series Ware line (see photo 12-6). Kingsware and the less-common Queensware are easily identified because the unique molding process makes the interior of a piece the same color as the background of the exterior.

12-6 *Kingsware was not specially marked, but is easily identified by examining the background color. Since the background color is solid throughout the article, the inside of the Kingsware mug (right) matches the exterior. The other mug is "airbrush brown" Series Ware, identified with a D5716 pattern number.*

12-7 *This Kingsware whiskey flask was made in 1936. Because the silver-topped stopper is hallmarked, the date of manufacture can be ascertained.*

DOULTON BURSLEM

Some of the most prized golf ceramics are the rare examples of Doulton Burslem, made between 1891 and 1902. The china pieces were marked "Burslem" for the town in Staffordshire in which they were made. Since the ceramics were individually decorated, it is possible to find one signed by "J. Littler" or other artists.

12-8 *Doulton Burslem ceramics are noted for their hand-painted, blue golf course scenes.*

SERIES WARE

Royal Doulton's Series Ware was a popular style. With standard blank shapes that were decorated with different themes, it was suited for mass production. The designs were applied by transfer printing and were hand tinted. Golf was just one of numerous subjects, which included: history, literature, pastimes, children's themes, legends and important events.

The series concept was geared to collectors. Not only were there different shapes within a series, there were a multitude of scenes and quotations. Because of this variety and the long length of production — most pieces were made from 1909 through the 1930s — Series Ware items are easily found today.

There are six types of Series Ware which have golf themes. All pieces are marked on the bottom with a pattern number to aid in identification.

GOLFERS

These ceramics have scenes done in the style of Charles Crombie. (Pattern numbers: D2296, D3394, D3395 and D5960) There were five sayings that appeared with the scenes:

- "Give losers leave to speak & winners to laugh."
- "He that complains is never pitied."
- "All fools are not knaves, but all knaves are fools."
- "He hath good judgment who relieth not wholly on his own."
- "Every dog has his day and every man his hour."

12-9 *"Golfers" style Series Ware is the most popular of the golf ceramics. Since the colorful pieces were made in complete place settings, it is likely that golf fanatics once bought them to use on special occasions.*

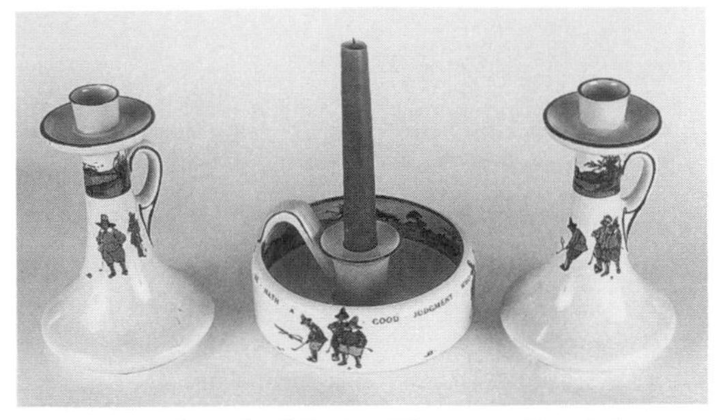

12-10 *Hard-to-find Series Ware candlesticks.*

PROVERBS PLATES

These rack plates have stylized floral or grapevine borders with one of the following proverbs surrounding the golfers who are dressed in Eastern attire. (Pattern numbers: D3391 and D3481)

- "If at first you don't succeed try again. A miss is as good as a mile."
- "Fine feathers make fine birds. Old saws speak the truth."
- "Hope springs eternal in the human breast. Hope deferred maketh the heart sink."
- "An Oak is not felled by one blow. Take the will for the deed."
- "Nothing venture nothing win. Count not your chickens before they are hatched."
- "Fine feathers make fine birds. Handsome is that handsome does."
- "Nothing venture nothing have. A bird in the hand is worth two in the bush."

GIBSON

The "Gibson Girl," created by noted American illustrator Charles Dana Gibson (see page 148) was featured on small ceramics, such as pin trays, cups, saucers and small vases. (Pattern numbers: E2766 and E2827)

One of the following quotes accompanied each scene:

- "Golf – a good game for two."
- "Is a caddie always necessary?"
- "Don't watch the player, keep your eye on the ball."
- "One difficulty of the game – keeping your eye on the ball."
- "Fore."
- "From 10 am to 6:45 pm this dog has been kept out. Where is the S.P.C.A.?"
- "The last day of summer."
- "Who cares?"

BATEMAN

Decorative pieces featured humorous scenes of Henry Mayo Bateman (see page 151), including "An Irate Golfer," "The Laughing Caddies" and "The Smug Golfer." Manufactured in the 1930s and '40s, the ceramics featured Bateman's facsimile signature. (Pattern number: D5813)

DIVERSIONS OF UNCLE TOBY

Uncle Toby was a character in Laurence Sterne's novel, Tristam Shandy, written in the 18th century. Uncle Toby's diversions consisted of 15 games, one of which was golf. (Pattern numbers: D3111, D3121 and D3197)

NINETEENTH HOLE

This series featured a scene of two golfers enjoying a post-round drink with a view of a golf course. (Pattern numbers: D3755 and D3770)

12-11 *Two miniature Gibson Series Ware vases — measuring less than 3 inches high.*

OTHER ROYAL DOULTON

12-13 *The Bunnykins line of Royal Doulton featured rabbits derived from watercolor paintings by Barbara Vernon. First made in the 1930s, the pieces often were given as baby presents. Bunnykins are still made today, although not with a golfing theme.*

12-12 *One of Royal Doulton's most amusing ceramics was this 10-inch-high stoneware golf bag vase, made in 1902. The base of the bag has numerous markings, including "Slaters Patent."*

12-14 *Part of a series of "Picturesque Scenes," this Royal Doulton plate combines a golf theme with a border depicting several scenes, including the abbey in Montrose, Scotland.*

COLLECTING TIP

■ **Because golf themes appeared on so many different styles of Series Ware, collectors can take several paths: try to assemble a complete set of plates, each with a different quotation; seek examples of many styles that were offered, such as mugs, bowls, plates, platters, jugs, candlesticks, large and small vases, ashtrays, pin trays, cups and saucers, sweets dishes, steins, playing card boxes and cigarette boxes.**

COPELAND SPODE

Copeland Spode golf stoneware was made in the early 20th century in the Stoke-on-Trent, an English town known for its pottery. Their distinctive style featured white relief decorations applied over a solid glaze of navy blue or olive green. The blue articles were made from a gray clay and the green ones from a tan clay.

12-15 *Copeland Spode specialized in making serving vessels, rather than dishes and other tableware. Shown from left are: a jug, quart mug, teapot and whiskey jug. Other items included three-handled mugs, creamers, biscuit barrels and jardinieres.*

12-16 *This advertisment dates to 1909. Note that the silver-rimmed cup cost more than two times the cost of a plain one.*

12-17 *Copeland ceramics were marked with a sailing ship and the words "Copeland Late Spode." This jug was produced for sale by Stearns of Boston.*

LENOX

The best-known American golf ceramics were produced by the Ceramic Art Company of Trenton, New Jersey, between 1894 and 1906. Although company co-founder Walter Scott Lenox did not officially change the firm's name to Lenox China Company until 1906, collectors still refer to the hand-painted pieces as "Lenox," even though they may be marked "CAC" on the bottom.

Similar golf course scenes with men or women golfers were featured on articles, which included toothpick holders, oil lamps, pitchers and mugs. Examples of Lenox are easily recognized by their dull green or blue monochrome color.

12-18 *A collection of three-handled Lenox mugs with various styles of silver rims. They range in size from 4 to 8 inches.*

COLLECTING TIP

■ **Golf ceramics are characterized as porcelain, stoneware or earthenware. Most delicate tableware is made of porcelain, noted for its translucent white appearance. Stoneware and earthenware are opaque objects. Because stoneware is fired at high temperatures, it is non-porous. Earthenware, or pottery, is fired at a temperature so low that the glaze hardens, but does not bond to the surface.**

12-19 *An unusual 3-inch-high oil lamp made by Lenox.*

OTHER CERAMICS

12-20 *Golf also was depicted on German stoneware. The stein (left) by an unnamed maker is marked "5043." The pitcher (above) is typical of the steins and other pieces made by Gerz at the beginning of the century. Gerz is marked with a small triangular symbol and the words "Ges. Gesch.," meaning the design is protected by law.*

12-21 *The Rookwood Pottery of Cincinnati, Ohio, was famous for its custom-made ceramics. The art deco cigarette holder (left) was mass produced in solid color glazes of blue, green and pink during the 1930s. The unique four-handled loving cup (above) was decorated with stick figure golfers for use as a tournament prize in 1899.*

12-22 *During the 1920s, many golf motifs appeared on glassware. The pitcher (left) features a cut-glass body fashioned after a mesh-patterned golf ball, while the corked jug (above) has a silver overlay. Heisey, Hawkes and Cambridge were prominent American glass companies.*

12-23 *Post-war mugs were mass produced in England by companies such as Dartmouth (right) and Eade (far right).*

12-24 *MacIntyre & Company of Burslem, England, made several differently shaped pieces at the turn-of-the-century with the same golfer that appears on this cream pitcher and sugar bowl.*

12-25 *Some plates were made for daily use, such as the one with a golf border (left) marked "Black Knight Hotel." Many, like the Warwick plate (right) with a Victor Venner scene, were intended primarily for decoration.*

12-26 *This unusual pair of 11-inch-high vases was made circa 1910. Although one is signed "P. Mitchell," it is possible that they were produced by an individual rather than a commercial pottery company.*

12-27 *This turn-of-the-century, foot-high vase marked "Utopian" was hand painted by the J.P. Owens Pottery Company. The company was located in Zanesville, Ohio — a hotbed of American art pottery production.*

12-28 *The Dickensware line of Weller Pottery was made in Zanesville, Ohio, using a method called sgraffito. Sgraffito was a process whereby outlines of the figures were created by scratching the soft surface layer of the object before firing it. The soft, earthtone background colors were sprayed and then the subjects were decorated with mostly solid colors. Vases and pitchers (left) were most common, and varied in height from 7 to 17 inches. Unlike other makers of golf ceramics, Weller made very few mugs (above).*

12-29 *An unusual golf collectible — a porcelain padlock, circa 1950.*

12-30 *The golfers featured in the porcelain figures currently produced by the Spanish firm of LLadro (left) appear happier than the bisque couple from the 1920s (right).*

12-31 *This early 20th-century sugar bowl, made in England by Jasperware, is similar in style to Copeland Spode.* *(See page 160)*

12-32 *Minton, of Stoke-on-Trent in Staffordshire, was a highly respected English ceramics firm. They only made a few pieces with golf scenes, such as this jug which dates from the 1890s.*

12-33 *Hundreds of unmarked golf ceramics have been produced during this century, including this sugar bowl (above) and tea cup (right).*

COLLECTING TIP

■ The nomenclature of ceramics can be confusing. In the United States, an open vessel with a handle and spout is referred to as a pitcher. In Great Britain, however, it is called a jug. And an American jug— often with a cork stopper for its small opening— is considered a flask by the British. It is proper to refer to an item based on its orgin.

12-34 *A small jug decorated with a humorous scene made by the Foley China Company of Staffordshire and marked "Late Foley, Shelley."*

12-35 *Two stylized pieces from countries not known for their golf ceramics — a Noritake humidor from Japan and a cup by Italian Richard Ginori.*

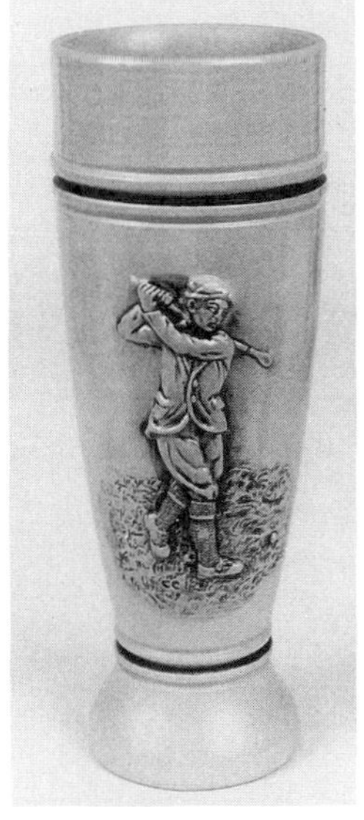

12-36 *Although A.J. Thewalt has been making stoneware for nearly a century in Germany, its old-looking golf steins and goblets are newly manufactured.*

12-37 *Schwarzburg ceramics featuring the style of Harrison Fisher were made in Germany in the early 20th century.* *(See page 148)*

12-38 *The O'Hara Dial Company, of Waltham, Massachusetts, was primarily in the business of making dials for watches and utility meters. However, in the late 1890s they sold ceramic mugs which featured custom-made enameled lids. Although the scenes were painted in the style of Lenox (see page 161), the craftsmanship and detail is of much lower quality.*

12-39 *The famous Limoges company of Paris is known to have made only one golf item, a hand-painted mug, circa 1900.*

12-40 *A Carlton Ware matchstick holder, made in England by Wiltshaw & Robertson, circa 1910.*

CHAPTER 13

SILVER

Years ago, champions of important golf tournaments or matches received prizes made of silver. Objects ranged from the full-size silver golf clubs of the mid-18th century and the British Open championship belt of the 1860s to simple loving cups and hole-in-one trophies from the early 20th century.

Long-standing competitions usually presented the winner with a medal or small trophy, along with an elaborate permanent trophy that was retained for a year (or until someone else earned the title). The old medals primarily were struck from silver, gold or a combination of the two and were adorned with crossed clubs or fancy trim. Some of the prizes featured elaborate hand engraving of names and designs that turned an otherwise ordinary object into a striking work of art.

By the end of the 19th century, golfers didn't have to be of championship caliber to possess golf-related articles of silver. Silversmiths produced various decorative items for personal and household use. Golf club-embellished toast racks joined golf ball salt-and-pepper shakers on the dining tables of well-to-do golfers. Cuff links, hatpins, buttons, belt buckles and other personal accessories were popular with golf fanatics up until World War II.

The following pages provide a glimpse at a few of the hundreds of different articles of silver and silver plate that were made on both sides of the Atlantic by both small craftsmen and large manufacturers. Also included are miscellaneous badges and other non-silver metalwares.

MEDALS

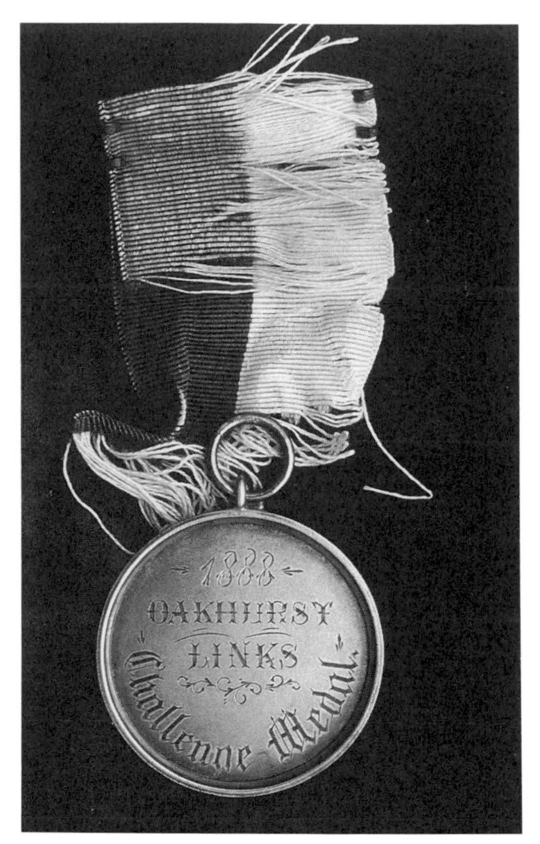

3-1 *A replica of the earliest known golf prize in the United States. Oakhurst Golf Links was founded in 1884 in White Sulphur Springs, West Virginia. Although this medal appears authentic, it is one of at least two duplicates made 60 or more years ago. One is owned by the James River Country Club Museum, the other by the USGA Museum.*

3-2 *A silver medal from the historic Royal Blackheath Golf club, near London. Dated 1870, the crest displays crossed clubs and balls, the royal crown, the Scottish thistle, St. Andrew's Cross and the club motto in Latin of "far and sure."*

13-3 *Women golfers won appropriate medals for their exemplary play. Originally presented by the Royal North Devon Golf Club in 1868, this silver medal is still being struck from the original dies for use as a modern day prize.*

13-4 *An alloy badge designed for gallery marshals at the 1929 U.S. Open, held at the Winged Foot County Club in Westchester County, New York. For years, spectators respectfully followed tournament players down the fairway. But by the 1920s, tournament officials found it necessary to rope off fairways and enlist marshals. They also saw fit to charge admission fees, beginning with the 1922 U.S. Open.*

13-5 *Winners of major championships traditionally receive permanent gold or silver medals for their accomplishments, while the trophy usually is kept only for the year. This medal, with a stylish "WP" engraved in the center, was awarded to Willie Park, Jr. for his 1887 British Open victory. It is made of silver and was plated with a gold wash.*

13-7 *Long-drive competitions are nothing new. This medal was awarded to the winner of a driving contest sponsored by* The Chicago Tribune *in 1927.*

13-6 *The U.S. Golf Association issues badges to all contestants who qualify for play in its national championships. Shown are examples from the 1920s, '30s and '40s.*

13-8 *This Bobby Jones medal was issued in 1932 as part of a fund-raising effort for those left unemployed by the Great Depression.*

13-9 *When the caddy corps became more structured in the early 20th century, numbered metal badges identified authorized caddies and simplified record keeping for caddy masters. Note on badge number 90 that even the municipal courses organized groups of caddies. Badges also were made of celluloid and plastic.*

Trophies

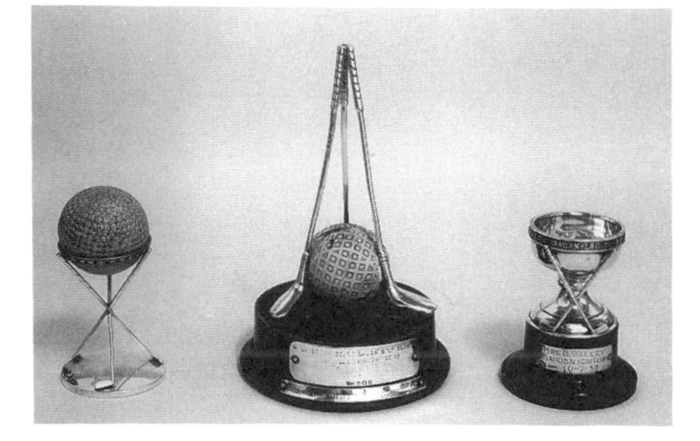

13-10 *Golf ball manufacturers, such as Dunlop, Spalding and Silvertown, furnished attractive hole-in-one trophies during the 1920s and '30s, that were made of silver.*

3-11 *Turn-of-the-century miniature loving cups, made of silver plate and measuring 4 inches high.*

13-13 *A drawing by 18th-century Scottish artist David Allan, depicting the procession of the silver club by members of the Company of Edinburgh Golfers. Presented in 1744, the silver club was golf's first trophy. Each year, a silver golf ball was inscribed with the club champion's name and was attached to the club.*

13-12 *John Olman exhibits two of the most distinguished prizes in golf: the original British Open championship belt used from 1860 until Young Tom Morris won the belt outright in 1870 after winning three successive championships and the silver claret jug that replaced it in 1873 and still is played for today.*

13-14 *An exquisitely engraved silver golf club presented to the Edinburgh Cleek Golf Club in 1888 as the permanent trophy for a competition that allowed the use of only one club.*

HOUSEHOLD & PERSONAL ITEMS

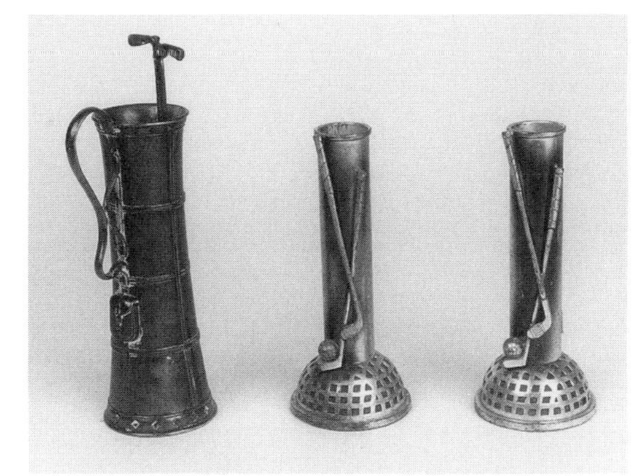

13-15 *Measuring about 6 inches high, bud vases often were made of pot metal or other alloy.*

13-16 *This spinning top, capped in sterling silver, looks old, but was produced by Gorham in the 1970s.*

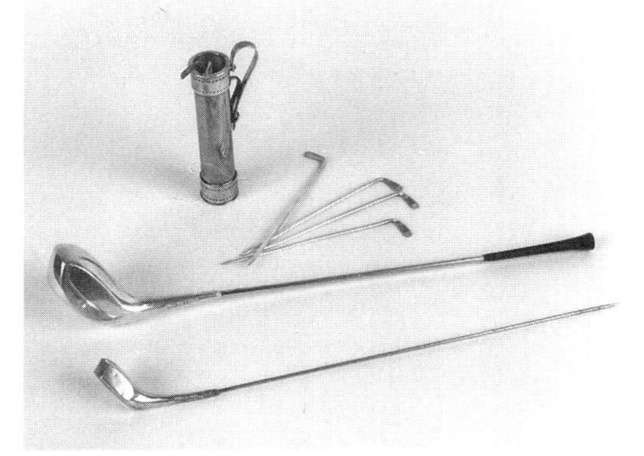

13-18 *Silver miniature golf clubs had various functions. The cocktail picks (above) came with a holder in the shape of a golf bag. After refrigerating the long club (center), it doubled as a swizzle stick and drink cooler. The pointed club (bottom) is a lady's hatpin.*

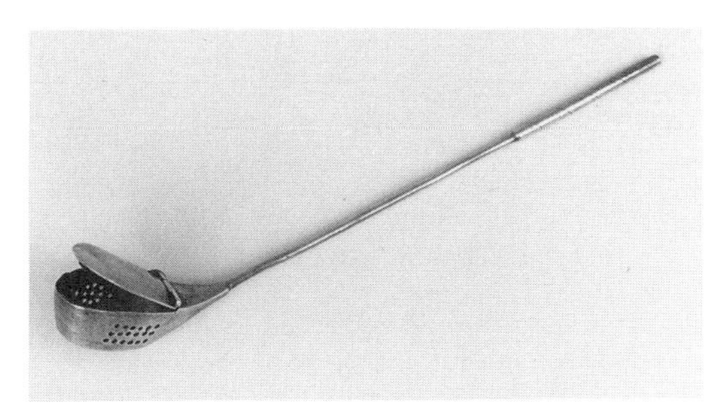

13-19 *A stylish American tea infuser, from the days before submersible tea bags became commonplace.*

13-17 *Golf items for the bar: a painted cocktail glass with a silver swizzle stick (left) and nesting brandy snifters that store inside a hinged golf ball (right). The stirring fingers of the swizzle stick retract into the slender club shaft.*

13-20 *Silversmiths found that the mesh pattern golf ball of the late 19th century was well-suited for a number of purposes, including salt and pepper shakers, condiment servers, inkwells, clocks and watch cases (left). The condiment caddy for salt, pepper and mustard (right) is ingeniously supported by three crossed long-nosed clubs. The mesh design continued to be used on these items until about 1920, when the line-type pattern gave way to the bramble, recessed mesh and dimple cover balls. In order to properly date a silver piece, it's best to research the hallmark.*

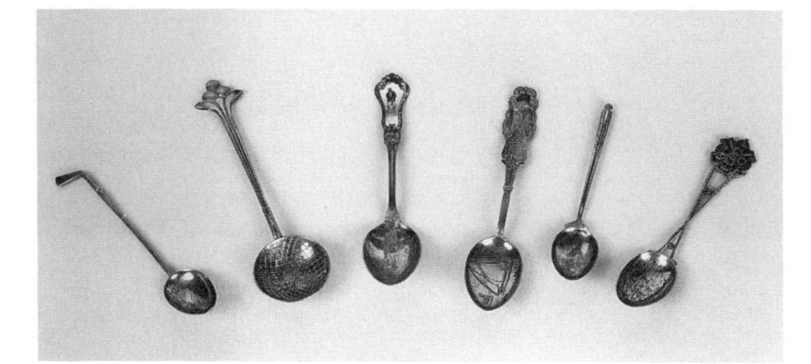

13-21 *Silver spoons were produced as gift items or by golf clubs to commemorate special occasions.*

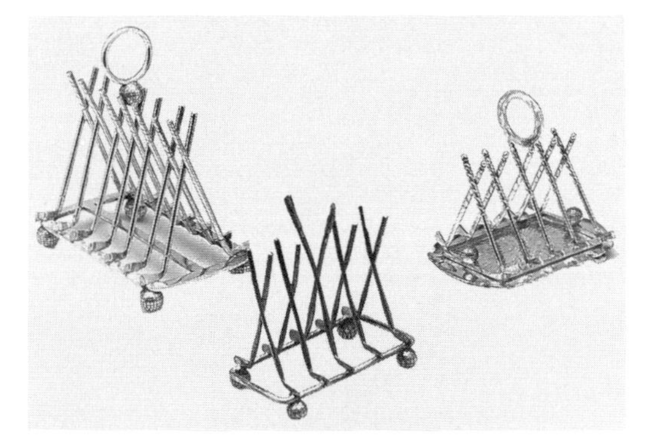

13-22 *The toast rack, formerly a popular breakfast table accoutrement, is more likely to be used today as a desktop letter file.*

COLLECTING TIP

■ **Unfortunately, a number of fraudulently altered silver items are being sold to golf collectors. These consist of antique match safes, cigarette cases and other small articles onto which vintage enameled golf scenes recently have been applied. Because the hallmarks are authentic, most collectors are fooled by the counterfeits. If you buy from a reputable source, you'll probably not be swindled.**

13-23 *An 1894 advertisement for enameled silver articles.*

13-24 *Beginning in the mid-19th century, pocket watches made stylish tournament prizes and presentation pieces. The gold or silver cases ranged from detailed relief engravings to simple inscriptions.*

13-25 *Before matchbooks, smokers protected their wooden matches in match safes — also called vestas. Dozens of elaborate styles were offered.*

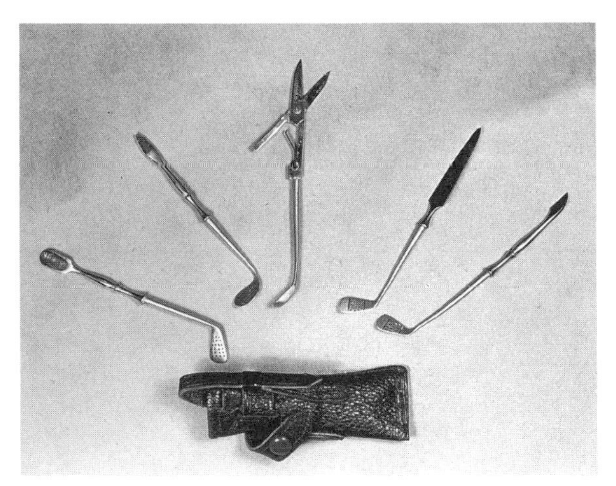

13-26 *A perfect gift for the golfer: a manicure kit, complete with a miniature leather golf bag.*

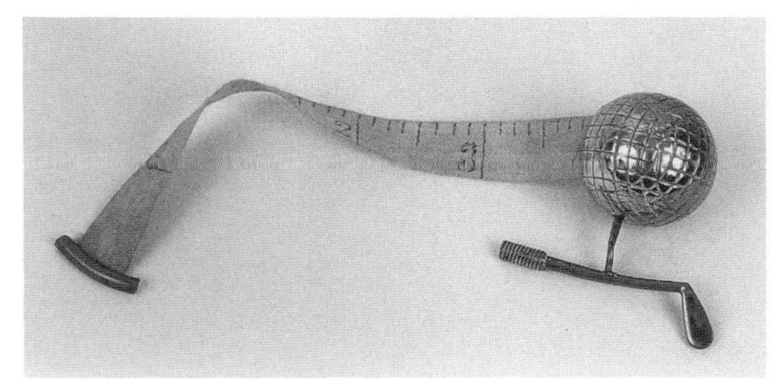

13-27 *For the golfing seamstress: a golf ball tape measure with handy club crank.*

13-28 *A silver coffeepot engraved with a scene of Old Tom Morris putting. The reverse side is elaborately engraved with an inscription to the Leith (Scotland) Thistle Golf Club, dated 1879.*

COLLECTING TIP

■ **British silver items were — and still are — carefully assayed to verify purity. They are stamped with a hallmark — a small series of letters and designs that indicate the maker, the year made and location of manufacture. The presence of a lion in the hallmark indicates solid silver on a British article. American silversmiths used a hallmark or "Sterling" stamp, but since plated pieces also may be marked, it is helpful to consult an identification guide. Plated items often are stamped with the letters "EP"— meaning electro-plate.**

13-29 *Coat buttons, frequently made of gold, provided the finishing touch to a golfer's wardrobe. Since golf clubs were first formed in the 18th century, members have sported custom-made buttons on playing and dining attire.*

13-30 *At the turn-of-the-century, jewelers and silversmiths on both sides of the Atlantic were advertising their golf wares in magazines.*

CHAPTER 14

BRONZES & STATUARY

Varying from delicate papier-mâché to hefty bronze, 3 inches to 6 feet in height, statuary is a minor — though artistically significant — category of golf antiques.

It is generally thought that a person has to be especially noteworthy to have his or her likeness cast in bronze. In the golf realm, however, this recognition once was limited almost exclusively to prominent amateur players. Only in the last 30 years have professionals become "worthy" of such an undertaking. Now it is possible to acquire a bronze of Ben Hogan, Tommy Armour, Gene Sarazen, Arnold Palmer or Jack Nicklaus, in addition to Horace Hutchinson, Bobby Jones and Harold Hilton.

Tabletop action figures of notable golfers first appeared in the late 19th century and featured such amateur stalwarts as John Ball, Harold Hilton and Horace Hutchinson. After winning four (of an eventual six) British Opens and a U.S. Open, Harry Vardon became the first professional to be portrayed in bronze.

Since famous golf personalities were first portrayed in bronze, all sorts of "generic" golfers have been cast for tournament prizes and decorations — even as hood ornaments for automobiles. These items are significant for their artistic merit even though they have no celebrity association. Golf businesses also developed advertising promotions around fictional characters; ball manufacturers Silvertown, Penfold and Dunlop and the Pinehurst Country Club resort all had well-recognized trademark figures that advocated a product or service.

Old golf statuettes range in value from several dollars for a simple ashtray to thousands for an exceptional bronze. Quality of workmanship, the artist's reputation, scarcity and type of material all contribute to the value of an item. The different materials include: bronze, brass, copper, silver, silver plate, pot metal, cast iron, pewter, wood, plaster, papier-mâché and even concrete.

CLASSIC BRONZES

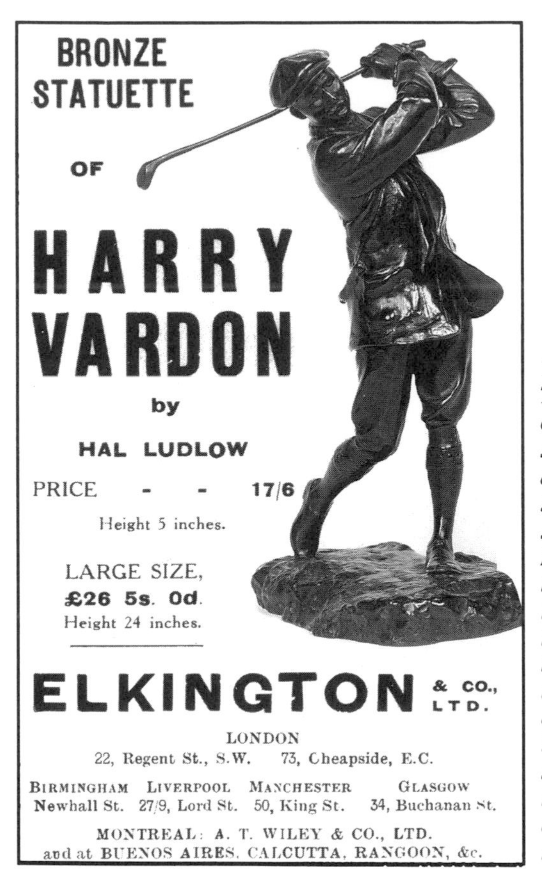

14-1 *HARRY VARDON*
This bronze of the immortal Harry Vardon is considered to be the pre-eminent example of golf statuary. It was produced by Elkington in 5-, 10- and 26-inch sizes in bronze, plaster and German silver (a silver-looking alloy). Hal Ludlow, the sculptor, was an accomplished amateur golfer. His keen awareness of the golf swing was described by Golf Illustrated *when the bronze made its debut in 1904: "[Ludlow] has given us Vardon to the life...Note the light folds of the Norfolk jacket, the belt loosely buckled at the back, the sleeve-wrists turned back, the tightly-locked thumb. Every trifling characteristic has been observed and fixed in enduring bronze, Vardon himself has expressed his entire satisfaction with the position as a whole. To put it is his own words: 'When I finish like that, I've hit one of the best.'" (See photo 14-13 regarding reproductions.)*

14-2 *JOHN LAIDLAY*
Thought to be John Laidlay, twice British Amateur champion, this 17-inch-high figure has appeared in two styles. The hand-painted originals were cast circa 1895 in a lightweight alloy and were signed and numbered by G. Gonnilla of Dundee. Recent unpainted copies have been made in bronze, all bearing the number "4."

14-3 *JOHN BALL*
Eight-time British Amateur champion John Ball, sculpted by Alex Macleay in 1893. Ball also won the British Open in 1890, the first of three amateurs to do so. The other two were Harold Hilton and Bobby Jones. This 19 1/2-inch high figure was cast in bronze and in iron.

14-4 *CECIL LEITCH*
This Cecil Leitch figure was fashioned by Sam Bugnatz and produced by Gorham in the late 1920s. She won 12 national championships in Great Britain, France and Canada. The other prominent women golfers depicted in bronze were Joyce Wethered and Glenna Collett Vare.

14-5 *HAROLD HILTON*
Hilton, featured in a 1901 bronze by Cassidy, was one of golf's greatest amateur players. He won the British Open in 1892 and 1897, four British Amateurs between 1900 and 1913 and was one of only three foreigners to win the U.S. Amateur. (The others were Canadians C. Ross Somerville and Gary Cowan.)

14-6 *This unclothed golfer was adapted from a 16th-century drawing by Renaissance artist Raphael. The original work depicted a male swinging some object other than a golf club in a manner much like a golf swing. Adolph A. Weinman employed his artistic license when he substituted a golf club in this 1901 bronze, cast by Gorham.*

COLLECTING TIP

■ **Just because some of the 19th-century golf statuary shows some wild-looking swings, don't think that the players depicted were duffers or that the sculptor was inaccurate.**

In comparing the 19th-century "St. Andrews" swing popularized by Young Tom Morris to the modern swing of Harry Vardon, a 1904 magazine article stated that "The [St. Andrews] swing itself was loose, dashing, and full of fire. Flinging after the club every ounce of youthful strength in his body, [Young Tom] would fall forward at the end of the stroke. Vardon's swing, on the contrary, is the very poetry of golf, full of concentrated ease and grace, of supple energy so applied as never to be obvious. It exemplifies the art of concealing the art. His play is the embodiment of smooth, even, machine-like accuracy . . ."

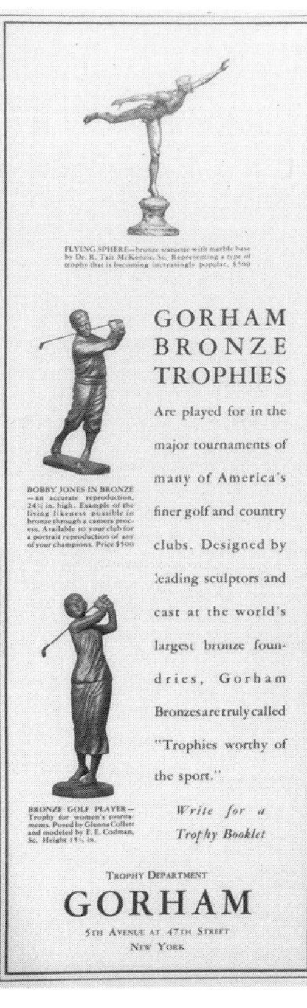

14-7 *Gorham was a prolific producer of golf trophies. This ad from 1928 shows examples of their bronzes of Bobby Jones (pre-Grand Slam) and Glenna Collett. These quality images were expensive — the statuette of Jones cost $500.*

14-8 *HORACE HUTCHINSON*
This 26-inch-high bronze features Horace Hutchinson, winner of back-to-back British Amateur Championships in 1886-87 and noted golf writer. William Tyler crafted this magnificent work in 1890, making it the first golf bronze to be issued.

OTHER FIGURES

14-9 *The Putter Boy has been associated with the historic Pinehurst (North Carolina) Country Club resort since the beginning of the century. It was created as a bronze sundial — with the shadow from the extra-long shaft indicating the hour — and stood on a pedestal near the practice putting green until it was transferred to the nearby PGA/ World Golf Hall of Fame in the 1970s. The Putter Boy frequently was personified in calendars and other vintage advertising for the resort. Reproductions of the original sundial were first made in the early 1970s as a real estate sales promotion and later as tournament prizes. They can be found in 5-, 7- and 9-inch sizes.*

14-10 *This golfer and caddy pair, originally cast in the 1920s, have graced decorative items such as ashtrays and bookends. The caddy even has been reproduced as a 4-foot-high concrete statue.*

14-11 *Hand-painted advertising figures made of papier-mâché, aluminum and plaster were fashionable in the 1920s. Usually 10 to 17 inches high, most were issued by golf ball manufacturers. The popular Penfold man (left) touts the Bromford ball alongside the North British Rubber Company's terrier, while the two crown-wearing, golf ball-headed "kings" publicize Silver King golf balls (below left). The Silvertown Company also distributed a companion "queen." The plaster figure (below right) was a pub display designed to encourage the sale of Plus Four whisky. Several figures have been recently reproduced.*

14-12 *A bronze $7^{1}/_{2}$-by-5-inch bas-relief plaque depicting King Charles I receiving news of the Irish Rebellion while playing golf on the Leith Links, near Edinburgh. The scene, originally painted by John Gilbert in 1875, was produced in metal circa 1900.*

COLLECTING TIPS

- **The term "bronze" often is used loosely to describe a metal statuette. If considering a purchase, it would be wise to learn about the different patinas and bronze finishes that are used. A "bronzed" figure can vary greatly in value from a true bronze.**
- **Old figures with worn or deteriorated paint should not be restored to an "as-new" appearance. This would destroy the character and warmth associated with an antique. If chipped paint bothers you, then consider buying a new reproduction.**

14-13 *More economical than the classic 100-year-old bronzes are the many silver-plated and bronzed golf figures that have been cast in recent decades, such as the items shown here. Collectors should be aware that modern reproductions have been made of Hal Ludlow's bronze of Harry Vardon (above, marked with arrows).*

14-14 *Six-inch high pewter ice cream molds — designed to create a unique sculpted dessert — were fashionable in the early 20th century. Shown are a golfing couple, golf bag and ball, along with samples cast in rubber.*

14-15 *Three golfer-adorned ashtrays, the one on the left being the much-produced, painted metal Dunlop advertising figure with movable head.*

14-16 *Desktop accessories were commonly made of inexpensive pot metal. Shown are a pencil holder (above) and an inkwell (right).*

14-17 *An appropriate cigarette lighter for a golfer. Disguised as a golf bag, a nudge to the putter causes the other clubheads to flip open and expose a flame. Made of bronzed pot metal, the lighters are a common novelty. However, it's rare to find one with the original box.*

CHAPTER 15

TOYS & GAMES

Before reading any further, take a few minutes to glance at the illustrations on the following pages.

Did you get a nostalgic feeling or smile a little?

If you answered yes, then you still must be a child at heart. If not, this chapter might be too frivolous for your tastes, and you probably would be more comfortable reading about serious art elsewhere in this book.

Toys and games have been part of our culture since ancient times. While most old toys related to golf were marketed toward youngsters, golf games and puzzles appealed to anyone with an interest in the sport. Many games, such as Rainy Day Golf and Wintre Golf, were designed to satisfy golfers' appetites for competition during inclement weather or during the off-season. Most of the board games and jigsaw puzzles, however, were intended for general amusement and required little hands-on knowledge of golf.

The first golf games were developed about a hundred years ago and involved putting on the lawn — a genteel after-dinner amusement similar to croquet. Card and board games soon evolved, and in the 1920s, wind-up golf toys became popular. Milton Bradley, Parker Brothers, Britains, Schoenhut, Ferdinand Strauss, McLoughlin Brothers and other prominent game and toy manufacturers acknowledged the universal appeal of golf and offered products with golf themes.

Many of these products featured attractive packaging with colorful lithography and elaborately embellished components that now make them highly desirable for use as decorations and conversation pieces.

An additional benefit is that some of the games and toys still can be utilized as originally intended: as a fun and challenging pastime. After all, you can never tell when the urge to play Teeny Weeny Golf or Goofy Golf may strike!

BOARD GAMES

15-1 *Hand-held manual dexterity games usually require an inordinate amount of skill to manipulate the small steel ball. (Anyone who has hands steady enough to master these games also must be an excellent putter.)*

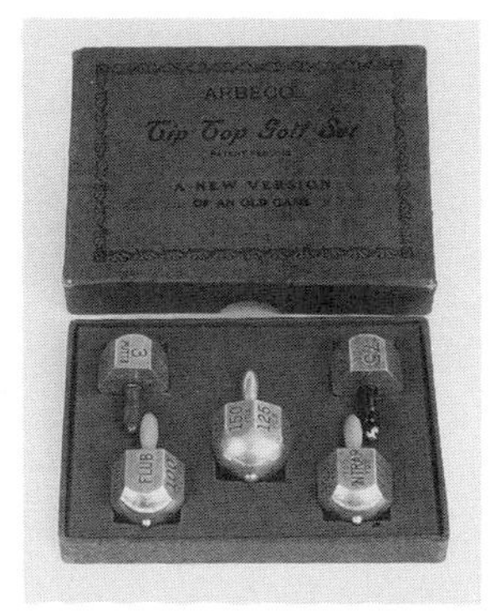

15-2 *Although the boards are missing from this game, the carton and playing pieces are interesting enough to be collectible in their own right. And if a matching board turns up someday, it'll be like finding a long-lost friend.*

15-3 *Celebrity golf games range from an Arthur Godfrey board game, introduced in 1954, to a radio-controlled Bob Hope golfer that appeared in toy stores in the mid-1980s.*

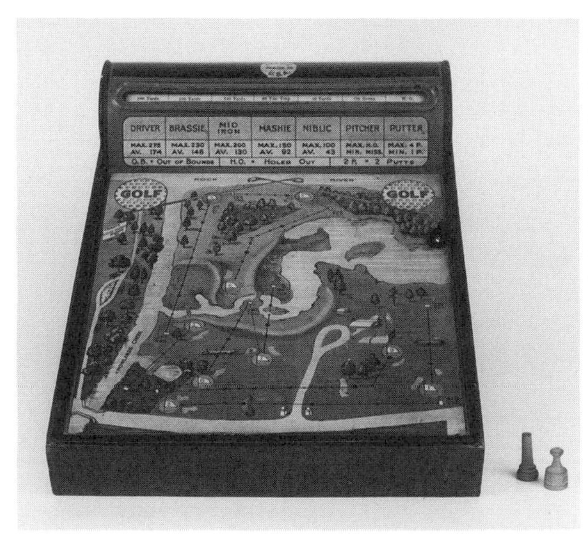

15-4 *The Frantz Company produced a number of sports games in the late 1920s, using the same tin housing with different artwork.*

Clockwork & Mechanical Toys

15-5 *The forerunners of today's battery-operated toys were wind-up toys that were propelled by a spring-wound clockwork mechanism. The Ferdinand Strauss Corporation, a pioneer in this concept, introduced Playgolf in 1927. After one player took a turn at activating the golfer to stroke the ball toward the holes, the mechanism automatically re-teed the ball for the next player. Originally retailing for $1, the tin games now are valued in the hundreds of dollars.*

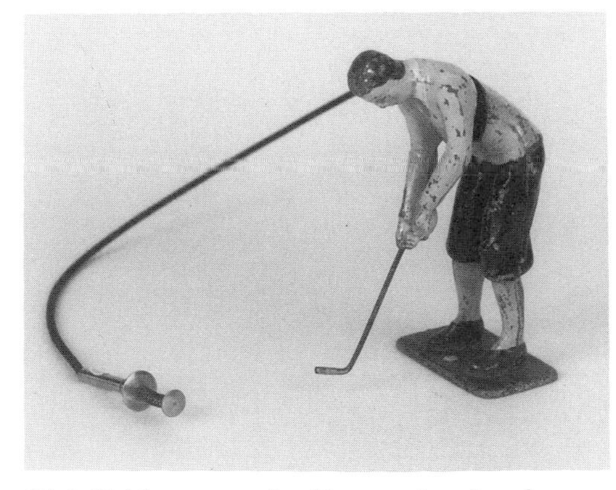

15-6 *Cable-operated golfers used a wire plunger or puff of air to initiate the swing. They generally were associated with tabletop or arcade games.*

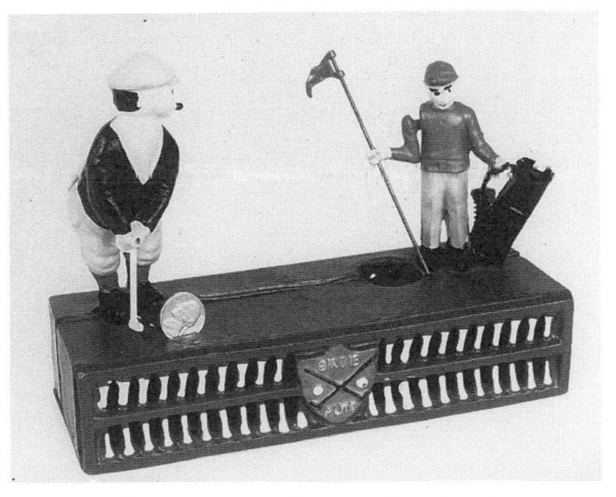

15-7 *Push a button on this cast iron bank and watch the golfer putt a coin to the hole as the caddy lifts the flagstick. Even though they look old, most banks of this style are relatively new.*

15-8 *The entertaining Mechanical Monkey Golfer. A good turn of the key gives the monkey a strenuous workout, as the ball repeatedly returns from the net to permit another practice shot. Imported from Japan by the Cragstan Company, circa 1950.*

15-9 *The Jocko mechanical golfer does not have a maker's label, but collectors have attributed its manufacture to the Behrend & Rothschild Company in the mid-1920s. The pull of a string enabled the little man to launch a ball across the room.*

15-10 *The Twistum golfer was similar to the Schoenhut golfers, except the player had to manually swing the figure's arms while holding his feet in place. The object of the game was to strike the ball into the hole on the cardboard green. (Although the box displays a 1920 patent date, the golfer did not debut until 1927; the 1920 date refers to a previously designed feature that was incorporated into the golf game.)*

SCHOENHUT'S INDOOR GOLF

15-11 *Albert Schoenhut's company, founded in 1903, was famous for its jointed wooden circus animals and musical toys. However, golf collectors are most familiar with their golf game. Introduced in 1921 and made for several years, it featured wooden club-swinging male and female figurines, mounted on the end of a shaft and operated by a remote control trigger. "Sissy Lofter" (right), the 5-inch-high wooden golf partner of "Tommy Green," stands at the first tee.*

15-12 *When Schoenhut introduced its golf game, it was an instant success, as explained in this 1921 magazine ad from* The Sporting Goods Dealer. *Directed toward retailers, Schoenhut boasted that "four thousand sets were sold to New York and Philadelphia golfers alone within three weeks of its introduction." It's still a big hit, even though a complete set can cost 100 times the original $10 price.*

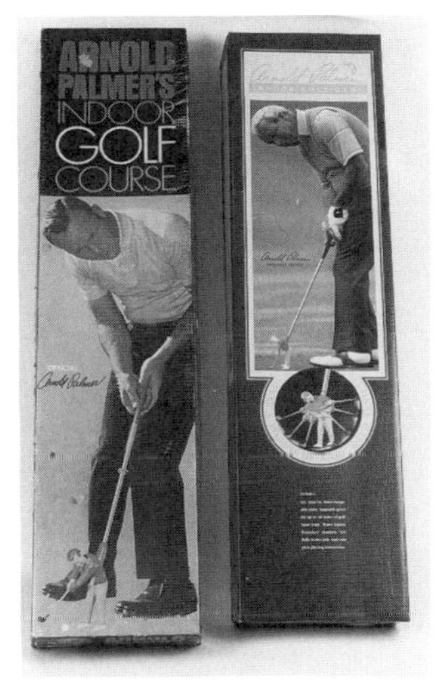

15-13 *Just as the Senior Tour can give new life to an aging golf pro, so can a toy company rejuvenate a product from the past. The Arnold Palmer Schoenhut-style golfer, initially marketed in the 1960s, recently staged a comeback in toy stores. (Also featured in the 1960s was similar toy named "Golfer Ike," after the golfing president.)*

Schoenhut's Indoor Golf was extremely popular as a game in the 1920s. Now it is one of the most desirable golf collectibles today. Sets were offered in several configurations. However, the basic single set consisted of:

"Tommy Green" or "Sissy Lofter"	**3 clubs (wood, iron, putter)**	**2 balls**
1 tee	**1 tee box (sand & water)**	**2 sand traps**
1 water hazard	**1 green**	**1 flag**
1 boundary marker	**box, instructions and scorecards**	

JIGSAW PUZZLES

15-14 *Although Richfield gave clever jigsaw puzzles away to encourage gasoline sales, they were quick to point out that there was no advertising on the puzzle. In addition to a "Goofy Golf" puzzle, customers also received a golf lesson on the envelope from Alex Morrison, a top teaching pro in the 1930s and '40s.*

15-15 *Taken from a painting by noted golf illustrator Charles Crombie, this puzzle could be extremely difficult for the assembler if he or she did not know that the golfer was in a horizontal position.*

15-16 *Joe Palooka, the popular comic strip character from the 1930s and '40s, takes an exasperating swing.*

COLLECTING TIPS

■ Golf collectors must recognize that antique toy and game collecting is a long-established hobby in its own right, so many desirable golf items have not yet worked their way into the realm of golfiana. And what may seem like an ordinary, but attractive, toy to a golf collector might be worth hundreds to a dedicated toy enthusiast. To become better informed about the overall hobby, consider contacting:

**American Game Collectors Assn.
4628 Barlow Drive
Bartlesville, Oklahoma 74006**

■ If you're not a perfectionist, it's possible to get a bargain by buying a game with missing parts. Even a discarded box cover or an orphaned game board can be framed to make an attractive display. (And there's always the chance that you might find the missing parts.)

MISCELLANEOUS

15-17 *Clock Golf, Garden Golf, Lawn Golf and Puttinshu were some of the outdoor putting games that were fashionable during the 1890s. The Lawn Golf set (top) included professionally-made scared-head putters. These games later evolved into commercial miniature golf course ventures: first the Tom Thumb variety in the 1920s, then Putt-Putt, and now the elaborate Jungle Golf and Mountain Golf complexes.*

15-18 *If you like old-fashioned board games and traditional hands-on toys, it's wise to acquire them now before they go entirely out of style. Today's trend is toward high tech computer games that feature realistic simulated play on famous golf courses from around the world.*

15-19 *Coin-operated games have been made in tabletop, arcade and slot machine styles. Rewards for good play included points, gumballs and real golf balls. (See slot machine, page 43.)*

15-20 *Some playing cards were decorated with golf themes, while others enabled players to create imaginary golf rounds in the palms of their hands.*

15-21 *Similar to toy soldiers, small golf figures were made of lead and other materials by manufacturers such as the noted English firm of Britains, Ltd. Usually hand-painted, they sometimes have jointed body parts. The highly detailed bronze animals, shown here, were made in Austria. The human lead golfers are recent reproductions of models originally made by Britains, Ltd. in the 1930s.*

15-22 *This 3-inch-high figure displayed the trump suit for card-playing golfers.*

15-23 *A vintage stationary golfer made of pot metal. The chipped paint shows signs of use, denotes age and gives the piece character. If offered for sale, a purist toy collector may pass on this one in hope of finding another figure in mint condition. A smart golf collector, however, probably would purchase it and then trade up if a nicer example comes along.*

CHAPTER 16

LITERATURE

Every serious golfer has at least one book on golf. It may be a golf course guide received at Christmas or an instruction book from Father's Day. There are probably some magazines lying around the house, too. Golfers like to read about the game, and publishers know it.

Since the first golf book (*The Goff*) was published in 1743 and the first golf magazine (*Golf*) appeared in 1890, golfers have been bringing the game into their homes. Poems, essays, instruction, histories, golf course reviews, novels, and other topics about the game have appeared in thousands of books.

Unfortunately, not all golf books are collectible. There are numerous poorly written instruction and hastily prepared history books that have little value — monetary or otherwise. But there are also the classics: works by Bernard Darwin, longtime golf correspondent for *The Times* of London and *Country Life* magazine; Herbert Warren Wind of *Sports Illustrated* and *The New Yorker* fame; Horace Hutchinson, a fine amateur golfer who first offered his wisdom in the 1890 golf volume of the Badminton Library series; and Bobby Jones, perhaps the most articulate championship golfer of all time.

The frequently overlooked, and perhaps the most fascinating, type of collectible golf literature is the magazine, such as the ones from 30, 50 or even 100 years ago. In the old issues of *Golf Illustrated* and *The American Golfer* you can read about history while it was being made, such as the advent of the rubber-core golf ball in 1898 or the grand slam play of Bobby Jones in 1930.

This chapter is not intended to be the "last word" on golf literature, but an overview of several prominent aspects. Remember that many of the noteworthy golf books and magazines are among the easiest golf collectibles to get your hands on and enjoy. Some are as close as the nearest public library. In addition to several golf libraries (see page 235), most big-city libraries have a surprisingly good collection of classic golf literature. (Smaller libraries often can acquire desired works via inter-library loans).

EARLY "FIRSTS"

Printed references to golf go back a long way. The first known mention of the game was contained in an act of Scottish Parliament in 1457 when King James II of Scotland decreed that citizens must no longer play "golfe" because it interfered with the more important practice of archery. Since the printing industry would not be born for several more years, this original reference was in the form of a handwritten entry. In 1566, when typesetting was available, this legislation then became the first printed mention of golf.

For the next two hundred years, the evolution of the game was at a standstill and only sporadic references appeared on the printed page. By the mid-18th century, however, there were hundreds of golfers in Scotland, and it was just a matter of time before an entire book devoted to golf would appear.

It finally happened in 1743, when a Scot named Thomas Mathison wrote *The Goff, An Heroi-Comical Poem in Three Cantos.* It consisted of 24 pages — a pamphlet by modern standards. The book was actually a poem about a mythical golf match between heroes of ancient Greece and Rome. *The Goff* was printed in limited quantities and although subsequent editions were produced in 1763 and in 1793, only a few dozen copies remain today. Written in a Scottish dialect, the text is difficult to understand. Like many collectible books, *The Goff* is prized more for its rarity than its content. An excellent translation, prepared over a half century ago by golf historian C.B. Clapcott, can be found in *The Clapcott Papers*, a 1985 reference work edited by prominent book collector, Alastair J. Johnston.

THE

GOFF.

AN

Heroi-Comical Poem.

IN

Three CANTOS.

Cætera, quæ vacuas tenuissent carmina mentes, Omnia jam vulgata. VIRG.

EDINBURGH:

Printed by J. COCHRAN and COMPANY. MDCCXLIII.

[*Price Four Pence.*]

16-1 *Title page from the first edition of* The Goff, *only 28 pages long, but considered to be the earliest book dedicated solely to golf. The three slightly different editions were published in 1743, 1763 and 1793.*

Although Mathison receives much attention for his premier work, there are a number of other notable "firsts" in golf literature, which follow. These authors were pioneers in their respective fields, and it is interesting to read their interpretations of the game.

First recorded mention of golf:
May 21,1457 — Act of Scottish Parliament

First printed mention of golf:
1566 — *Actis and Constitutiounis of the Realme of Scotland . . .*

First book devoted to golf:
1743 — *The Goff* by Thomas Mathison

First instruction book:
1857 — *The Golfer's Manual* by A Keen Hand (Henry Farnie)

First book written by a woman:
1896 — *The Sorrows of a Golfer's Wife* by Mrs. Edward Kennard

First biography:
1900 — *F.G. Tait: A Record* by John L. Low

First novel:
1893 — *Won at the Last Hole* by M.A. Stobart

First book about golf courses:
1897 — *British Golf Links* by Horace Hutchinson

First book by a professional golfer:
1896 — *The Game of Golf* by Willie Park, Jr.

First golf magazine:
1890 — *Golf, A Weekly Record of "Ye Royal and Ancient Game"*

First printed American mention of golf:
1772 — *Sermones to Gentlemen upon Temperance and Exercise* by Dr. Benjamin Rush

First American golf publication:
1893 — *Golf* by J.Stuart Balfour (a pamphlet published by the Spalding Athletic Library)

First golf book published in America:
1895 — *Golf in America* by James P. Lee

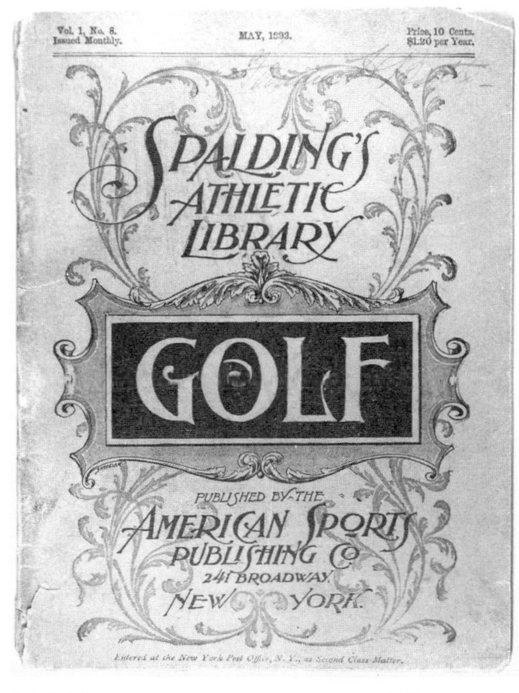

16-2 *This Spalding pamphlet, dated 1893, was the first text on golf published in the United States.*

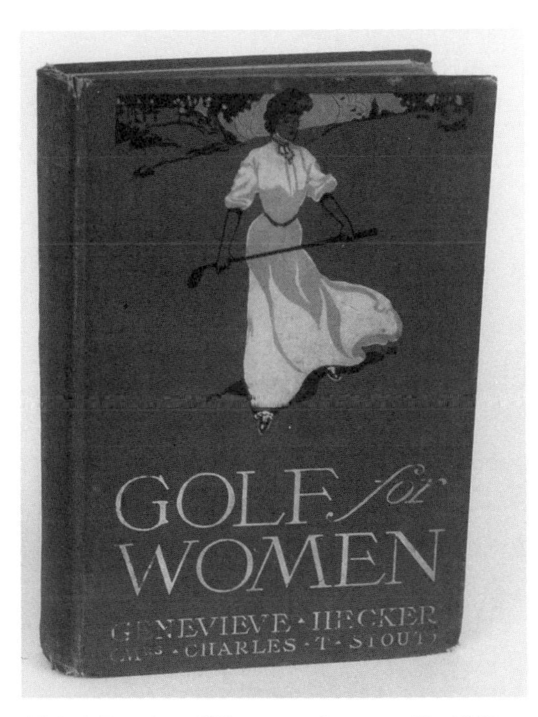

16-3 *A first in golf literature happened in 1902: a book written by a woman for women golfers.*

GOLF BIBLIOGRAPHIES

Collecting golf books is by no means a recently developed hobby. In 1910, Harry B. Wood of Manchester, England, included a golf bibliography with more than 500 entries in his *Golfing Curios and "The Like"*. A later bibliography, *Collecting Golf Books 1743-1938* by London book dealer Cecil Hopkinson, did not list as many titles but offered collecting guidelines and precise descriptions, known as collations. Golf magazines also have published short bibliographies over the years; the oldest list, by a Mr. Chapman, appeared in 1892.

A half century passed after Hopkinson's work before another major bibliography appeared. In 1968, after years of research, Joseph S.F. Murdoch's *The Library of Golf–1743-1966* came on the market. Murdoch's work was complete with straightforward annotations, a history of golf literature and a system of reference numbers (abbreviated "MRN" by book collectors for "Murdoch Reference Number"). Murdoch, a founder of the Golf Collectors' Society, updated his bibliography in a 1978 addendum and collaborated with Janet Seagle in 1979 to produce *Golf – A Guide to Information Sources*, which contains a section on golf-related books.

Murdoch since has worked with New York bookseller Richard Donovan in compiling the consummate golf bibliography, titled *The Game of Golf and The Printed Word, 1566-1985*, which was published in 1988. Murdoch's latest work of interest to the golf book collector is *The Murdoch Golf Library*, in which he takes the reader down the collecting trail that led to Murdoch's own immense collection of golf literature.

16-4 *Jack Level was a prolific golf book collector and dealer. He also compiled a never-published golf bibliography in the 1940s. He is pictured above in his Elmhurst, New York library, circa 1953.*

It is interesting to note that when Murdoch's first bibliography first came out, it was not an immediate success. It took more than 14 years to sell out the fewer than 4,000 copies printed. Now that there is tremendous interest in collecting old golf books, *The Library of Golf* is not an easy find. Originally selling for about $12, the book now brings several hundred dollars.

Another bibliography, containing basic information and 1985 values, was included in *The Encyclopedia of Golf Collectibles* by John M. and Morton W. Olman. The book also contains excellent reading recommendations by noted golf book specialists.

COLLECTING TIP

■ **Books about golf literature are collectibles in their own right. Refer to page 257 for further information on these references.**

LIMITED EDITION RARE BOOKS

Many outstanding golf books also were offered in special editions. Almost all were numbered in limited editions, and certain ones had deluxe bindings or were printed on large paper. Publishers often solicited prepublication orders, called subscriptions, to help offset their costs. (See photo 16-7) The subscribers were acknowledged with a listing of their names in the book.

Limited editions generally have a page before the title page that describes the quantity of the edition, along with a numeral designating the book's sequential number. This page usually is signed by the author, although some authors, such as Robert Clark just initialed the page.

Certain books were offered in several editions, which can be confusing. Clark's *Golf: The Royal and Ancient Game*, for instance, was printed in several formats: a large paper, signed edition of 50 copies; a large paper, presentation copy; and three regular trade editions. *The Golf Book of East Lothian* by Rev. John Kerr was published in a large paper, signed edition of 250 copies, a small paper, signed edition of 500 copies, and NO regular edition.

Limited edition golf books are not just a thing of the past. Almost every golf book published today that is of interest to the collector (this book included) is also offered in a specially bound edition.

16-5 *The unique limitation statement from what is often referred to as* The Golf Greens of Scotland. *The book, done in 1893, consists of scenes etched by George Aikman from original watercolors painted by John Smart.*

16-6 *Limitation statement from the rare* Golf Book of East Lothian, *written by John Kerr in 1896.*

Author	Title	Date	Qty.	Numbered	Signed
Aikman, George & Smart, John	*A Round of the Links: Views of the Golf Greens of Scotland*	1893	100	yes	yes
Boomer, Percy	*On Learning Golf*	1942	500	yes	yes
Clapcott, C.B.	*Rules of the Ten Oldest Golf Clubs From 1754-1848*	1935	500	no	no
Clark, Robert	*Golf: A Royal and Ancient Game*	1875	50^{LP}	yes	"R.C."
	(special presentation edition)	1875	?	yes	"R.C."
Darwin, Bernard	*A Golfer's Gallery by Old Masters*	c1920	500	yes	yes
Evans, Jr., Chick	*Chick Evans' Golf Book*	1921	999	yes	yes
Haultain, Theo. A.	*The Mystery of Golf*	1908	440	yes	yes

Author	Title	Date	Qty.	Numbered	Signed
Hilton, Harold H.	*The Royal and Ancient Game of Golf*	1912	100[D]	yes	no
& Smith, Garden C.		1912	900	yes	no
Hutchinson, Horace	*British Golf Links*	1897	250[LP]	yes	no
Hutchinson, Horace & Others	*Golf, The Badminton Library*	1890	250[LP]	yes	no
Jones, Jr., Robert T. & Keeler, O.B.	*Down the Fairway*	1927	300	yes	yes
Kerr, John	*The Golf Book of East Lothian*	1896	250	yes	yes
		1896	500	yes	yes
MacDonald, Charles	*Scotland's Gift, Golf*	1928	260	yes	yes
Martin, H.B.	*Fifty Years of American Golf*	1936	355	yes	yes
Martin, H.B. & Halliday, Alexander	*St. Andrews Golf Club, 1888-1938*	1938	500	no	no
Martin, John Stuart	*The Curious History of the Golf Ball*	1968	500	yes	yes
Ouimet, Francis	*A Game of Golf*	1932	550	yes	yes
Wethered, H.N. & Simpson, T.	*The Architectural Side of Golf*	1929	50[LP]	yes	yes
Wood, Harry B.	*Golfing Curios and the Like*	1910	150[LP]	yes	no

FOOTNOTES: [LP] Large paper edition [SP] Small paper edition [D] Deluxe edition

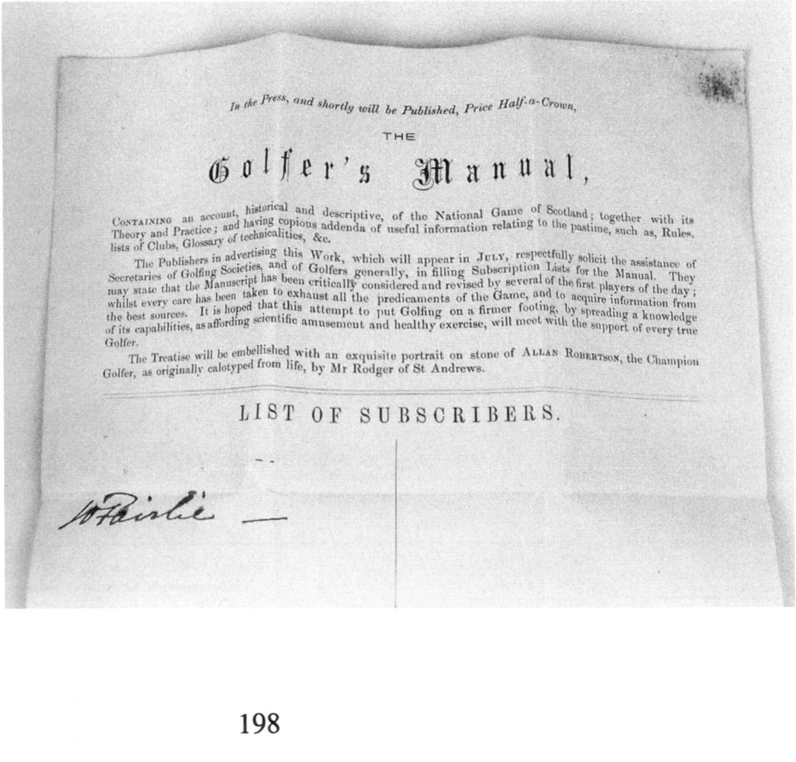

In the Press, and shortly will be Published, Price Half-a-Crown,

THE

Golfer's Manual,

Containing an account, historical and descriptive, of the National Game of Scotland; together with its Theory and Practice; and having copious addenda of useful information relating to the pastime, such as, Rules, lists of Clubs, Glossary of technicalities, &c.

The Publishers in advertising this Work, which will appear in July, respectfully solicit the assistance of Secretaries of Golfing Societies, and of Golfers generally, in filling Subscription Lists for the Manual. They may state that the Manuscript has been critically considered and revised by several of the first players of the day; whilst every care has been taken to exhaust all the predicaments of the Game, and to acquire information from the best sources. It is hoped that this attempt to put Golfing on a firmer footing, by spreading a knowledge of its capabilities, as affording scientific amusement and healthy exercise, will meet with the support of every true Golfer.

The Treatise will be embellished with an exquisite portrait on stone of Allan Robertson, the Champion Golfer, as originally calotyped from life, by Mr Rodger of St Andrews.

LIST OF SUBSCRIBERS.

16-7 *In the mid 18th century, the audience for golf books was limited, so often the publisher would solicit advance sales to help offset production costs. The subscription form shown was used to finance the 1857 publication of* The Golfer's Manual, *the first "how-to" book on golf.*

REPUBLISHED BOOKS

Prior to the 1970s, much of golf's outstanding literature had gone unread by collectors and others interested in the history of the game. This was because many of the early books were difficult to obtain or sold for hundreds, or sometimes thousands, of dollars.

Book dealers, collectors and even the U. S. Golf Association have dealt with this dilemma by reprinting these hard-to-obtain golf books. The reprinted version of a book can be either a facsimile of the original work, where the actual pages are reproduced, or it can be a newly typeset version of the original text. Since most reprints are produced in limited quantities, many already have become collectors' items in their own right. As a result, the eloquent prose of Bernard Darwin, Grantland Rice, John Kerr and Walter Simpson has been preserved and brought into the limelight once again.

Even old magazine articles are worthy of reissue. A collection of stories written during the last twenty years for *The New Yorker* magazine by Herbert Warren Wind was published in 1985 under the title, *Following Through*. In 1954, Charles Price edited *The American Golfer*, a selection of articles from the 1920's and 1930's from the magazine of the same name. And recently, Tom Stewart has compiled *A Tribute to Golf*, which contains all sorts of classic literature and artwork.

Although numerous new golf books are published each year, an increasing number of golfers are discovering the classic works. The available biographies enable the reader to compare today's superstars with those of the past such as Tom Morris, Harry Vardon, Bobby Jones, Walter Hagen, Francis Ouimet and Gene Sarazen.

The following list of republished books, considered classics, constitutes an excellent "want list" for a personal golf library. There are, of course, hundreds of other fine books in the marketplace designed to satisfy the reading tastes and interests of every golfer. Following the author, title and original date of publication is the name of the new publisher and the year of reissue.

A Keen Hand (Pseud. for Henry Brougham Farnie). *The Golfer's Manual*, 1857, (Dropmore Press, 1947 and Vantage Press, 1965).

A Member. *St. Andrews to the Play*, 1854, (Dufner and Dezieck, 1983).

Aikman George & Smart, John. *A Round of the Links: Views of the Golf Greens of Scotland*, 1893, (Heritage Press, 1980).

Armour, Tommy. *How to Play your Best Golf All the Time*, 1953, (Classics of Golf, 1984).

Balfour, James. *Reminiscences of Golf on St. Andrews Links*, 1887, (Dufner, 1982; Classics of Golf, 1987).

Bateman, H.M. *Adventures at Golf (reprint titled H.M. Bateman on Golf)*, 1923, (Whittet, 1977).

Bennett, Andrew. *The Book of St. Andrews Links*, 1898, (Ellesborough, 1984).

Boomer, Percy. *On Learning Golf*, 1942, (Classics of Golf, 1989).

Browning, Robert H.K. *A History of Golf: The Royal and Ancient Game*, 1950, (Classics of Golf, 1984).

Chambers, Robert. *A Few Rambling Remarks On Golf*, 1862, (USGA, 1983).

16-8 *Nearly 100 classic and rare golf books have been reproduced as facsimile or reprinted editions. Shown are* Golf in America, Down the Fairway, Swing the Clubhead, *and* Golfing Reminiscences.

Clark, Robert. *Golf: A Royal and Ancient Game*, 1875, (EP Publishing, 1975; Lang Syne, 1984).

Collett, Glenna. *Golf for Young Players*, 1926, (Old Golf Shop, 1984).

Colt, Harry S. & Alison, C.H. *Some Essays On Golf Course Architecture*, 1920,(Grant Books 1990).

Crombie, Charles. *The Rules of Golf Illustrated,* circa 1905, (Ariel, 1966; Taplinger, 1966).

Cundell, James. *Rules of the Thistle Club*, 1824, (USGA, 1983).

Darwin, Bernard. *The Golf Courses of the British Isles*, 1910, (Classics of Golf, 1988).

Darwin, Bernard. *Golf Between Two Wars*, 1944, (Classics of Golf, 1984).

Darwin, Bernard. *A History of Golf in Britain*, 1952, (Classics of Golf, 1990).

Darwin, Bernard. *James Braid*, 1952, (Old Golf Shop, 1981).

Darwin, Bernard. *Tee Shots and Others*, 1911, (USGA, 1984).

Dunn, Seymour. *Golf Fundamentals: Orthodoxy of Style*, 1922, (Golf Digest, 1977).

Edgar, J. Douglas. *The Gate to Golf*, 1920, (Ellesborough, 1983).

Evans, Jr., Chick. *Chick Evans' Golf Book*, 1921, (Wilson Sporting Goods, 1969; Old Golf Shop, 1978; Memorial Tournament, 1985).

Flint, Violet. *A Golfing Idyll*,1892, (Grant Books, 1978).

Forgan, Jr., Robert. *The Golfers Manual*, 1897, (Robert Kuntz, 1973).

Hagen, Walter & Heck, Margaret Seaton. *The Walter Hagen Story*, 1956 (Memorial Tournament, 1977).

Haultain, Theodore Arnold. *The Mystery of Golf*, 1908, (Serendipity Press, 1965; Classics of Golf, 1986).

Hogan, Ben & Wind, Herbert Warren. *Five Lessons, The Modern Fundamentals of Golf*, 1957, (Golf Digest, 1985).

Hopkinson, Cecil. *Collecting Golf Books, 1743-1938*, 1938, (Grant Books, 1980).

Hutchinson, Horace. *Hints on the Game of Golf*, 1886, (Classics of Golf, 1986).

Hutchinson, Horace. *After Dinner Golf*, 1896, (Ellesborough, 1986).

Hutchinson, Horace. *Fifty Years of Golf*, 1919, (USGA, 1985).

Hutchinson, Horace and Others. *Golf, The Badminton Library*, 1890, (Ashford Press, 1987).

J.A.C.K. (Pseud. for J. McCullough). *Golf in the Year 2000, or What Are We Coming To?*, 1892, (Old Golf Shop, 1984).

Jones, Ernest & Eisenberg, David. *Swing the Clubhead*, 1952, (Golf Digest, 1977).

Jones, Jr., Robert Tyre & Keeler. O. B. *Down the Fairway: The Golf Life and Play of Robert T. Jones, Jr.*, 1927, (Classics of Golf, 1983).

Jones, Jr., Robert Tyre. *Bobby Jones on the Basic Golf Swing* (reprint is *The Basic Golf Swing*), 1969, (Classics of Golf, 1990).

Jones, Jr., Robert Tyre. *Bobby Jones On Golf,* 1930, (Golf Digest, 1976).

Kerr, John. *The Golf Book of East Lothian*, 1896, (Spa Books Ltd., 1987).

Lee, James P. *Golf in America: A Practical Manual*, 1895, (USGA, 1986).

Low, John L. *F.G. Tait – A Record*, 1900, (Classics of Golf, 1989).

MacDonald, Charles Blair. *Scotland's Gift, Golf,* 1928, (Classics of Golf, 1985).

Mackenzie, Alister. *Golf Architecture*, 1920, (Classics of Golf, 1988).

Mackenzie, Alister. *Golf Architecture* (reprint is *Dr. Mackenzie's Golf Architecture*), 1920, (Grant Books, 1982).

Martin, H.B. *Fifty Years of American Golf*, 1936, (Argosy, 1966).

Mathison, Thomas. *The Goff, An Heroi-comical Poem in Three Cantos*, 1743-1763-1793 (USGA, 1981).

Ouimet, Francis. *A Game of Golf,* 1932, (Old Golf Shop, 1978; Ouimet Scholarship Fund, 1963).

McPherson, Rev. J. Gordon. *Golf and Golfers – Past and Present,* 1891, (USGA, 1991)

Peter, H. Thomas. *Reminiscences of Golf and Golfers*, circa, 1890, (Dufner, 1985).

Price, Charles. *The American Golfer,* 1964, (Classics of Golf, 1987).

Rice, Grantland & Briggs, Clare. *The Duffer's Handbook of Golf,* 1926, (Classics of Golf, 1989).

Rice, Grantland. *The Bobby Jones Story: from the writings of O.B. Keeler*, 1953, (Old Golf Shop, 1980).

Robb, George. *Historical Gossip About Golf and Golfers*, 1863, (USGA, 1991).

Robbie, J. Cameron. *The Chronicle of the Royal Golfing Society of Edinburgh, 1735-1935*, 1936, (Alna Press, 1983).

Robinson, W. Heath. *Humors of Golf,* 1923, (Duckworth, 1975).

Sarazen, Gene & Wind, Herbert Warren. *Thirty Years of Championship Golf,* 1950, (Old Golf Shop, 1979; Classics of Golf, 1987; A & C Black, 1990).

Simpson, Sir Walter G. *The Art of Golf,* 1887, (Classics of Golf, 1991; USGA, 1982).

Smith, Charles. *Aberdeen Golfers: Record and Reminiscences*, 1909, (Ellesborough, 1982).

16-9 *Robert Clark's* Golf: A Royal and Ancient Game *originally was published in regular (left) and large paper (right) versions in 1875. There also were later editions and modern reprints of this first comprehensive documentation of golf history. His work has been a standard reference for virtually all subsequent writings on the subject.*

16-10 *Most golf history books are rewrites of previous works, however these older books with a geographical slant on golf history were well researched at the time they were written. The books shown are histories of golf in Canada, Great Britain, and the United States written by Kavanagh, Darwin, and Wind respectively. (If a certain aspect of golf history needs to be positively ascertained, it is advisable to confirm facts stated in older texts with several modern works.)*

Sutphen, W.G. Van T. *The Golfer's Alphabet*, 1898, (Charles E. Tuttle, 1967).

Sutton, Martin A.F., et al. *Golf Course Design, Construction and Upkeep*, 1933, (Sutton & Sons, 1950).

Thomas, Jr., George C. *Golf Architecture in America*, 1927, (USGA, 1990).

Tulloch, W.W. *The Life of Tom Morris*, circa 1908, (Ellesborough, 1982).

Vardon, Harry. *The Complete Golfer*, 1905, (Golf Digest, 1977).

Vardon, Harry. *My Golfing Life*, 1933, (Memorial Tournament, 1981; Ellesborough, 1985;).

Vardon, Harry. *The Complete Golfer*, 1905, (Golf Digest, 1977).

Wethered, H.N. & Simpson, T. *The Architectural Side of Golf*, 1929, (reprint is *Design for Golf*, Sportsman's Book Club, 1952).

Wethered, Joyce. *Golfing Memories and Methods*, 1933, (Sportsman's Book Club, 1954).

Wind, Herbert Warren. *The Complete Golfer*, 1954, (Classics of Golf, 1991).

Wind, Herbert Warren. *The Story of American Golf*, 1948, (Knopf, 1975).

Wodehouse, P.G. *The Clicking of Cuthbert*, 1922, (Classics of Golf, 1986).

Wodehouse, P.G. *The Heart of a Goof*, 1927, (Classics of Golf, 1990).

Wood, Harry B. *Golfing Curios and the Like*, 1910, (Pride, 1980).

COLLECTING TIPS

- **There are two primary sources for "born again" golf books. Each year since 1981, the U.S. Golf Association (USGA) has republished a notable golf book, presented in an attractive slipcase. The most prolific of these publishers is Classics of Golf (65 Commerce Road, Stamford, Conn. 06902), which operates a mail-order book club for its titles.**

- **Books produced by other publishers may be difficult to find, so it's best to check with one of the old book specialists mentioned in Appendix A.** **(See page 243.)**

Golf Architecture Books

Avid golf fans have a true appreciation for the game's finest courses. Unfortunately, the closest most golfers get to a top-rated course — such as Augusta National or Pebble Beach — is their television set. The next best way to experience these masterpieces is by reading some of the books devoted to golf courses and their design.

16-11 *Because of the current revival of classic golf course design, older books on the subject have become very desirable.*

Golfers are forever critiquing golf courses and the architects responsible for them. Highly respected author and noted amateur golfer Horace Hutchinson was the first to produce a substantive assessment of golf course design a century ago when he assembled the comments of noted golf authorities in *Famous Golf Links*.

Although Hutchinson's work is credited with being the first on golf course architecture, Bernard Darwin's *Golf Courses of the British Isles*, published in 1910, is thought by many to be the finest. Even though it is illustrated with paintings by golf artist Harry Rountree, Darwin's prose alone beautifully illustrates the popular courses of the day. His description of the venerable links at Prestwick — site of the first British open in 1860 — as exhibiting "pleasurable uncertainty" is typical of his vivid style.

One of the most amusing treatises on design was written by Dr. Alister Mackenzie in 1920, prior to the creation of his masterpieces at Cypress Point and Augusta National. Mackenzie's forthright, and often humorous manner is illustrated in the following passage: "There is a yarn about two rival constructors of golf courses: one of them was admiring the other's greens, and remarked that 'he never managed to get his green-keeper to make the undulations natural looking.' The other replied that 'it

Golf Architecture in America

Its Strategy and Construction

By GEO. C. THOMAS, Jr.

THIS is the first book ever written on Golf Architecture as it is scientifically interpreted and carried out today on the American continent. Nothing quite so comprehensive in its particular sphere has ever been published anywhere during the entire history of this, the world's greatest sport.

The author writes from a very practical experience gained in many years devoted to the designing and remodeling of golf courses, from the Atlantic to the Pacific.

"Golf Architecture in America" will be sent postpaid, for $5.00. Send in your order to

GOLFERS MAGAZINE

506 So. Wabash Ave. CHICAGO

16-12 *Upon publication in 1927,* Golf Architecture in America *was heavily advertised. The print run appears to have been substantial as the book was readily available in the 1970s for under $20. Because of increased interest in golf course design, this book now sells for several hundred dollars. The U.S. Golf Association offered a reprint edition in 1991 as part of their rare book program.*

was perfectly easy; he simply employed the biggest fool in the village and told him to make them flat."

From the time of the Great Depression until the 1970s, very few books were written about golf courses. Bill Davis, founder of *Golf Digest*, then compiled *Great Golf Courses of the World* in 1974, which was the first modern attempt to identify and rank the top courses. Pat Ward-Thomas, Herbert Warren Wind and other prominent writers went into further detail in *The World Atlas of Golf* (1976). Finally the evolution of both the profession of golf course architect and of the golf course itself were chronicled in *The Golf Course* (1981) by Geoffrey S. Cornish and Ronald E. Whitten.

In recent years, beautifully illustrated coffeetable books on the subject have been the publishing rage. Any large bookstore is sure to have at least one of the many titles available.

CLASSIC BOOKS

The cream of the crop. Most of these books are valued in the hundreds of dollars.

Colt, Harry S. and Alison, C.H. *Some Essays on Golf Course Architecture*, 1920.

Darwin, Bernard. *The Golf Courses of the British Isles*, 1910 (also modern reprint).

Darwin, Bernard. *The Golf Courses of Great Britain*, 1926. Reprint of above.

Hunter, Robert. *The Links*, 1926.

Hutchinson, Horace. *British Golf Links*, 1897.

Hutchinson, Horace and others. *Famous Golf Links*, 1891.

Hutchinson, Horace. *Golf Greens And Greenkeeping: The Country Life Library of Sport*, 1906.

Mackenzie, Alister. *Golf Architecture*, 1920 (also modern reprints).

Miller, Rev. T.D. *Famous Scottish Links and other Golfing Papers*, 1911.

Pennink, Frank. *Homes of Sport: Golf*, 1952.

Sutton, Martin A.F. and others. *Golf Courses: Design, Construction and Upkeep*, 1933.

Sutton, Martin H.F. and others. *Book of the Links: A Symposium on Golf*, 1912.

Thomas, Jr., George C. *Golf Architecture in America*, 1927 (also modern reprint).

Wethered, H.N. and Simpson, T. *The Architectural Side of Golf*, 1929.

Wethered, H.N. and Simpson, T. *Design For Golf*, 1952. Reprint of above.

Wethered, Joyce and others. *The Game of Golf: The Lonsdale Library*, 1931.

COLLECTING TIP

■ **If you get the chance to play a famous old course, you will appreciate its timelessness by reading a classic description, before and after your round. You'll be astounded at how the accounts written by Bernard Darwin and Horace Hutchinson nearly a century ago still hold true. If you don't own any of the classic golf course books, check with a library or collector and have photocopies made of the appropriate passages.**

16-13 *Some of the hard-to-find golf architecture books are small enough to be considered pamphlets.* Golf Course Architecture *(top row, center) was written by Robert Trent Jones in 1936, long before he became the most recognizable name in his profession.*

NEWER BOOKS

Color photography and detailed research make these excellent references for a golf library.

Cornish, Geoffrey S. and Whitten, Ronald E. *The Golf Course*, 1981.

Davis, William H. and the Editors of *Golf Digest*. *Great Golf Courses of the World*, 1974.

Grant, Donald. *Donald Ross of Pinehurst and Royal Dornoch*, 1973. A pamphlet.

Hawtree, F.W. *The Golf Course: Planning, Design, Construction & Maintenance*, 1983.

Hawtree, Fred. *Colt & Co.: Golf Course Architects*, 1991.

Jones, Robert Trent. *Golf's Magnificent Challenge*, 1988.

Lyle, Sandy. *Sandy Lyle Takes You Around the Championship Golf Courses of Scotland*, 1982.

Peper, George. *The Golf Courses of the PGA Tour*, 1986.

Peper, George. *Grand Slam Golf*, 1991.

Strawn, John. *Driving the Green*, 1991.

Ward-Thomas, Pat and others. *The World Atlas of Golf*, 1976.

OLD PAMPHLETS & SMALL BOOKS

These are some of the rarest and most unique works on golf architecture.

Bauer, Aleck. *Hazards: The Essential Elements in a Golf Course . . .*, 1913.

Jones, Robert Trent. *Golf Course Architecture*, circa 1938.

Langford, William B. *Golf Course Architecture, The Chicago District*, 1915.

Sutton, Martin H.F. *Laying Out and Upkeep of Golf Courses and Putting Greens*, 1906.

Tillinghast, A.W. *Planning a Golf Course*, circa 1917.

Tull, A.H. *The Relation of the Design of the Golf Course To Low Maintenance Cost*, 1934.

CLUB HISTORIES

History books about individual golf and country clubs provide interesting accounts of the development of golf from the grass-roots level. Hundreds of books — varying from mimeographed pamphlets to full color productions — have been published to commemorate important anniversaries in clubs' histories. And with many clubs approaching their centenaries, the number of available histories will grow considerably.

Most accounts are personal in nature and may have little appeal to an outsider. The members and golf professionals of certain clubs, however, have been such major influences in the game's evolution that the accounts of their deeds are must reading for anyone interested in golf history. **The following list recognizes some exceptional club history books.**

GREAT BRITAIN

Aberdeen Golfers by Charles Smith, 1909.

Chronicles of the Blackheath Golfers by Charles Hughes, 1897.

Royal Blackheath by Ian T. Henderson and David I. Stirk, 1981.

History of the Edinburgh Burgess Golfing Society by the club, 1906 (reprinted circa 1984).

The Chronicle of the Royal Burgess Golfing Society of Edinburgh, 1735-1935 by J. Cameron Robbie, 1936 (reprinted 1983).

Reminiscences of the Old Bruntsfield Links Golf Club 1866-1874 by Thomas S. Atchison and George Lorimer, 1902.

The Glasgow Golf Club 1787-1907 by James Colville, 1907.

The Honourable Company of Edinburgh Golfers 1744-1944 by R.M. McLaren, 1944.

Muirfield and the Honourable Company by George Pottinger, 1972.

The Honourable Company of Edinburgh Golfers at Muirfield, 1891-1914 by Stair A. Gillon, 1946.

Five Open Champions and the Musselburgh Golf Story by George M. Colville, 1980.

Prestwick Golf Club by James E. Shaw, 1938.

Prestwick, Birthplace of the Open by David Cameron, 1989.

A History of the Royal and Ancient Golf Club, St. Andrews from 1754-1900 by H.S.C. Everard, 1907.

The Story of the R & A by J.B. Salmond, 1956.

The Royal and Ancient by Pat Ward-Thomas, 1980.

Royal Musselburgh Golf Club 1774-1974 by the club, 1974.

Royal North Devon Golf Club, A Centenary Anthology, 1864-1964 by J.W.D. Goodban, 1984.

The History of the Royal Perth Golfing Society by T.D. Miller, 1935.

Troon Golf Club, Its History from 1878 by Ian M. Mackintosh, 1974.

UNITED STATES

The Story of Augusta National Golf Club by Clifford Roberts, 1976.

Fifty Years of Mostly Fun: The History of Cherry Hills Country Club by Jim Norland, 1972.

Chicago Golf Club Diamond Jubilee, 1892-1967 by Charles Bartlett, 1967.

Chicago Golf Club 1892-1992 by Ross Goodner, 1992.

Congressional Country Club 1924-1984 by Anne Dolan Reilly, 1984.

Golf at Merion by Desmond Tolhurst, 1991.

75 Years at Oakland Hills by the Club, 1991.

Oakmont County Club: The First Seventy-Five Years by Edwin B. Foote, 1980.

Short History of Pine Valley by John Arthur Brown, 1963.

Pine Valley Golf Club, A Chronicle by Warner Shelly, 1982.

St. Andrew's [New York] Golf Club, 1888-1938 by H.B. Martin and A.B. Halliday, 1938.

St. Andrew's [New York] Golf Club, 1888-1963 by the Club, 1963 (includes the above book in its entirety).

St. Andrew's Golf Club, The Birthplace of American Golf by Desmond Tolhurst, 1989.

Some facts, Reflections . . . of the Shinnecock Hills Golf Club by Samuel Parrish, 1923.

16-14 *Detailed anecdotes and vintage photos make this history of America's best recognized golf club a pleasure to read. The commentaries on Bobby Jones and President Eisenhower are especially entertaining.*

The 75 Year History of the Shinnecock Hills Golf Club by Ross Goodner, 1966.

Winged Foot Story by Douglas Larue Smith, 1884.

CANADA

The Royal Montreal Golf Club 1873-1923 by the Club, 1923.

The Royal Montreal Golf Club 1873-1973 by Duncan C. Campbell, 1973.

Toronto Golf Club 1876-1976 by Jack Batten, 1976.

MAGAZINES

Old magazines don't get much respect. With thin paper covers and an abundance of advertisements, it's easy to see why they're frequently discarded, whereas a hardcover book has a good chance of finding a permanent home in a personal library. As a result, old magazines — especially bound volumes of continuous runs prior to World War II — are scarce.

Golf magazines got their start in 1890, when *Golf: A Weekly Record of "Ye Royal and Ancient" Game* was created to serve the interests of the increasing number of British golfers. It featured articles about famous golfers, competition results, openings of new courses, along with advertisements of the latest clubs, balls and accessories for the golfer.

Other magazines soon entered the marketplace, but most were short-lived. *Golf*, on the other hand, persevered. The format continued until 1899, when it became *Golf Illustrated*, a magazine which is still published. Another excellent periodical with the same name, *Golf Illustrated* (American), was published in New York from 1914 until 1935. Golfers in the United States were

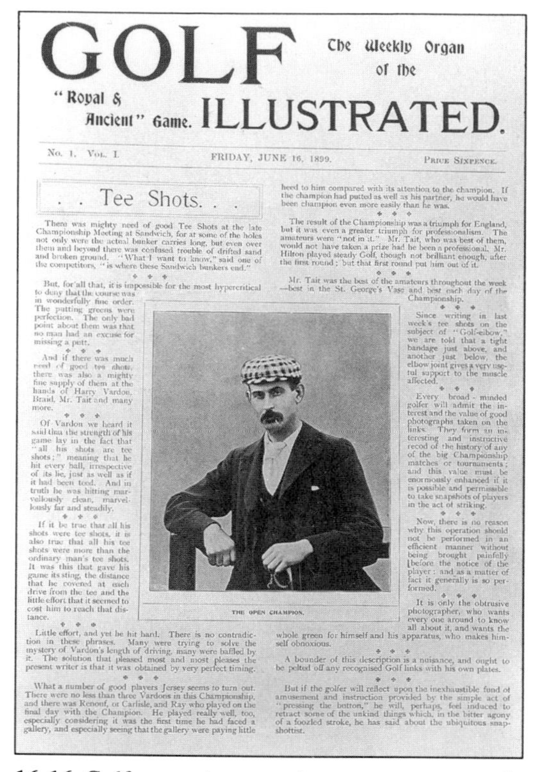

GOLF The Weekly Organ of the "Royal & Ancient" Game. ILLUSTRATED.

No. 1. Vol. I. FRIDAY, JUNE 16, 1899. Price Sixpence.

. . Tee Shots. . .

There was mighty need of good Tee Shots at the late Championship Meeting at Sandwich, for at some of the holes not only were the actual bunker carries long, but even over them and beyond there was confused trouble of drifted sand and broken ground. "What I want to know," said one of the competitors, "is where these Sandwich bunkers end."

But, for all that, it is impossible for the most hypercritical to deny that the course was in wonderfully fine order. The putting greens were perfection. The only bad point about them was that no man had an excuse for missing a putt.

And if there was much need of good tee shots, there was also a mighty fine supply of them at the hands of Harry Vardon, Braid, Mr. Tait and many more.

Of Vardon we heard it said that the strength of his game lay in the fact that "all his shots are tee shots;" meaning that he hit every ball, irrespective of its lie, just as well as if it had been teed. And in truth he was hitting marvellously clean, marvellously far and steadily.

If it be true that all his shots were tee shots, it is also true that all his tee shots were more than the ordinary man's tee shots. It was this that gave his game its sting, the distance that he covered at each drive from the tee and the little effort that it seemed to cost him to reach that distance.

Little effort, and yet he hit hard. There is no contradiction in these phrases. Many were trying to solve the mystery of Vardon's length of driving, many were baffled by it. The solution that pleased most and most pleases the present writer is that it was obtained by very perfect timing.

What a number of good players Jersey seems to turn out. There were no less than three Vardons in this Championship, and there was Renouf, of Carlisle, and Ray who played on the final day with the Champion. He played really well, too, especially considering it was the first time he had faced a gallery, and especially seeing that the gallery were paying little heed to him compared with its attention to the champion. If the champion had putted as well as his partner, he would have been champion even more easily than he was.

The result of the Championship was a triumph for England, but it was even a greater triumph for professionalism. The amateurs were "not in it." Mr. Tait, who was best of them, would not have taken a prize had he been a professional. Mr. Hilton played steady Golf, though not brilliant enough, after the first round; but that first round put him out of it.

Mr. Tait was the best of the amateurs throughout the week—best in the St. George's Vase and best each day of the Championship.

Since writing in last week's tee shots on the subject of "Golf-elbow," we are told that a tight bandage just above, and another just below, the elbow joint gives a very useful support to the muscle affected.

Every broad-minded golfer will admit the interest and the value of good photographs taken on the links. They form an interesting and instructive recod of the history of any of the big Championship matches or tournaments; and this value must be enormously enhanced if it is possible and permissible to take snapshots of players in the act of striking.

Now, there is no reason why this operation should not be performed in an efficient manner without being brought painfully before the notice of the player: and as a matter of fact it generally is so performed.

It is only the obtrusive photographer, who wants every one around to know all about it, and wants the whole green for himself and his apparatus, who makes himself obnoxious.

A bounder of this description is a nuisance, and ought to be pelted off any recognised Golf links with his own plates.

But if the golfer will reflect upon the inexhaustible fund of amusement and instruction provided by the simple act of "pressing the button," he will, perhaps, feel induced to retract some of the unkind things which, in the bitter agony of a foozled stroke, he has said about the ubiquitous snapshottist.

THE OPEN CHAMPION.

16-16 Golf *magazine was given a new name and format when this first issue of* Golf Illustrated *hit the newsstands in 1899.*

also fond of *The American Golfer*, edited first by noted amateur golfer Walter Travis and later by Grantland Rice, sports writer extraordinaire.

These old magazines contain a treasure trove of information waiting to be rediscovered. The ads alone provide insight into the game's evolution. The letters to the editors often are a continuing debate on golf club design or slow play. The feature articles provide a thrilling account of the exploits of golfing greats such as Harry Vardon, Walter Hagen, Gene Sarazen and Bobby Jones, as they were taking place.

Although most of the oldest magazines are permanent fixtures in libraries and private collections, they sometimes surface

NOTICE.

GOLF is published every Tuesday and Friday. Price Twopence. All editorial communications to be addressed to the Editor of GOLF, 80, Chancery Lane, W.C. Advertisements to Greenberg & Co., at the same address.

In order to make the Tuesday and Friday issues distinctive, and to accentuate the bi-weekly character of the paper, we have arranged to publish Tuesday's paper in a red, and Friday's in a green cover.

Note.—Tuesday, **Red;** Friday, **Green.**

16-15 *Golf was so popular in Great Britain in the 1890s that* Golf, *the foremost golf magazine tried publishing twice weekly for a period in 1894. After less than a year, they returned to a weekly format.*

at golf auctions. If bound volumes are out of your price range, consider loose issues. Past issues of modern magazines, such as *Golf Digest*, *Golf Monthly* and *GOLF*, are less expensive and much easier to find. The stories about Hogan, Palmer and Nicklaus from the 1950s and 1960s are a pleasure to read and will undoubtedly become treasures in the future.

The following golf magazines were the most popular when first published and continue to be most desirable:

The American Golfer, New York: 1908-1936.

Golf, New York: 1897-1917.

Golf, London: 1890-1899; continued as ***Golf Illustrated*** from 1899 to present.

Golf Digest, Evanston, Ill.; then Norwalk, Conn.; then Trumbull, Conn.: 1950 to present.

Golf Illustrated, London: 1899 to present. Formerly ***Golf***.

Golf Illustrated, New York: 1914-1935. Not to be confused with the current magazine with the same title.

Golf Journal, New York, then Far Hills, N.J.: 1948 to present.

Golf Magazine, New York: 1959 to present.

Golf Monthly, Glasgow: 1910 to present.

Golf World, London: 1962 to present.

Golf World, Pinehurst, N.C.: 1947 to present.

Golfdom, Chicago: 1927-1978.

The Golfer, New York: 1894-1903.

Golfers Magazine, Chicago: 1902-1931.

Golfing, London: 1898-1970.

GOLF.
A Weekly Record of "ye Royal and Auncient" Game.
"Far and Sure."
[Registered as a Newspaper.]

No. 26. Vol. 1. FRIDAY, MARCH 13TH, 1891. Price Twopence.

J. & G. STEWART'S
OLD VATTED SCOTCH WHISKIES
ARE THE BEST. FOUNDED 1779.
GOLD MEDAL, International Exhibition, Edinburgh, 1886.
Sole Address—111 and 113, HIGH STREET, EDINBURGH.
Telegrams—"Stewart, Edinburgh." Telephone No. 685.

If you want A GOOD CLUB get A GOOD GOLFER to make it.
PARK'S PATENT LOFTER,
PARK'S PATENT DRIVING CLEEKS,
A. M. ROSS'S PATENT PUTTING CLEEK.
PRICE 7s. 6D. EACH.
W. PARK, Jun., Ex-Champion Golfer (1887-8), MUSSELBURGH.

ALEX. PATRICK,
Golf Club and Ball Maker,
LEVEN, FIFESHIRE, and WIMBLEDON, SURREY.

P. PAXTON,
GOLF CLUB AND BALL MAKER, EASTBOURNE.

TOM MORRIS,
GOLF CLUB AND BALL MANUFACTURER, ST. ANDREWS.

BORTH HYDROPATHIC HOTEL,
BORTH, R.S.O., CARDIGANSHIRE.
MISS DILLY.
BEST GOLF LINKS SOUTH OF THE BORDER

R. FORGAN & SON,
Golf Club Makers to H.R.H. the Prince of Wales, St. Andrews, Fife.

D. McEWAN & SON,
GOLF CLUB & BALL MAKERS,

16-17 *This 1891 cover of* Golf *carried advertisements from almost every top clubmaker of the period: Park, Morris, Paxton, Morris, Forgan and McEwan.*

16-18 *Several American publications in the 1890s claimed to be "official." This ad appeared in a British magazine in 1899.*

Gene Sarazen's

Common Sense

GOLF TIPS

The book is practical, easy to follow, clear, concise and to the point. A pocket guide for the man who would correct his faults and better his game.
—*New York Sun*

THIS new book will help your game. Written by a player who ranks today as one of the greatest golfers of all time. A highly practical, easy to follow book on golf. It has been wisely devoted to correct and effective methods, and is somewhat unique in that it deals more with *how* to play than with how Sarazen plays.

Clear, concise and to the point, the reader feels that he can intelligently follow the tips; feels that he is receiving instructions from one of the world's most famous golfers; feels that he *can do it!*

Gene Sarazen has kept away from long drawn out theories and hair splitting arguments, and his book is just what it is named—*Common Sense Golf Tips*.

Here is indeed a pocket guide for the man who would correct his faults, better his game, and come in with a card that need not be buried.

Price $1.00

Sent postpaid upon receipt of a dollar bill

ADDRESS

GOLFERS MAGAZINE

48th and Grand Blvd. CHICAGO

16-19 *With two PGA Championships and a U.S. Open to his credit, 22-year-old Gene Sarazen was also hailed as an author. Although modern golf books by professional golfers are usually written in conjunction with a golf writer, this 1924 text was actually "ghost-written" for Sarazen by an unnamed writer.*

16-20 *Two of golf's finest writers — Bernard Darwin (left) and Grantland Rice (right) — observe play at a golf tournament.*

16-21 *If you insist on having top-grade specimens in your golf library, then try to obtain books with their original dust jackets. If the content of the book is your prime concern, then don't worry about the jacket; most old books are without them anyway.*

COLLECTING TIP

■ **If you appreciate well-written books and articles, keep your eyes open for anything written by the following authors:**

Henry Cotton
Peter Dobereiner
Bernard Darwin
H.S.C. Everard
Horace Hutchinson
Robert Tyre Jones, Jr.
Henry Longhurst
Charles Price
Pat Ward-Thomas
Herbert Warren Wind
Harry Vardon

CHAPTER 17

STAMPS & POSTAL ITEMS

Postal items with a golf theme — stamps, postcards, first-day covers and cachets — are convenient collectibles. Since they are small, an extensive collection requires little storage space and being relatively inexpensive, you don't need a second mortgage to finance your hobby. Even the "hunt" can be an entertaining adventure.

Postage stamps pertaining to golf are generally issued to promote tourism or to commemorate a special event. Temporary post offices often are set up at major golf events, such as the U.S. and British Opens, to serve the postal needs of spectators and to issue commemorative postmarks and cachets. This practice is also observed at other relevant occasions, such as the opening of the World Golf Hall of Fame. One unusual facility was the "Calamity Jane, Georgia" station, a small wooden structure erected at the 1976 U.S. Open in Atlanta as a tribute to Bobby Jones and his famous putter.

Although golf stamps are relatively new collectibles — the first ones were issued in the 1950s — golf postcards have been around for nearly a century. In addition to their golfing significance, they afford golfers an intriguing look at foreign cultures and world geography.

STAMPS

At last count, there were more than 100 different golf stamps, issued by almost 60 different postal authorities. . . and the number continues to grow.

Each time a stamp is released, additional specialty items also are offered, including souvenir sheets, gutter pairs, plate blocks and overprints. Such an extensive array of material makes it exhaustively difficult to obtain everything associated with each stamp. Therefore, it's best to specialize by acquiring only those things that appeal to you.

Stamp dealers and collectors in the United States regularly identify stamps with the reference numbers contained in the *Scott Standard Postage Stamp Catalogue*. Referred to simply as *Scott's*, this multi-volume catalog is updated annually and can be accessed at a public library or stamp shop. Some stamps, however, only can be found in the no-longer-published *Minkus* catalog. The British use a numbering system and catalog prepared by *Stanley Gibbons*.

The following list includes each known golf stamp with the issuing country, date of release, description, and *Scott's Catalog* number (shown in parentheses). If no *Scott's* number is available, thena Minkus number appears.

ALDERNEY
1983 Two of the first stamps issued by Alderney, showing course on map (Minkus AK1) and view of course (Minkus AK11).
1989 Survey map showing golf course location.

AUSTRALIA
1974 Golf swing (592).
1989 Man showing a boy how to putt (1112).

BAHAMAS
1968 Drawing of golfer and caddie (272).

BERMUDA
1971 A series featuring views of different golf courses: Ocean View (284), Port Royal (285), Castle Harbour (286), Belmont (287).

BHUTAN
1984 Donald Duck playing golf, issued for his 50th birthday (462).

BOPHUTHATSWANA
1980 Sun City Hotel Casino C.C. (64).
1980 Sun City Gary Player C.C. (65).

CAPE VERDE
1962 A square stamp printed off axis to give diamond effect (325).

CAYMAN ISLANDS
1987 View of green with golfers (574).

CHINA
1979 Olympic issue showing a golf club in the margin of souvenir sheet (1497).
1986 Ancient sports issue showing two old figures with some sort of club (2072).

17-1 *An assortment of recently issued golf stamps.*

CHRISTMAS ISLAND
1980 Commemorating 25 years of golf on the island: Ninth green (93) and Clubhouse (94).
1986 Santa Claus playing golf with reindeer in background (192).

COCOS (KEELING) ISLANDS
1987 Scene showing the 5th green. (161).

COLOMBIA
1980 Issued for the 1980 World Cup Golf Championship (C695).

COOK ISLANDS
1969 An attractive triangular shape stamp with gold border (263).
1985 Issued with soccer and tennis stamps for the 1985 South Pacific Mini Games (880).

DOMINICAN REPUBLIC
1974 Two sets of stamps commemorating the World Amateur Golf Championship (729-30, C222-3).

ECUADOR
1975 One of a series on sports showing ancient Indian figure swinging a club (922).

FRANCE
1962 Promoting golf, tourism and the resort of Le Touquet (1027).
1980 A stylish golfer swinging to honor the French Golf Federation (1714).

FRENCH POLYNESIA
1971 Issued for the South Pacific Games (C75).
1974 A bikini clad native golfer (275).
1974 View of the golf course (276).

FRENCH WEST AFRICA
1958 Commemorates 100th anniversary of Dakar with a sports theme (C27).

GAMBIA
1976 The Banjul Golf Course is shown in this series celebrating the independence of Gambia with a female golfer (332), a male golfer (333), and the president playing golf (334).

GREAT BRITAIN
1979 Aerogramme showing the R & A clubhouse, Bob Hope and Bing Crosby.

GREECE
1979 Part of a sports series commemorating the World Golf Championship, showing a golfer's follow-through (1325).

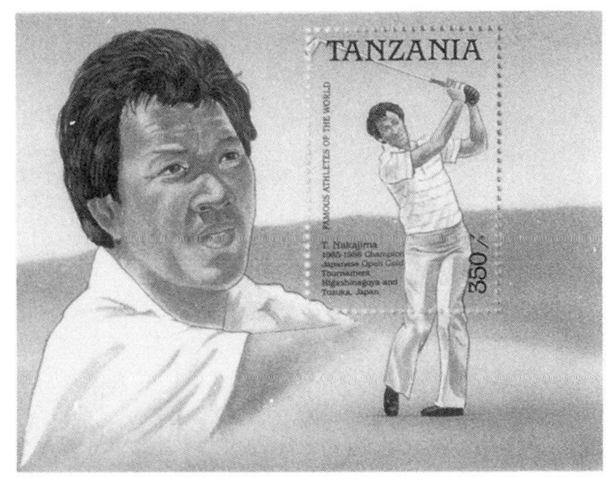

17-2 *Two recently issued souvenir sheets. Note the incorrect caption on the Tanzanian issue: the golfer shown is Isao Aoki, not Tommy Nakajima.*

GRENADA
1976 View of St. Georges Golf Course (704).
1979 Donald Duck playing golf, one of a series of Disney characters (954).

GUERNSEY
1985 Shows golf course at L'Ancresse with ancient stone tower near a green (302).

ISLE OF MAN
1990 Aerogramme only.

INDONESIA
1977 Golf is shown as one of 11 recreational emblems (1002).

IRELAND
1975 Photographic views issued for the 9th Annual European Amateur Team Championship showing "Chipping" (371) and "Putting" (372).

ITALY
1988 "Sport Il Golf " small golfer silhouetted on top of large ball (1741).

JAMAICA
1979 Golfer as part of a sports set (466).
1986 Tourism issue for Ameripex '86. One of four themes is "Holiday Resorts" and shows a small golf scene (626).

JAPAN
1953 Shows view of Mt. Unzen from the Sasebo Golf Course. This is the earliest stamp related to golf (592).

JERSEY
1978 A set of four stamps honoring Jersey native Harry Vardon and centenary of the Royal Jersey Golf Club: golf course plan (183), grip and swing (184), grip and putt (185) and accomplishments (186).
1989 Royal Jersey Golf Course. (480)
1990 Festival of Tourism showing various recreational activities including golf. Also aerogramme (537).

LUXEMBOURG
1980 Sports issue showing various sports equipment including a golf club and ball (643).

MALDIVES
1990 Souvenir sheet with Disney characters playing golf (1407).

MALI
1973 Officially cataloged as astronaut Alan Sheperd on the moon with a golf club. He is actually holding a soil sampler (C200).

MONTSERRAT
1967 Golfer and caddie, with the Queen's picture in the margin (192).
1970 View of the "5th tee" at Montserrat Golf Club (251).
1986 Green at Montserrat Golf Club (640).

MOROCCO
1974 International Golf Gran Prix commemorative with vignettes of a club, ball and swing (310).

NAURU
1984 Golfer addressing ball (288).

NEW CALEDONIA
1987 Closeup of golfer inset on view of course for VIII Pacific Games (568).
1988 Shows coat of arms of Dumbea that has a golf club and ball (C214).

NICARAGUA
1963 Part of a set commemorating the 1964 Olympics (C535).

NORFOLK ISLANDS
1974 U.P.U. Centenary with golfer on adhesive side (184a).
1975 Three sheets issued that have a golfer on adhesive side: 150th anniversary of settlement, Girl Scouts, and Boy Scouts.
1986 Queen Elizabeth celebrates her 60th birthday at the opening of the Norfolk Island Golf Club. Shows the Queen unveiling a plaque (387).

PHILIPPINES
1988 A series of four stamps for Philippine Olympic Week with one depicting a golfer lining up putt (1937).

RAS AL KHAIMA
1971 Alan Sheperd shown hitting the first golf ball on the moon. Only moon stamp to actually show the golf ball. (Minkus 539).

REDONDA
1989 Issued for Christmas. Shows Santa playing golf with Mickey and Minnie Mouse in MGA automobile.

SAMOA
1983 Issued for the 1983 South Pacific Games showing a golfer with a strange looking left-handed swing. (598)

ST. KITTS NEVIS ANGUILLA
1975 Commemorating the opening of Frigate Bay Golf Course in St. Kitts in a stop-action golf swing series of four stamps, each with a different denominations and colors (308-311).
1978 Royal St. Kitts Hotel and Golf Course (364). Same view reissued as Nevis overprint in 1980 and St. Kitts overprint in 1980.
1988 Frigate Bay Beach Hotel clubhouse
1988 Royal St. Kitts Casino and Jack Ter Village, with view including golf course.

17-3 The U.S. Postal Service has a policy that persons, other than U.S. presidents, must be dead for 10 years before their image can appear on a postage stamp. Three Americans have been honored thus far: Bobby Jones and Babe Zaharias in 1981 and Francis Ouimet in 1988.

ST. VINCENT

1975 Scene with golfers putting on Aquaduct Golf Course (431).

SCOTLAND

1989 Not a stamp, but a booklet of stamps with photo of Gleneagles Hotel Golf Course.

SHARJAH

1972 Golfer's follow-through (Minkus 755).

SINGAPORE

1981 Golfer shown in lower righthand corner of a grid of sports figures (375).

SOUTH AFRICA

1976 Drawing of Gary Player finishing his swing (459).

1979 A rose named in honor of Gary Player in a set of four stamps issued for the World Rose Convention (525).

SOUTH KOREA

1986 A souvenir sheet for the 10th Asian Games that shows a golfer in a border of 25 different athletes (1473).

SRI LANKA

1989 Two stamps celebrating centenary of Nuwara Eliya Golf Club (942-3).

SWITZERLAND

1986 Not really golf view but a Volkswagen "Golf" automobile (786).

TANZANIA

1989 Part of a Famous Athletes of the World series. Stamp shows Tommy Nakajima and souvenir sheet shows Isao Aoki, however the captions are reversed (495).

TONGA

1990 Economic development issue showing golf as one of serveral activities.

TUNISIA

1979 Abstract tourism issue with golfer, club, and ball (738).

UMM AL-QIWAIN

1968 What was once thought to be a golf club in a still-life painting is actually a smoking pipe. (Minkus 188).

UNITED STATES

1977 A postal envelope offered in four styles with a printed golf club stamp. (U583)

1981 Bobby Jones swinging (1933).

1981 Babe Zaharias with trophy (1932).

1988 Francis Ouimet portrait and swing (2377).

YUGOSLAVIA

1971 Shows an astronaut possibly playing golf on the moon (1050).

FIRST-DAY COVERS AND CACHETS

17-5 *Postmarked 1901, this stationery belonged to an early American ball and club maker. While not necessarily valuable, it is a rarity since envelopes are usually discarded.*

A first-day cover is an envelope that bears a special postmark indicating a postage stamp's first day of issue. Most first-day covers consist of special envelopes called cachets, which are decorated with designs that range from elaborate handmade drawings to simple rubber-stamped motifs.

Several of the desirable first-day covers feature well-known golfers. The Isle of Jersey in the English Channel commemorated the 100th anniversary of the Royal Jersey Golf Club in 1978 by honoring Harry Vardon, its most distinguished native golfer, with a series of four stamps and a special cover.

The memorable 1930 Grand Slam of Bobby Jones and his subsequent retirement from competition were recognized in 1980 with a set of five illustrated covers depicting his successes. These privately marketed cachets were postmarked in each city where the triumphs occurred, 50 years to the day after the victory.

When the 18¢ Jones commemorative stamp was issued by the U.S. Postal Service the following year in Pinehurst, North Carolina, the cachets were delivered there to receive the additional first-day cancellation. In order to produce these unique first-day covers, the cachet maker had to send the covers to post offices in St. Andrews, Liverpool Minneapolis, Atlanta, Pinehurst, and Ardmore, Pennsylvania in order to attain the appropriate cancellations.

If you think the Jones covers traveled a lot, consider the ones carried around the world by Arnold Palmer in 1976 while setting a speed record for a small corporate jet. These commemorative covers traveled 22,984.55 miles in just under 58 hours as part of an "Official United States Bicentennial Activity." They were produced by the Aviation Historical Foundation and show Palmer's plane and route, plus they were autographed by the golf hall-of-famer.

An ongoing series of commemorative covers with special cancellations have been

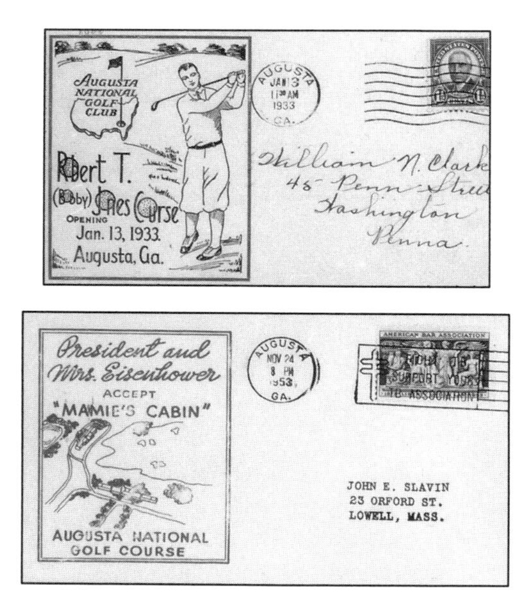

17-4 *Four different golf cachets were issued in Augusta, Georgia between 1933 and 1953. One of them (not shown above) illustrates President Dwight Eisenhower visiting the golf course and the other commemorates the 20th anniversary of air mail service (1938) from the "Winter Golf Capital of the World."*

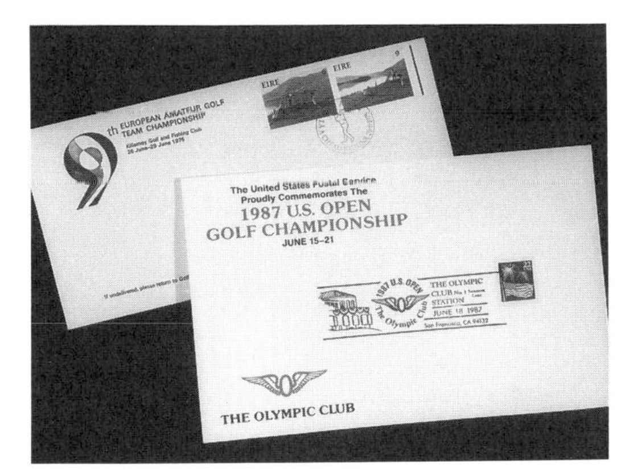

17-6 *Postal issues sometimes are produced in conjunction with a golf tournament. Ireland released two golf stamps during the 1975 European Amateur Team Championship, while the U.S. Postal Service recognized the 1987 U.S. Open with a special cancellation, shown here on a souvenir card.*

issued by the British Royal Mail at every British Open since 1968. Only those covers purchased and mailed during the championship enter the marketplace, so it's best to advise a friend in attendance to satisfy your collecting needs.

Although governments throughout the world print first-day and commemorative covers, those sold in the United States are printed by private parties, not the Postal Service. Therefore, when the Bobby Jones, Babe Zaharias and Francis Ouimet stamps were issued by the Postal Service, hundreds of different cachets were forwarded by dealers to the specific issuing post office to receive first-day cancellation.

17-7 *The inaugural issue of the popular cachets issued annually at the British Open.*

POSTCARDS

During the last 100 years, thousands of different golf postcards have been published that depict a variety of golf-related themes. Topics include: golf course views, famous golfers, cartoons, greeting cards and artwork.

The first postcards originated in Austria in 1869. They were an inexpensive and simple vehicle for relaying messages that quickly became popular in other countries. Eventually private publishers were permitted to print postcards that featured a preprinted message or illustration. Some were actual photographic prints, while others featured hand-colored illustrations. Postcards became the rage from the turn of the century until the beginning of World War I.

17-8 *A hand-tinted postcard, circa 1902, showing British Open champions Old Tom Morris, Harry Vardon, and Alexander "Sandy" Herd on the first tee of the Old Course at St. Andrews. The publisher neglected to list Morris' four Championship victories in 1861, 62, 64 and 67. After the card was issued, Vardon went on to win the event three more times.*

17-9 *Postcards illustrated by two popular artists at the beginning of the 20th century: Tom Browne (left) and Lance Thackeray (right).*

Throughout this period, hardly a home was without an album or collection of postcards. These albums were entertaining and educational. When the postman delivered a card, there usually was a commotion as the family gathered to view the picture on the front and to read the message from a friend or relative.

Famous illustrators from the United States and Great Britain provided much of the art for the illustrated golf postcards. Some of the better-known artists included: Tom Browne, F. Earl Christy, Charles Crombie, Harrison Fisher, Charles Dana Gibson, John Hassall, George Studdy, Lance Thackeray, Louis Wain and Lawson Wood.

There are postcards to please the taste of every golf collector. For just a few dollars, it is possible to obtain an old postcard featuring famous players, golf courses you have played or artwork you admire. (One of the authors of this book actually looks for picture postcards that show golf courses with sand greens — a nearly forgotten feature from the past.)

Buy cards because they are fun and you like them. Condition is a mater of personal taste. Some collectors only want cards in mint condition, while others prefer ones that have traveled through the mail. These often are the most interesting since they sometimes bear an amusing message and can be dated by their postmark.

COLLECTING TIPS

■ **To learn more about golf postal issues, consider joining the International Philatelic Golf Society (P.O. Box 2183, Norfolk, Virginia 23501). Their newsletter, *Tee Time*, deals with new releases, postal stationery, postmarks and other matters related to the hobby.**

■ **Instead of just storing postal collectibles in a binder, have a group of stamps, covers, or postcards put into a picture frame. It's an inexpensive way to decorate with a golf theme.**

CHAPTER 18

CIGARETTE CARDS

Americans claim that cigarette cards with a golf theme are the British version of baseball cards. The British, however, maintain that American baseball cards are a type of cigarette card.

Actually, neither side is totally correct . . . or incorrect. Cigarette cards got their start in the United States in the 1870s when tobacco companies realized that the paper boards used to stiffen the soft pack of cigarettes also could be used for advertising. The British followed suit in the mid-1880s. The small illustrated cards commonly feature royalty, actors, sports, transportation, travel and other popular topics along with an advertisement for the particular brand of cigarette. As for the baseball versus golf controversy, baseball cards were issued in the United States in 1887, about a decade before golf cigarette cards appeared in Liverpool, England. The baseball issues were primarily produced by the tobacco industry until the 1930s, when candy and chewing gum companies became the dominant distributors.

Because cigarette cards have not been commercially exploited to the extent of other sports cards, they have retained their charm and distinctiveness. Only about three dozen golf series — each containing 12 to 127 cards — have been produced.

Most of the golf cards were issued from 1923 to 1939, but an increased popularity in the hobby — known as cartophily — has resulted in the reprinting of six different series during the past decade. Several attractive new series also have been introduced in recent years.

Golf Cigarette Card Sets

COMPANY	SET QTY.	SIZE/ COLOR	DATE	DESCRIPTION
ARDATH	50	A/C	c1935	Cricket, Tennis & Golf Celebrities
FELIX BERLYN	25	A/C	c1902	Humorous Golfing Series (Also reprinted in 1989)
BIRCHGREY	25	B/C	1989	Panasonic European Open
BRINDLEY	25	B/C	1987	Old Golfing Greats
W.A. & C.A. CHURCHMAN	50	A/U	1927	Famous Golfers
	12	B/U	1927	Famous Golfers – 1st edition
	12	B/U	1928	Famous Golfers – 2nd edition
	50	A/C	1931	Prominent Golfers (Also reprinted in 1989)
	12	B/C	1931	Prominent Golfers (Also reprinted in 1989)
	36	A/C	1934	Three Jovial Golfers in Search of the Perfect Golf Course (English issue)
	72	A/C	1934	Three Jovial Golfers in Search of the Perfect Golf Course (Irish issue)
	55	A/C	1934	Can You Beat Bogey at St. Andrews?– 1st edition
	58	A/C	1934	Can You Beat Bogey at St. Andrews?– 2nd edition
WM. CLARKE & SON	12	D2/C	1902	Golf Terms (part of a set of 50 sporting cards)

SIZE/COLOR KEY
A = 36mm x 68mm
B = 62mm x 80mm
D = 37mm x 62mm
1 = slightly larger
2 = slightly smaller
C = color
P = photograph
B = black & white
U = monochrome

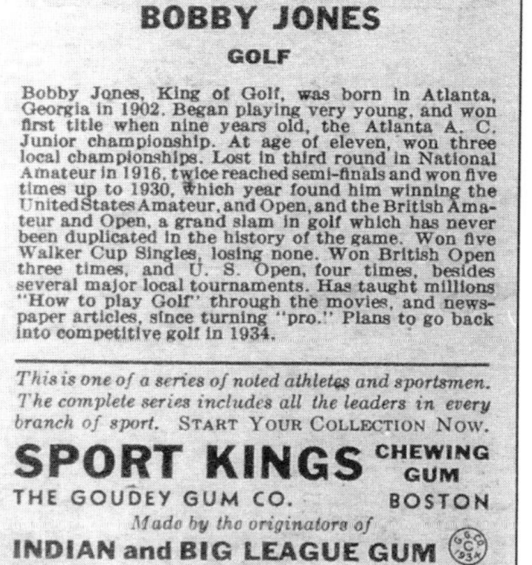

18-1 Chewing gum card from a series of sports greats. Issued in 1937 by the Boston-based Goudey Gum Company, known primarily for their baseball cards.

COPE BROS. & CO. LTD.	50	A/C	c1897	Cope's Golfers (Also reprinted in 1983)
	50	A2/C	c1897	Cope's Golfers (cut narrow)
	32	B/B	1923	Golf Strokes
JOHN COTTON LTD.	50	A/U	1936	Golf Strokes: a & b
	50	A/U	1937	Golf Strokes: c & d
	50	A/U	1938	Golf Strokes: e & f
	50	A/U	1939	Golf Strokes: g & h
	50	A/U	1939	Golf Strokes: i & j
W. & F. FAULKNER	12	A/C	c1901	Golf Terms

18-2 *Troon (now Royal Troon) clubhouse featured on a 1924 "Golfing" card by Wills.*

18-3 *Freddie Tait, noted amateur champion, and Old Tom Morris are part of an 18-card photographic series published by Ogden's in the late 19th century.*

COLLECTING TIPS

■ **Cigarette cards can be obtained from golf memorabilia dealers and at stamp shows. The premier source for cards and publications about them, however, is The London Cigarette Card Company (Sutton Road, Somerton, Somerset TA11 6QP, England).**

■ **Several dozen card sets comprised of famous celebrities or sports figures contain golf subjects. These single cards are becoming difficult to obtain since dealers generally will not break up a set to sell one card.**

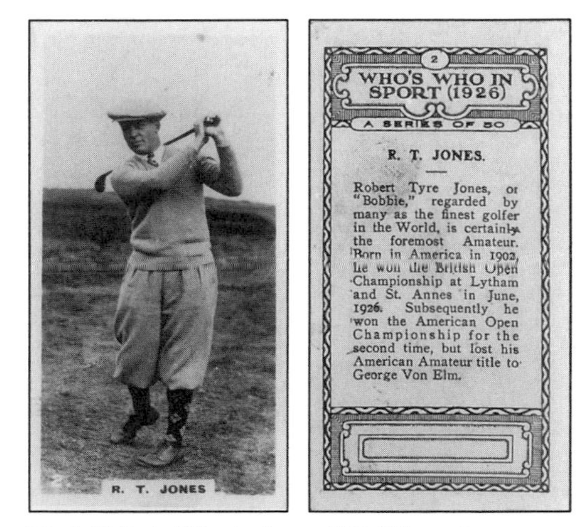

18-4 *"Who's Who in Sport (1926)" card referring to Bobby Jones as "Bobbie."*

IMPERIAL PUBLISHING	25	B/C	1990	American Golfers
IMPERIAL TOBACCO CO.	50	A/B	1925	How to Play Golf
	127	A/C	1926	Smokers Golf Cards
MARSUMA LTD.	50	A/B	1914	Famous Golfers and Their Strokes
MECCA CIGARETTES	6	60x75/C	1930	Champion Golfers (Published in New York)
J. MILHOFF & CO. LTD.	27	A/P	1928	Famous Golfers
B. MORRIS & SONS LTD.	25	D/U	1923	Golf Strokes Series
OGDEN'S LIMITED	18	D2/P	c1897	"Guinea Gold" Series - Golfers
	15	D/P	c1897	"Tabs" Series - The Golfers are a Subset of a 420 card series.
JOHN PLAYER & SONS	25	B/C	1936	Championship Golf Courses
	25	B/C	1939	Golf (Also reprinted in 1986)
	25	B/C	1939	Golf (Same as above but without Imperial Tobacco notation)
W.D. & H.O. WILLS	25	B/C	1924	Golfing
	25	B/C	1930	Famous Golfers (Also reprinted in 1987)

18-6 Two of the non-golf issues containing golf cards are "The Nose Game" by Carreras (left) and the second "Did You Know" series by Wills (below).

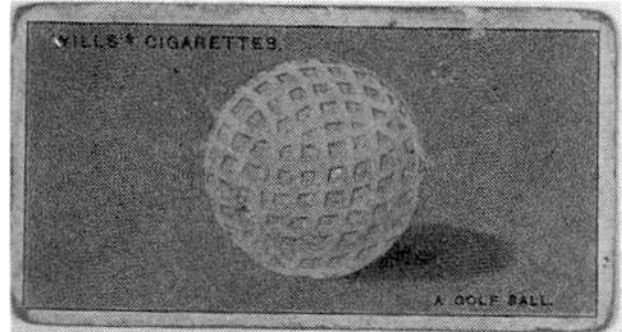

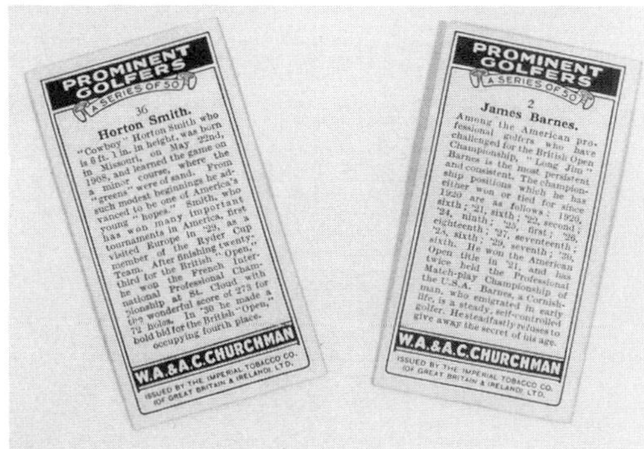

***18-5** Caricatures of fifty golfers are portrayed in Churchmen's "Prominent Golfers" series. The original set, done in 1931, was reproduced in 1989.*

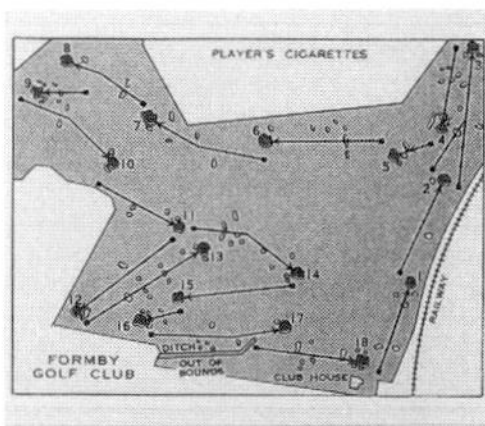

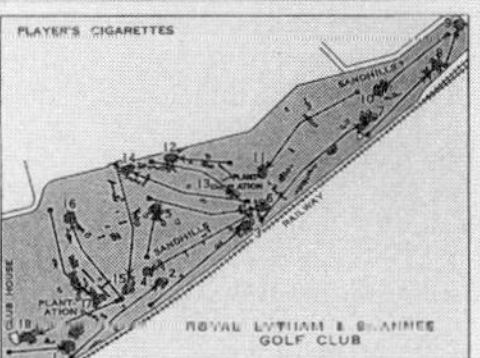

***18-7** Published in 1936 by Player's, the "Championship Golf Course" series shows layouts that are still popular today.*

CHAPTER 19

AUTOGRAPHS

Just as no two signatures are identical, no two autograph collectors are alike. Some collectors may have a few autographs obtained in person from touring golf professionals. Well-known players are easy to approach during a tournament at practice areas and around the clubhouse, and it's easy to solicit a quick signature. Unlike many athletes, golfers do not charge a signing fee.

Other collectors practice hero worship by seeking autographs of prominent figures from the past, such as Tom Morris. But since most of these golfers are no longer alive, their signatures are not free for the asking. Instead, they are usually procured through a golf memorabilia dealer or autograph specialist. Because of their scarcity, these signatures usually cannot be purchased "off the shelf." You may have to express your "wants" and be patient — sometimes for as long as several years. Prices vary from a few dollars for the autograph of an insignificant player from the 1930s to several thousand dollars for the signature of a 19th-century luminary.

Prized signatures can be found on documents, letters, receipts, golf balls, books, photographs, pairing sheets, ticket stubs, scorecards — virtually any article that will accept ink. Arnold Palmer — probably the game's most prolific signer — handles the multitude of requests by carrying his own special marking pens that will write on anything. His staff estimates that he signs an incredible 25,000 autographs a year.

WHAT NAMES TO COLLECT

Most collectible golf autographs belong to famous players. A good starting point are the four dozen golfers who have been inducted into the PGA/World Golf Hall of Fame. Other "shopping lists" include winners of the U.S. and British Opens, the PGA Championship and The Masters Tournament. If you are a fan of the senior's, women's or other tours, seek out winners of their respective major championships. Lists of these players can be found in golf reference books or in the annual compilation of tournament results and records published by several major golf magazines.

There also are a number of other individuals whose signatures are desirable because of their significant contributions to the game. This group includes golf course architects (Donald Ross, Robert Trent Jones), writers (Bernard Darwin, Henry Longhurst), artists (Thomas Hodge, A.B. Frost) and administrators (Joe Dey, Deane Beman). Signatures of golf writers often are found inscribed in books and artists' signatures usually appear on their paintings or prints.

If funds allow, collect examples of deceased or older individuals. As the autograph hobby expands, these autographs are becoming increasingly scarce and expensive. A comprehensive autograph collection should feature the infamous British triumvirate of Harry Vardon, James Braid and J.H. Taylor, as well as Americans Francis Ouimet, Walter Hagen, Bobby Jones and "Babe" Zaharias. Older players who no longer compete on a regular basis include: Gene Sarazen, Ben Hogan, Byron Nelson and Sam Snead.

Since signatures from the 19th century or earlier are so difficult to locate, collectors shouldn't be too particular about their condition. It's wise to buy any piece you can afford and then upgrade if a better one becomes available. The most sought after of the early autographs is the legendary "Old Tom" Morris (1821-1908). Having spent more than 60 years in the golf business, he was the first golfer to regularly sign autographs. While his signature most often appears on photogravures and postcards, it also has been found on scorecards, personal letters, and even a bank draft.

Although signatures of current professionals, such as Curtis Strange and Nick Faldo, as well as seniors Lee Trevino, and Gary Player, are relatively easy to obtain, don't procrastinate. It's better to solicit a free autograph at a tournament now than pay a dealer for the same one in a few years. And don't forget the rookies and top amateurs; they may become superstars.

19-1 *The most desirable golf autograph belongs to Bobby Jones. These four signatures were made at various times throughout his life. Even though afflicted with a muscular disorder in the 1950s, he continued to sign for his appreciative fans.*

19-2 *The first golfer to be actively solicited for autographs was Scotsman Old Tom Morris (1821-1908). This signature is from the 1890s.*

Types Of Autographs

Although nearly any object can be autographed, common sense can make the difference between an exceptional autograph and a poor one. A pencil-signed dinner menu or an autographed, sweat-stained hat are far less desirable than a handwritten letter or an inscribed action photo.

The following terms and abbreviations are used within the autograph hobby:

Signed Photographs (SP) are the most popular type of golf autograph because they are easily displayed when matted and framed. Press and publicity photos are the most common forms, especially ones 8" x 10" or larger. The best signed photographs are ones with the signature placed in an uncluttered, light colored area so that it can be read easily. A permanent marker, such as the Extra Fine Point Sharpie, is the best pen to use since it will not smear or tear the picture. When an inscription precedes the signature, the photo becomes a **Signed Document Inscribed (SDI)**.

An **Autograph Letter Signed (ALS)** is a letter entirely handwritten by the signer. The content of the letter greatly affects its value. A letter from Tom Morris to Allan Robertson about ballmaking, for instance, would be much more valuable than an **Autograph Note Signed (ANS)** from Morris confirming receipt of a package.

A **Typed Letter Signed (TLS)** is the modern version of the ALS. Content and letterhead are important in determining the value of the piece. Be aware that signatures on these letters may not always be authentic. Many active golfers receive a tremendous amount of correspondence and spend most of their time on the road, so their correspondence is sometimes signed on their behalf by a secretary or "signer" who often is capable of producing a convincing imitation of the person's signature.

A plain **Signature (SIG)** on a standard 3" x 5" card, album page or cutout from a document is the most common form of autograph. A clean cut has nice square corners with no extraneous writing, whereas an irregular cut is from a letter or other document and has uneven edges.

19-3 Gene Sarazen, the first golfer to win all four majors, has been signing autographs for more than 70 years — longer than any other golf celebrity. He typically includes a date after his name.

19-4 *First-day covers often are appropriate for autographs. Tom Watson signed this U.S. postal envelope issued at the 1977 Masters. Gary Player's autograph appears on a cachet featuring the postage stamp with a rose named in his honor.*

COLLECTING TIP

■ **Autographs require special care or are likely to discolor or deteriorate with time. See page 21 for details on the care and preservation of paper goods.**

AUTHENTICITY

Authenticity is the name of the game when it comes to autographs and, unfortunately, forgeries exist. Luckily for the golf collector, the automatic signing machine — routinely utilized by politicians — is not a factor . . . yet. These devices, known as Autopens, enable an ordinary pen to perfectly reproduce a person's signature time after time. And that's their giveaway. All the signatures are identical — a human impossibility. An Autopen signature is not really a forgery, though. It's just not authentic and therefore has little, if any, value.

Deliberate forgeries, however, are a collector's nightmare. Forged pieces often are produced by disreputable dealers or others looking for a quick profit. Some are quite realistic and only can be detected by a handwriting expert. Secretarial signatures also fall into the forgery classification, although some are so unconvincing that an untrained eye can detect their phoniness.

Advances in desktop publishing recently have made it possible for a personal computer to scan a signature and reproduce it via a laser printer. Laser signatures can be detected by their intense black color and lack of impression in the paper. However, if the item is behind glass in a picture frame, it can look real.

What's the best way to guarantee authenticity? First and foremost, only deal with reputable sources. (A written guarantee is not necessarily adequate protection, especially when legal expenses for recovery might exceed the amount of the purchase.) It also is essential that you study other examples, either actual signatures or ones reproduced in collecting guides or dealer catalogs. Often a fellow collector can help by providing a photocopy of a signature known to be genuine.

GOLF: MY LIFE'S WORK

To my friend
"Alf" Durnford
With gratitude and affection
From the
Author
J H Taylor
Open Champion Golfer
1894. 1895. 1900. 1909. 1913
French Champion
1908. 1909
German Champion
1912

19-6 *This inscription appears in a copy of* Golf: My Life's Work, *J.H. Taylor's autobiography written in 1943. The statement of his championship victories adds a desirable personal touch.*

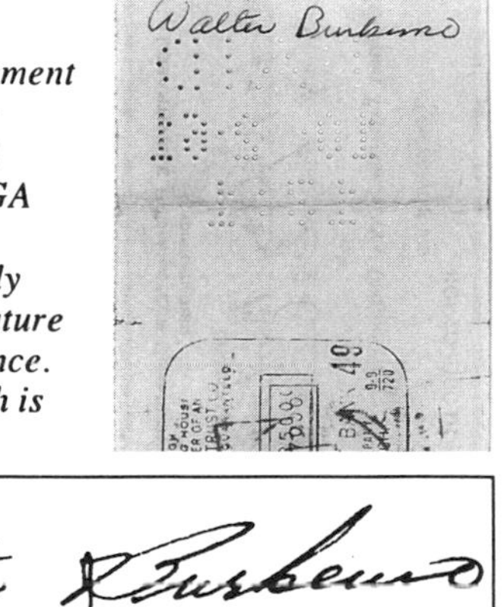

19-5 *The endorsement of this tournament prize check (right) written to 1953 PGA Champion Walter Burkemo is actually a secretarial signature signed in his absence. His real autograph is shown below.*

HOW TO OBTAIN AUTOGRAPHS

IN-PERSON

Attending a golf tournament or other appearance by a golf celebrity is the best approach. The autograph is free, the memory is everlasting and the authenticity is unquestionable. If possible, bring an autograph album, photograph, scrapbook, magazine cover, program or other suitable item. Although it might be inconvenient, the effort will be well worth the trouble, especially if you can get a personalized inscription. And don't forget your manners; as long as golf fans perpetuate their reputation for being polite, players will continue to oblige the incessant requests for autographs. (A policy initiated at the 1991 Masters Tournament specifically limits autograph seeking to the parking lot and practice tee portion of the property. Time will tell if restrictions at other events will be imposed.)

GOLF MEMORABILIA & AUTOGRAPH DEALERS

In addition to the golf memorabilia dealers listed in Appendix A (see page 243), there are dozens of full-time autograph dealers throughout the world. A reputable

19-7 *This Nicklaus autograph dates from the early 1960s, when he signed at a pace slow enough to form each letter.*

BEN HOGAN

July 19, 1949

Bert Heizmann
Reading, Pennsylvania

Dear Bert:

The very kind message received from you just after my accident was truly appreciated. I must ask you to forgive my failure to acknowledge it sooner, but until recently I haven't felt equal to the job of getting at my mail, and I hope you will understand.

Again thanking you, and with all good wishes, I am

Sincerely,

Ben Hogan

BEN HOGAN

s

19-8 *This TLS (Typed Letter Signed) from Ben Hogan to noted golf collector Bert Heizmann is significant. It was written just after Hogan's near fatal auto accident, when it was doubtful whether he would ever play golf again. Not only did he recover, but went on to add three U. S. Opens, one British Open and two Masters titles to the three majors he won before the accident. Hogan autographs have been difficult to obtain in recent years.*

19-9 *Best known for winning 11 tournaments in succession in 1945, Byron Nelson's signature is a must for a golf autograph collection.*

dealer always offers a money-back guarantee on authenticity. To locate these specialists, consult the journals and guidcs described below in the collecting tip. Most dealers their inventory through a descriptive catalog and do business through the mail and over the phone. You have to act quickly when a new catalog comes out because the desirable autographs sell quickly. Most dealers allow a few days to examine a purchase, so don't be concerned about obligating yourself based on a catalog description.

OTHER DEALERS

Autographs also may be purchased from autograph galleries and sports memorabilia dealers. It is important to exercise caution when doing business with someone other than an established specialist. Although these sources are generally legitimate, some have been known to offer items of questionable origin and may have tremendous profit margins built into the prices of picture frames and accompanying artifacts.

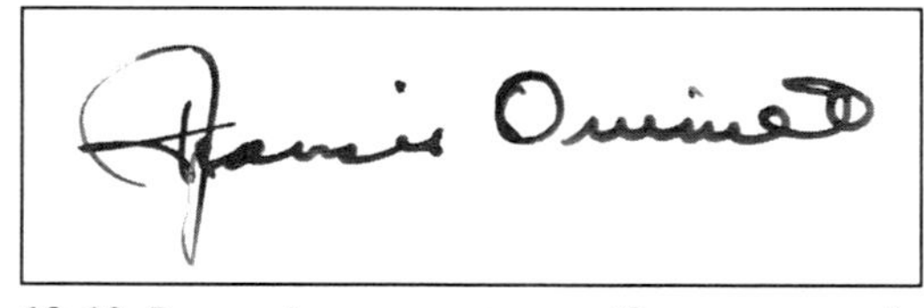

19-10 *Possessing an amateur golf career second only to Bobby Jones, Francis Ouimet first made headlines at the age of 20, when he won the 1913 U.S. Open. This signature dates is from the 1940s.*

19-11 *Tony Lema is perhaps one of the most difficult post-war British Open autographs to secure. Winner of the 1964 championship by five strokes at St. Andrews, he was killed two years later in an airplane crash.*

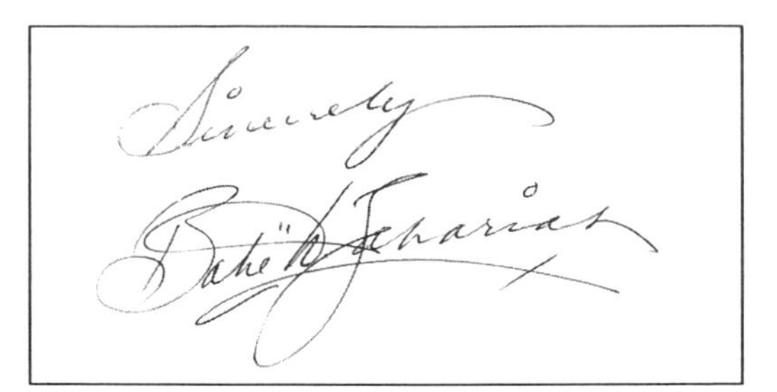

19-12 *Because Mildred "Babe" Didrikson Zaharias is the most sought after female golf autograph, it is prized by general autograph collectors and sports collectors.*

WRITING

It is possible to obtain an autograph by sending a brief request to a golfer in care of his or her agent, equipment manufacturer or upcoming tournament site. This method sometimes results in a phony autograph executed by a secretary or "designated signer," so avoid mailing a prized possession that could be ruined by a forgery. Make sure that the packaging for your photo or other memento is suitable for a round trip, and don't forget to include a shipping label and sufficient postage.

COLLECTING TIPS

- **Two excellent references on autographs are *Collector's Guide to Autographs* and *The Price Guide to Autographs,* both by George Sanders, Helen Sanders and Ralph Roberts.**
- **For up-to-date information on collecting trends and buy-sell advertisements, consult *The Pen and Quill,* published by the Universal Autograph Collectors Club (P.O. Box 6181, Washington, D.C. 20044) or *Autograph Collector's Magazine* (P.O. Box 55328, Stockton, California 95205).**

CHAPTER 20

EPHEMERA

Ephemera — *Webster's Dictionary* defines it as "items designed to be useful or important for only a short time." Simply stated, ephemera consists of items destined for the landfill. But tell that to a collector, and he'll tell you that "one man's trash is another's treasure."

The intrigue of collecting ephemera is the uncertainty of what you may discover. Golf ephemera usually is in the form of printed matter, ranging from scorecards, tournament programs and memorabilia to advertising and product packaging. Most articles of sentimental value or special significance are unearthed purely by coincidence from a pile of papers or a dealer's cluttered shelf.

Because golf has enjoyed such a great following for the last century, advertisers have found golf themes to be an effective means of portraying products unrelated to the game. Golf scenes and motifs have been used to promote candy, automobiles, clothing, canned food, razor blades, soap and other commodities.

The following pages provide a sampling of a wide variety of golf ephemera. Several categories — autographs, postcards and cigarette cards — are such popular golf collectibles that they warrant discussion in separate chapters, found elsewhere in this book. After reviewing these pages, it will become evident that virtually every old printed item related to golf has an interesting story behind it. The challenge for the collector is to find out what that story may be.

ADVERTISING

20-1 *Although attractive golf calendars currently are in vogue, the concept is far from novel. The 1931 Pinehurst Country Club calendar (above) is especially desirable. Not only does it depict the popular Carolina resort, it also shows the club's famous golf course architect, Donald Ross, teeing off. The British* Golf Illustrated *calendar (below) from 1949 shows the 17th and 18th holes at the Old Course, St. Andrews.*

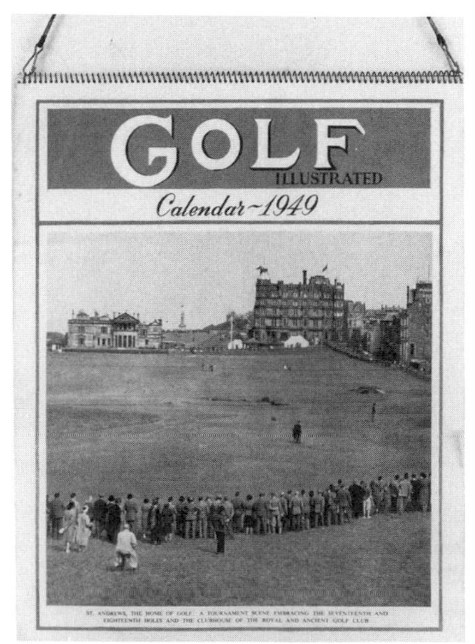

20-2 *Movie theaters displayed posters and lobby cards which were supplied by the filmmakers. This counter-top lobby card was part of a set of eight issued in 1953 to promote* The Caddy. *Shown, from left to right, are Dean Martin, Jimmy Thomson, Ben Hogan, Jerry Lewis, Byron Nelson, Sam Snead and Julius Boros. Other significant golf movies include* Follow The Sun, *the 1953 epic about the comeback of Ben Hogan, and the* Caddy Shack *comedies of the 1980s.*

20-3 *Tom Thumb miniature golf courses opened across America in the 1920s and '30s. This porcelain sign measures 43 inches in diameter.*

20-4 *Hinds skin cream advertisement printed on a sticker similar to a postage stamp.*

20-5 *Since ads clipped from magazines can be bought for only a few dollars, you shouldn't feel bad about cutting out a desirable portion and having it framed. This 1950s' scene of the Campbell Soup kid was a minor feature of a full-page ad, but to display the entire ad is not nearly as effective as showing just the part pertaining to golf.*

20-6 *If you ever come across a case of old printing type at a flea market or antiques shop, take a few minutes to rummage through it. You might come across an old copper printing block with a golf scene. This 2-inch-high block shows a golfer and a tee box, probably from the 1920s.*

20-7 *Golf themes in product advertising have been popular over the years. This colorful turn-of-the-century bookmark promoted Libby's food products.*

20-8 *Matchbooks can be found imprinted with a golf product advertisement or club name (above). The monogrammed matches (below) were made for President Dwight D. Eisenhower.*

20-9 *As far back as the early 1900s, car companies included golf themes in their advertising. Although Cadillac currently is a major sponsor of professional golf — with Arnold Palmer and Lee Trevino as spokesmen — the company once relied on an artist's brush to take their 1928 LaSalle to St. Andrews.*

PRODUCT PACKAGING

20-10 *Handkerchief packaging using a golf theme.*

20-11 *Lowney's packed their chocolates in decorated boxes at the turn of the century.*

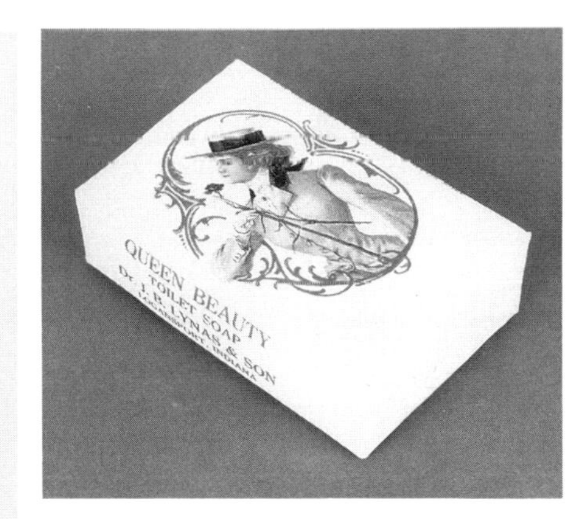

20-12 *Golf items showed up in all rooms of the house, including the bathroom. The soap carton (left) was fashioned after a package of golf balls.*

COLLECTING TIP

■ What can be done with golf ephemera? Some pieces are suitable for framing, others can be displayed on a shelf and large quantities are best stored in binders. Or you can modify the filing system developed by Bert Heizmann, who collected for more than half a century. He stored mementos and other ephemera between the pages of related golf books. For instance, when Heizmann traveled to Troon, Scotland, for the British Open, he would file tickets, pairing sheets and newspaper clippings inside his copy of the Troon club history. Because the acid content of most paper ephemera can destroy the pages of a book, this method is not encouraged. But if modified, its not such a bad idea.

20-13 *Fifty-year-old containers with golf decorations may not be valuable, but they are scarce because most people would not think of keeping an empty tomato or paprika can.*

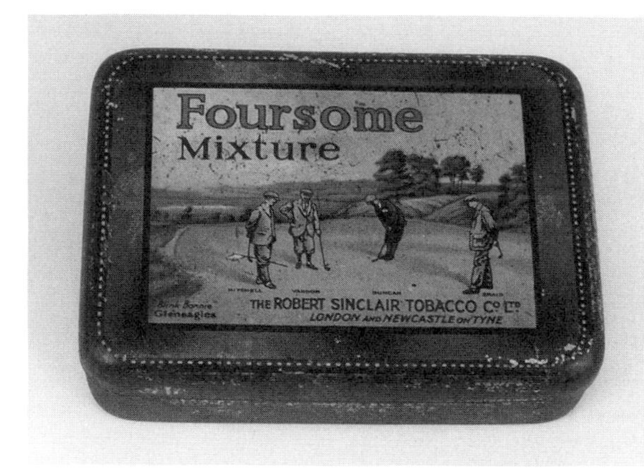

20-14 *Early 20th-century tobacco (above) and cigar containers (right) are prized by collectors of vintage advertising tins.*

Golf Memorabilia

20-15 *Byron Nelson's golf play in 1945 was inconceivable. He won 11 tournaments in a row, 18 for the year and scored under 70 for 19 consecutive rounds. This admission ticket (above) was from an exhibition match played prior to the fifth victory of his amazing streak. Nelson returned to his former home course in Pennsylvania to team with noted amateur Dot Germain in a match against local pro Henry Williams and hall-of-famer Patty Berg, who was stationed nearby in the U.S. Marine Corps Reserve.*

Non-Transferable 1931 No. 130
SEASON TICKET
AVON FIELD GOLF COURSE
Cincinnati, Ohio
This School Ticket
permit entitles Morton Olman
to the privileges of AVON FIELD GOLF COURSE for the season of 1931. Any violation of the rules of the COURSE, or the USE of this card by ANY OTHER than the ONE to whom it was issued will result in the revoking of the permit and the cancelling of this card.
Signed W. R. Reeves
Director of Recreation.
Fees Paid $ 5

20-16 *This season ticket entitled one of the authors of this book to play unlimited golf in 1931. The annual fee for high school students was $5.*

George Anderson Esq. Aberdeen 18
To Ludovic G. Sandison
Turner, Fishing Rod & Golf Club Maker.
King Street
1875
July 8 4 Balls
20 Play Club
Sept 21 Splicing Shaft
Dec 2 1875 —
Paid

20-17 *Ludovic Sandison (1825-1884) was club-maker to the Aberdeen Golf Club in Scotland. This bill of sale, dated 1873, also indicates his ability to make fishing rods.*

20-18 *Tournament tickets make excellent mementos, such as a 1941 Masters ticket signed by Ben Hogan (far left) or a 1935 U.S. Open tag (left). The winners of those particular events: Craig Wood won the Masters and Sam Parks won the Open.*

August 1864

To the Committee
of the Prestwick
Golf Club
as I leave Prestwick
in November to go
to St Andrews to tak
charge of the Links there
I bege to thank the
Members of the Club
for ther kindness to
me for the last 13 years
that I have had the
Pleasure of serveing
them and I will

be happy to serve
them at any time
I ame Gentleman
your
Humble Servant
Thomas Morris

20-19 *Handwritten personal notes often are discarded after a short period. Fortunately, this note of historical importance never made it to the wastebasket. It was written in 1864 by Old Tom Morris to inform the Prestwick Golf Club that he was ending his 13-year relationship with the club as course designer, greenkeeper and professional to return to his native home of St. Andrews. Morris won all four of his British Open Championships at Prestwick during the 1860s.*

20-20 *Golf course yardage books generally are regarded as a modern convenience. However this booklet contains hole-by-hole drawings of the Pasadena (California) Municipal Golf Course and is dated 1947. Located next to the Rose Bowl Stadium, the course — now known as Brookside Golf Course — is closed during major college football games.*

20-21 *Famous golfers and golf illustrations have graced the covers of virtually every major magazine. The covers are excellent for framing and the text provides amusing reading. When* Life *magazine ran this cover story in 1955, Ben Hogan already had won all of his major championships (and just had lost a U.S. Open playoff to Jack Fleck). In the article, he revealed his secret method to eliminate a hook: a weak grip and an open clubface at the top of the backswing.*

20-23 *Sam Snead fishes with baseball great Ted Williams on this 1959 Fleer bubble gum card, which was part of a set of 80 cards that illustrated Williams' career. Fleer, famous for their Dubble Bubble chewing gum, had stayed away from baseball card promotions until signing Williams to an exclusive contract that resulted in this well-known issue.*

SHELL'S WONDERFUL WORLD OF GOLF

MATCH SCHEDULE

PLAYERS	LOCATION	BROADCAST DATE
Gene Littler Eric Brown	Gleneagles (Scotland)	Jan. 20
Dow Finsterwald Peter Alliss	Tryall (Jamaica, B. W. I.)	Jan. 27
Dave Ragan Celestino Tugot	Wack-Wack (Philippines)	Feb. 3
Art Wall Stan Leonard	Royal Quebec (Canada)	Feb. 10
Doug Sanders Arne Werkell	Halmstad (Sweden)	Feb. 17
Jack Nicklaus Sam Snead	Pebble Beach (California)	Feb. 24
Byron Nelson Gerry de Wit	Hague (Holland)	Mar. 3
Phil Rodgers Frank Phillips	Royal Singapore (Singapore)	Mar. 10
Bill Casper [illegible]	Portmarnock (Ireland)	Mar. 17
Bob Goalby Bob Charles	Paraparaumu Beach (New Zealand)	Mar. 24
Bob Rosburg Roberto De Vicenzo	Los Leones (Chile)	Mar. 31

See them in color on the N. B. C. Network
Starting January 20, 1963

20-24 *The back side of a pocket calendar that details the 1963 schedule of the Shell Oil televised golf matches from around the world. Note the match between Jack Nicklaus and Sam Snead at Pebble Beach— the 22-year-old Nicklaus sunk a clutch putt on the final hole to beat the veteran by one stroke.*

NINTH INTERNATIONAL MATCH

FOR THE

WALKER CUP

PINE VALLEY GOLF CLUB

Pine Valley, New Jersey

September 2nd and 3rd, 1936

OFFICIAL SCORE CARD

20-22 *Scorecards are inexpensive and fun to collect, especially ones from historic events. Most new cards are free for the asking at a golf course, but older ones may have to be obtained from a dealer. This card was issued for the 1936 Walker Cup Match, noted for being the event's only shutout, accomplished when the United States defeated the team of Great Britain and Ireland by a score of 9-0.*

MISCELLANEOUS EPHEMERA

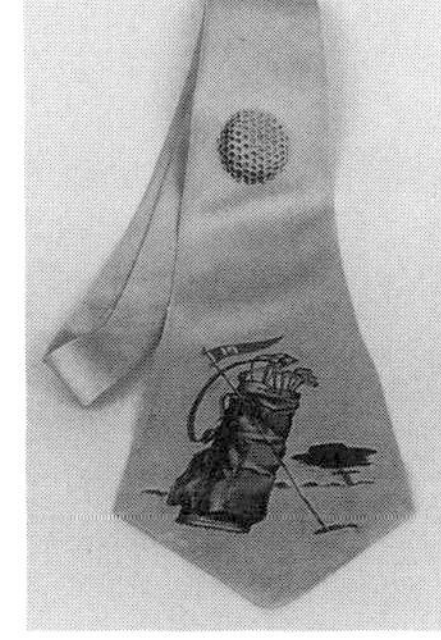

20-25 *The bold graphics now considered fashionable for neckties make this silk tie from the 1920s look conservative.*

20-26 *Although personalized license plates are now the rage, the concept goes back a few years, as seen on this special issue.*

20-27 *Die-cut golfers were used for valentines and advertising during the early 20th century.*

20-28 *Dozens of sheet music covers have been decorated with a golf scene, as shown in this example from 1901. Sometimes the music has a golfing song such as Bing Crosby's "Right Down the Middle," while others such as Dean Martin's "That's Amore" from* The Caddy *contain unrelated lyrics.*

20-29 *A cast iron muffin tray designed to form edible golf shapes, circa 1930.*

20-30 *Woven silk patches issued as a premium by the Murad Cigarette Company as an alternative to the traditional cigarette cards (see page 219). The issue feaured major American universities.*

CHAPTER 21

GOLF COURSE EQUIPMENT

A newcomer to the spectrum of golf antiques is the category of golf course tools and implements. Much of this attention is due to the current fascination with golf course architecture. Golfers critique golf course designs as an art enthusiast would an art exhibit. The golf architect has become a celebrity — from Willie Park to Donald Ross to Arthur Tillinghast to Robert Trent Jones to Pete Dye

Golfers' interest in the features of their playing arenas also has carried over to the items associated with the golf course. Like many aspects of the past, the old-fashioned methods of greenkeeping are fascinating to study in today's high-tech environment.

Books on golf architecture have become prized collector's items (see page 203). And now, golfers are searching through storage buildings on golf courses in hopes of discovering a vintage flagstick, sign, tee box or even a horse-drawn mower. These artifacts add variety to a golf collection and make wonderful conversation pieces.

21-1 *Three old-fashioned golf course mowing methods in use at the turn-of-the-century. The scythe (top left) was traditionally used during the 19th century to compensate for the inefficiencies of sheep and other grazing animals. Horse-drawn equipment (left) was the preferred method for mowing fairways and roughs from the 1890s until the 1920s, when the gasoline engine became the standard provider of horsepower. Early attempts at mechanization included steam-powered mowing machines (above).*

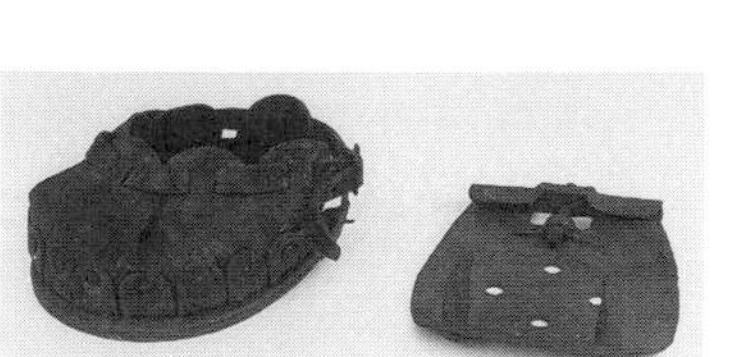

21-2 *Horses that pulled mowers and wagons over golf courses frequently wore special shoes or boots to minimize damage to the turf. Constructed of leather, rubber and steel in various styles, they were popular until about 1930, when gasoline-propelled equipment took over from true horsepower. The advertisement (right) from 1926 extols the virtues of Pattisson's Lawn Boots.*

21-3 *The first golf course irrigation systems consisted of underground pipes with exposed hose bibs or concealed quick coupling valves to which hoses and portable sprinklers could be attached. Although pop-up sprinklers, such as this one patented in 1928 by the Dayton (Ohio) Irrigation Company, had been available since the beginning of the century, they were not used extensively on golf courses until the 1960s.*

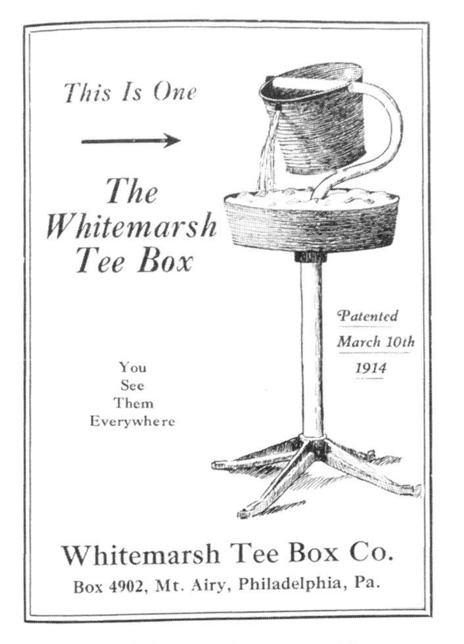

21-4 *Hole markers have evolved from a tin sign or cloth remnant attached to a pole or stick to the modern nylon flag with its fancy silks-screen printing. The collectible markers shown are an actual flag used at the 1990 British Open and an antique type marker of steel and tin that was still being advertised in the 1930s.*

21-5 *Until the wooden peg golf tee became the standard teeing device in the 1930s, a small mound of moistened sand had been the preferred method for centuries. Contraptions like the Whitemarsh Tee Box simplified the process of wetting the sand.*

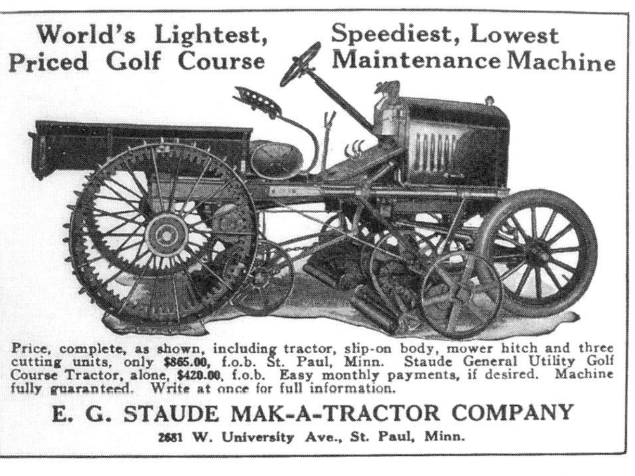

21-6 *Steel-studded driving wheels helped propel this three-gang mower in 1926.*

21-7 *A Ransome's Patent Chain Drive non-motorized greens mower, circa 1899.*

21-8 *A hand operated hollow-tine aerifier.*

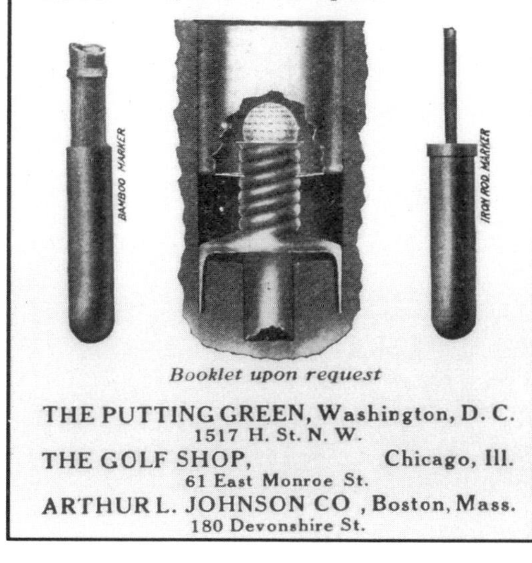

21-9 *Metal liners specifically designed for golf holes were popularized during the 1890s. Earlier methods included cans, clay pots or no liner at all.*

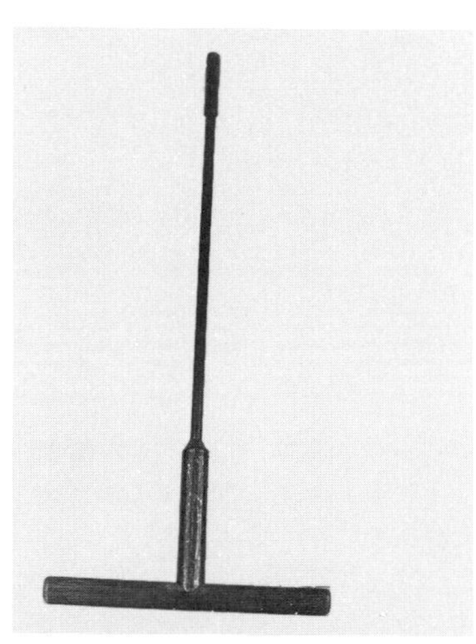

21-10 *Van's Sand Green Smoother, patented by C.E. Van Patten of Holstein, Iowa, was a device for smoothing the sand prior to putting on the oiled sand greens used throughout much of the Midwest and South, where it was difficult to maintain grass greens. The end of this 33-inch long implement retracts so it can be stored in a golf bag.*

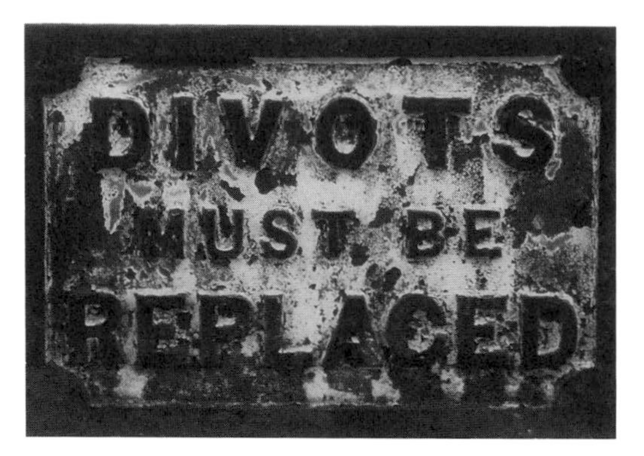

21-11 *Early 20th-century golf course signs often were made of cast iron, such as this one that measures 9 x 13 inches.*

COLLECTING TIPS

■ **Several extensive collections of golf course equipment have been established and can be viewed at:**

Golf House
U.S. Golf Association
Far Hills, New Jersey

Turf Equipment Museum
Valentine Turfgrass
Research Center
Penn State University
University Park, Pennsylvania

Vintage Turfgrass Tools
Collection
Department of Crop &
Soil Sciences
Michigan State University
East Lansing, Michigan

■ **No definitive research on golf course equipment has been undertaken, however there is a small booklet that may be of interest to collectors: *Old Lawnmowers*, by D.G. Halford (Princes Risborough, England: Shire Publications, 1982).**

APPENDIX A

DEALERS & AUCTIONEERS

As the field of collecting golf-related items has expanded, so have the number of businesses that buy and sell such items. Most transactions are done through a golf memorabilia dealer or an auction house that conducts golf specialty sales. Some firms are one-person operations, while others have a large staff or are part of a multifaceted business operation.

The full-time dealers mentioned in this chapter do most of their business over the telephone and through the mail. Some have elaborate showrooms. They should not be confused with "collector/dealers" who usually display golf merchandise for sale at collectors' meetings and flea markets. Some "collector/dealers" are excellent sources, but since most are not established business enterprises, they are not listed in this book.

All three of the leading British auction firms traditionally conduct major golf sales in July during the week of the British Open. The auctions take place near the Open venue, in a branch office salesroom or in a rented facility. Sales of lesser importance are held in January or at other times during the year.

Although the two primary American auction firms are relative newcomers to the scene, they have no difficulty acquiring top quality consignments. Since both are located in New England, sales often coincide to accommodate out-of-town buyers.

The following establishments are known to be reputable within the golf collecting hobby, however the inclusion (or exclusion) of any business is not to be construed as a recommendation by the authors. As the saying goes: "Caveat emptor: Let the buyer beware."

DEALERS

Burlington Gallery Limited
10 Burlington Gardens
London W1X 1LG
England

Phone: 01-734-9228
Contact: Nick Potter or Angus Lloyd
Catalog: One per year, sometimes a charge.
Showroom: 9:30 a.m.-5:30 p.m. Monday-Friday;
10 a.m.- 5 p.m. Saturday
Specialty: Prints, paintings, ceramics and other artwork. Also other sporting art.

Richard E. Donovan Enterprises
P.O. Box 7070
305 Massachusetts Ave.
Endicott, New York 13760

Phone: 607-785-5874
Contact: Dick Donovan
Catalog: Two or three per year, no charge.
Showroom: None; Office by appointment only.
Specialty: An extensive selection of new golf books, as well as old titles.

A-1 *Like most full-time dealers, Dick Donovan sets up a display at meetings of the Golf Collectors' Society. He sells old and new golf books.*

J.C. Furniss
Crossway House
Torthorwald
Dumfries DG1 3PT
Scotland

Phone: 0387-75-624
Contact: John Furniss
Catalog: Four times per year, no charge.
Showroom: By appointment only.
Specialty: Secondhand and antiquarian books. Also postcards and cigarette cards.

Golf Art and Imports
P.O. Box 6208
Dolores at 6th
Carmel, California 93921

Phone: 408-625-4488
Contact: Mike Roseto
Catalog: One per year, no charge.
Showroom: 9 a.m.-5 p.m. Monday-Saturday, 10 a.m.-3 p.m Sunday
Specialty: Golf gifts, featuring both new and old artwork and collectibles. Also arranges custom golf travel.

Golf Gap
3435 Yonge St.
Toronto, Ontario M4N 2N1
Canada

Phone: 416-485-5316
Contact: James Heffernan or Tony Kent
Catalog: None.
Showroom: 10 a.m.-6 p.m. Monday-Saturday
Specialty: The Canadian source for contemporary golf art, books, videos and gifts.

Golf Interest
P.O. Box 1226
Eastbourne
East Sussex BN20 9DH
England

Phone: 0323-422075
Contact: David Neech
Catalog: None.
Showroom: By appointment only.
Specialty: Full line with emphasis on clubs. Exhibits in the tented village at the British Open.

The Golf Shop Collection
P.O. Box 14609
2409 Spring Grove Ave.
Cincinnati, Ohio 45214
Phone: 513-241-7789
Contact: Jim Olman
Catalog: Available to wholesale accounts only.
Showroom: 9 a.m.-5 p.m. Monday-Friday
Specialty: Artwork, framing, and tournament prizes, primarily sold through dealer network of pro shops and art galleries. (Operated as part of Old Golf Shop prior to 1988.)

Golf's Golden Years
2929 N. Western Ave.
Chicago, Illinois 60618
Phone: 708-934-4108
Contact: David Berkowitz
Catalog: Mailings only.
Showroom: 10 a.m.-6 p.m. seven days. Located in an antiques mall.
Specialty: All types of golf collectibles, with emphasis on old balls.

A-2 *Most golf dealers offer their products by mail-order catalog. A nominal subscription fee usually is charged.*

COLLECTING TIPS

■ Prior to contacting golf dealers or auction firms, consult Chapter 3 (page 13) to learn some of the "ins and outs" of the golf collectibles business.

■ All of the auction houses (and some of the dealers) offer descriptive catalogs, some of which are lavishly illustrated. There often are charges, but once you become an established customer, the fees usually are waived. Even if you don't have plans to make a purchase, it's worth obtaining a few catalogs to see what is available.

Golfiana Gallery
Grays-in-the-Mews, B10
Davies Mews
London W1
England

Phone: 071-408-1239
Contact: Sarah Fabian-Baddiel
Catalog: Occasionally, no charge.
Showroom: 10 a.m.-6 p.m. Monday-Friday
Specialty: Decorative items, including: silver, ceramics, prints, postcards and ephemera. Also old books.

Grant Books
Victoria Square
Droitwich
Worcestershire WR9 8DE
England

Phone: 0905-778155
Contact: Bob Grant or Maureen Jones
Catalog: Antiquarian books, 2-3 per year. New books, regularly. No charge.
Showroom: 9 a.m.-5 p.m. Monday-Friday. Other times by appointment.
Specialty: Antiquarian, out-of-print and new books. Also publishes limited edition golf books, reprints and club histories.

Greg and Barbara Hall Antiques and Golf Memorabilia
24717 E. Oakland Road
Bay Village, Ohio 44140

Phone: 216-871-9319
Contact: Greg Hall
Catalog: Mailings of show dates.
Showroom: 373 Detroit Road, Avon, Ohio 44011
10 a.m.-5 p.m. Monday-Saturday,
12 p.m.-5 p.m. Sunday
Specialty: The Halls are antiques dealers who exhibit at about 30 shows annually.

George Lewis Golfiana
P.O. Box 291
Mamaroneck, New York 10543
Phone: 914-698-4579
Contact: George Lewis
Catalog: At least one annually, $5.
Showroom: By appointment only.
Specialty: A PGA Master Professional and former head pro, George handles mostly decorative golf antiques and old books.

Maxwell's Bookmark
2103 Pacific Ave.
Stockton, California 95204
Phone: 209-466-0194
Contact: Bill Maxwell
Catalog: One or two per year.
Showroom: 9:30 a.m.-6 p.m. Monday-Saturday
Specialty: Primarily a general new and used book dealer, but maintains a large selection of out-of-print golf books.

Old Golf Shop, Ltd.
325 West Fifth St.
Cincinnati, Ohio 45202
Phone: 513-241-7797
Contact: Morton W. Olman and John M. Olman
Catalog: Periodic mailings.
Showroom: By appointment only.
Specialty: High-grade golf antiques, consulting services and historical research. Also golf art by Arthur Weaver.

Old St. Andrews Gallery

9 Albany Place		10 Golf Place
St. Andrews	**and**	St. Andrews
Fife KY16 9H4		Fife KY169JA
Scotland		Scotland

Phone: 0334-77840
Contact: David Brown
Catalog: Annually, no charge
Showroom: 10 a.m.-5 p.m. Monday-Saturday
Specialty: Broad range of golf memorabilia and gifts.

A-3 *The Old St. Andrews Gallery, operated by David Brown, is just a wedge shot from the 18th green of The Old Course.*

Old Troon Sporting Antiques
49 Ayr St.
Troon
Ayrshire KA10 6EB
Scotland

Phone: 0292-311822
Contact: Bob Pringle
Catalog: Periodic mailings.
Showroom: 9:30 a.m.-5 p.m. Monday-Saturday
Specialty: Golf paintings and prints, along with other items of golfing interest.

Quarto Bookshop
8 Golf Place
St. Andrews
Fife KY16 9JA
Scotland

Phone: 0334-74616
Contact: Margaret Squires
Catalog: None.
Showroom: Hours vary with season.
Specialty: New and used golf books offered as part of a general line bookshop, especially hard-to-find British titles.

Manfred Schotten Antiques
The Crypt
109 High St.
Burford
Oxfordshire OX18 4RG
England

Phone: 099382-2302
Contact: Manfred Schotten
Catalog: None.
Showroom: 9 a.m.-5:30 p.m. Monday-Saturday.
Specialty: All kinds of golf antiques, in addition to items pertaining to tennis, polo, cricket and other sports.

A-4 *Newer golf books are just one of the specialties offered by Margaret Squires at the Quarto Bookshop on Golf Place in St. Andrews. Her selection of books about the historic golf town make it a must stop for the visiting golfer.*

Eldon P. Steeves, Rare Books Limited
P.O. Box 188
Colvin Station
Syracuse, New York 13205

Phone: 315-428-1437
Contact: Eldon Steeves
Catalog: Three or four yearly, $5.00 charge.
Showroom: By appointment only.
Specialty: Rare and old golf books, primarily in exceptional condition.

The Wooden Putter
1441 Grandview Ave.
Columbus, Ohio 43212

Phone: 614-488-7888
Contact: Joanie Johnson
Catalog: Periodic mailings.
Showroom: 11 a.m.-6 p.m. Monday-Friday,
10 a.m.-5 p.m. Saturday
Specialty: Golf gifts, artwork and antiques.

MAJOR GOLF AUCTION FIRMS

Christie's
164-166 Bath St.
Glasgow G2 4TG
Scotland
Phone: 041-332-8134
Contact: Edward Monagle
Auction frequency: January and July

Oliver's Auction Gallery
P.O. Box 337
Route 1, Plaza 1
Kennebunk, Maine 04043
Phone: 207-985-3600
Contact: Tim Melanson
Auction frequency: One or two per year

A-5 *Bob Gowland of Phillips has been conducting golf auctions regularly since 1981. He is shown here at their New York branch running the First International Golf Auction, held in conjunction with Old Golf Shop in 1988.*

A-6 *Illustrated catalogs for each sale are issued by the auction houses so that potential bidders can assess the merchandise in advance. Most one-day auctions offer 400 to 600 lots for sale.*

Phillips
New House
150 Christlcton Road
Chester
Cheshire CH3 5TD
England
Phone: 0244-313936
Contact: Bob Gowland
Auctions: Main sales in January and July, secondary sales in April and October

Sotheby's
34/35 New Bond St.
London W1A 2AA
England
Phone: 071-408-5205
Contact: Jon Baddeley
Auctions: July, and sometimes one other sale

Sporting Antiquities
P.O. Box 1386
47 Lconard Road
Melrose, Massachusetts 02176
Phone: 617-662-6588
Contact: Kevin McGrath
Auctions: One per year.

NOTE: All firms publish descriptive illustrated catalogs. Prices vary, so it is advisable to write or call in advance. Catalogs and prices realized sheets also may be available from prior sales.

A-7 *Christie's held their 1990 golf auction in St. Andrews during the week of the British Open. They erected a large tent on the grounds of Strathtyrum, an estate owned since the 18th century by the prominent Cheape family.*

APPENDIX B

REFERENCE SOURCES

The golf memorabilia hobby is so diverse that it is impossible to become an overall expert in the field. Some collectors try to learn as much as they can about a single aspect of the hobby, while others are content with knowing a little about a lot of areas. The key to being successful with either philosophy is to broaden your knowledge by studying and researching.

For some, reading this book may be a first attempt to learn about the heritage of golf through its artifacts. It is a good starting point because the goal of *Olmans' Guide to Golf Antiques* is to indoctrinate interested readers without intimidating them. Hopefully, veteran golf collectors will discover a new slant or theory that will enhance their enjoyment of the hobby.

More than 40 recommended references are listed on the following pages. To own every book, magazine and catalog would make a fine collection in its own right, but these references are not intended to be a shopping list. Numerous books duplicate information from earlier works. Also, many of the items described are out of print, difficult to locate or are cost prohibitive. Therefore, you might want to seek assistance from a golf book dealer or visit a library.

Don't be surprised to see conflicting facts in these books; most of golf's history occurred generations ago and historians must rely on prior accounts, some of which may be inaccurate. You may want to check several sources and then decide which you feel has the most credibility.

GOLF HISTORY BOOKS

***The PGA World Golf Hall of Fame Book* by Gerald Astor, (New York: Prentice Hall Press, 1981).** A well-illustrated history of golf related through the resources and memorabilia collection of the PGA/World Golf Hall of Fame in Pinehurst, North Carolina.

***A History of Golf* by Robert H.K. Browning, (London: Dent, 1955; reprint edition: New York: Classics of Golf, 1985).** The first complete "modern" golf history — long on text, short on pictures.

***The Glorious World of Golf* by Peter Dobereiner, (New York: McGraw-Hill, 1973).** Nicely illustrated text by one of the most knowledgeable golf writers.

***The PGA* by Herb Graffis, (New York: Crowell, 1975).** Written by a legend in the golf industry, this book gives a detailed account of the Professional Golfers Association from its inception in 1916.

***The Golf Book of East Lothian* by John Kerr, (Edinburgh: Constable, 1896; reprint edition: Scotland: Spa Books Ltd.).** With the republication of this rare text, an excellent account of early golf in Scotland is now within the financial reach of the average collector.

***The Clapcott Papers* by Alastair J. Johnston, (Edinburgh: Privately Printed, 1985).** A compilation of research by golf historian C.B. Clapcott from the early 20th century, much of which was never previously published.

***Golf In America* by George Peper, Robin McMillan, and Jim Frank, (New York: Harry N. Abrams, 1988).** Extensively researched coffee-table book, produced by the editors of *GOLF* Magazine.

The Encyclopedia of Golf* by Donald Steel and Peter Ryde, (New York: Viking Press, 1975). UK edition: *The Shell International Encyclopedia of Golf. Gives concise encyclopedic listings of the events, places, and personalities of golf.

***Early Golf* by Steven J.H. van Hengel, (Bentveld, Holland: Privately Printed, 1982; revised edition: Liechtenstein: van Eck, 1985).** A comprehensive explanation of the Dutch influence on the development of golf.

B-1 *In 1948, the publisher must have envisioned that this extensive volume would someday become a classic work, because the first edition was furnished with a protective slipcase (left). It is considered by many to be the most significant treatise on American golf. Later revised editions (1956 and 1975) came with dust jackets (right).*

***The Story of American Golf* by Herbert Warren Wind. (New York: Farrar, Strauss, 1948; revised editions: New York: Simon & Schuster, 1956 and New York: Knopf, 1975).** Written by America's foremost golf historian, this book has been considered one of the best for more than four decades.

General Golf Collecting

Golf: The Golden Years **compiled by Sarah Baddiel, (London: Bracken Books, 1989).** An anthology of classic golf stories, illustrated with attractive color photos of golf memorabilia.

Golfing Bygones **by Dale Concannon, (Princes Risborough, England: Shire Publications, 1989).** A 32-page booklet that gives a brief glimpse into the field of golf antiques.

Golf in the Making **by Ian T. Henderson and David I. Stirk, (Crawley, England: Henderson & Stirk, 1979; supplement added in 1982, reprinted in 1986).** A very detailed account of the development of golf equipment and those who made it.

The Compleat Golfer **by Ian T. Henderson and David I. Stirk, (London: Victor Gollancz, 1982). Later revised as: *The Heritage of Golf* (Crawley, England: Henderson & Stirk, 1985).** A collection of excerpts from *Golf in the Making*.

The Encyclopedia of Golf Collectibles **by John M. Olman and Morton W. Olman, (Florence, AL: Books Americana, 1985; later printings by Old Golf Shop, Cincinnati, Ohio).** The most comprehensive reference work available for the golf collecting hobby.

Golf: History of an Obsession **by David Stirk, (Oxford: Phaidon, 1987).** An attractively illustrated history of the game showing many items of interest to the collector.

Golf Collectors Price Guide **by John L. Taylor, (Milton Keynes, England: St. Giles Publications, 1983; supplement added 1984).** A recounting of the British golf auction results from the early 1980s. Prices and descriptions are not very accurate.

Golfing Curios and The Like **by Harry B. Wood, (London: Sherratt & Hughes, 1910; reprint edition: Manchester, England: Pride, 1980).** An amusing, but not comprehensive, book written by one of the early golf collectors about his own collection.

B-2 *Two of the classic works on the hobby of golf collecting.*

Golf Art

Shortspoon **by Ian T. Henderson and David I. Stirk, (Crawley, England: Henderson & Stirk Ltd., 1984).** A limited edition collection of golf paintings by Major F.P. Hopkins.

Golfing Art **edited by Phil Pilley, (London: Stanley Paul, 1988; Boston: Salem House, 1988).** An attractive work with full-page color plates of golf prints and paintings, along with the artists' biographies.

Decorative Golf Collectibles **by Shirley and Jerry Sprung, (Coral Springs, Fla.: Glentiques, Ltd., 1991).** A price guide showing golf ceramics, silver, and other decorative items.

GOLF CLUBS

***Classic Golf Clubs, A Pictorial Guide* by Joe Clement, (Jackson, Miss.: Classic Golf Clubs Joint Venture, 1980).** A softbound limited production book that shows the collectible golf clubs of the 1950s, '60s and '70s.

***A.G. Spalding & Bros. Pre-1930 Clubs* by Jim "The Spalding Man" Cooper, (Kannapolis, N.C.: Privately Printed, 1985; also later addenda).** Magazine style publications assembled by the expert on old Spalding clubs.

***The History of the Golf Pride Grip* by Bill Junker, (Newark, Ohio: Maltby Enterprises, 1989).** An amusing booklet that details the evolution of the modern slip-on grip, but gives little credit to the pioneers of the rubber grip back in the 1890s.

***Golf Club Trademarks – American: 1898-1930* by Patrick Kennedy, (South Burlington, Vermont: Thistle Books, 1984).** A detailed listing of trademarks registered with the U.S. Patent Office.

***Golf Club Design, Fitting, Alteration & Repair* by Ralph Maltby, (Newark, Ohio: Maltby Enterprises, 1982).** A thorough review of modern clubmaking and repair.

***The Club Makers* by Janet Seagle, (Far Hills, N.J.: U.S. Golf Association, 1989).** A list of clubmakers, manufacturers, and golf professionals whose names appear on old clubs cataloged by the U.S. Golf Association.

***Collecting Old Golf Clubs* by Alick Watt, (Alton, England: A. A. Watt, 1985; revised edition, 1990).** A specialized account of the old clubmakers and their work.

***Antique Golf Club Price Guide* by Peter Georgiady. (Endicott, New York: Castalio Press, 1991).** Contains prices from various sources that indicate value ranges of collectible clubs.

***The Golf Club Identification and Price Guide* by Mark Wilson. (Newark, Ohio: Maltby Enterprises, 1989).** Descriptions and values of used modern golf clubs, intended for use by the club professional.

CATALOG REPRINTS:

These three books each contain a brief company history along with facsimiles of old catalogs. Compiled in the early 1980s by Jim Kaplan, they can be obtained from a golf book dealer.

Hillerich & Bradsby: History – Catalogs
MacGregor Golf: History – Catalogs
Wilson Golf: History – Catalogs

The following booklets are reprinted full-line equipment catalogs that do not indicate the modern reprint date, so don't assume that one obtained secondhand is old. (Available from The GolfWorks, Newark, Ohio.)

Burke Golf Company – 1922
Burke Golf Company – 1927
Crawford, McGregor & Canby Company – 1913
Spalding Golf Guide – 1891 (Date shown on cover of this book is incorrect. Contents were assembled from several later publications.)

B-3 *Numerous pamphlets and equipment catalogs have been reproduced in recent years for the benefit of collectors. They are both amusing to read and are a great help when trying to date certain products.*

GOLF LITERATURE

***Turfgrass Bibliography from 1672 to 1972* by James B. Beard and Harriet Beard and David P. Martin, (Ann Arbor, Mich.: Michigan State University Press, 1977).** An extensive 730-page bibliography of turf articles and books that includes entries on golf course architecture and construction.

***The Game of Golf and the Printed Word* by Richard E. Donovan and Joseph S.F. Murdoch, (Endicott, N.Y.: Castalio Press, 1988).** The most complete golf bibliography assembled, along with commentary on golf books from different eras.

***Collecting Golf Books 1743-1938* by Cecil Hopkinson, (London: Constable, 1938; reprint edition with added footnotes and comments: Worcestershire: Grant Books, 1980).** An interesting discussion of the different categories of golf books. Does not include a comprehensive bibliography.

***C.B. Clapcott and His Golf Library* by Alastair J. Johnston and Joseph S.F. Murdoch, (Worcestershire: Grant Books, 1988).** A 300-copy limited edition book about one of the most notable golf book collections and the documents concerning its sale in 1956.

***The Library of Golf, 1743-1966* by Joseph S.F. Murdoch, (Detroit: Gale Research Co., 1968). Supplement with 1967-1977 added, (Lafayette Hill, Penn.: Privately Printed, 1978).** A classic bibliography, complete with the authors amusing insights on the literature of golf.

***The Murdoch Golf Library* by Joseph S.F. Murdoch, (Worcestershire: Grant Books, 1991).** The most recent of the Murdoch works, this book tells how the author's phenomenal golf library was formed.

***Golf–A Guide to Information Resources* by Joseph S.F. Murdoch & Janet Seagle, (Detroit: Gale Research, 1979).** An annotated guide to golf books and other sources of information within the golf industry.

COLLECTING TIPS

- **Out of print books can be obtained from sources listed in Appendix A. (See page 243)**
- **Golf history is brought to life on videotapes, such as *History and Traditions of Golf in Scotland* (Sherry Productions, 1990); *Tom Morris: Keeper of the Green* (Quadrant Video, 1991); and *Legacy of the Links* (Paramount Pictures, 1987).**

B-4 *These three reference books are a must for the collector of golf books.*

GOLF BALLS

***The Curious History of the Golf Ball* by John Stuart Martin, (New York: Horizon Press, 1968).** An enlightening, but not entirely accurate, description of the development of the golf ball.

PERIODICALS AND CATALOGS

Catalogs — current and old — issued by golf dealers and auction firms contain informative descriptions and photographs. Beware that prices and descriptions may not always be accurate. (See Chapter 22 for a list of sources.)

Golfiana, a quarterly magazine that provides an in-depth look golf history and collecting, (Golfiana Productions, P.O. Box 668, Edwardsville, Illinois 62025)

The Golf Collectors Society Bulletin, published six times per year for the members of the Golf Collectors Society (P.O. Box 491, Shawnee Mission, Kansas 66201). Contains collecting news and articles of interest.

Tee Time is provided with membership in the International Philatelic Golf Society (P.O. Box 2183, Norfolk, Virginia 23501). A quarterly newsletter that reports and details all golf related postal items.

Through The Green, the quarterly newsletter of the British Golf Collectors' Society describes the golf collecting happenings in the United Kingdom. (B.G.C.S., Robin Hill, Smedley Street West, Matlock, Derbyshire DE4 3LF, England)

COLLECTING TIPS

- **Old golf magazines — preserved by the several golf libraries (see page 27) and numerous public libraries — are a wonderful source of information about an event or item from the past.**

- **Don't forget to consult specialized periodicals such as *Golfiana* and *The Golf Collectors Society Bulletin,* which contain detailed information not recorded elsewhere.**

B-5 Golfiana *magazine deals exclusively with the history of golf.*

INDEX

Bold type indicates entire chapters.